Eugenie de Guerin, Guillaume Stanislas Trebutien

**Letters of Eugénie de Guérin**

Eugenie de Guerin, Guillaume Stanislas Trebutien

**Letters of Eugénie de Guérin**

ISBN/EAN: 9783337249458

Printed in Europe, USA, Canada, Australia, Japan

Cover: Foto ©ninafisch / pixelio.de

More available books at **www.hansebooks.com**

*LETTERS OF*
# EUGÉNIE DE GUÉRIN

Edited by G. S. TREBUTIEN

ALEXANDER STRAHAN, PUBLISHER
LONDON AND NEW YORK
1866

# CONTENTS.

|   |   | PAGE |
|---|---|---|
| Letter to Mdlle. Louise de Bayne | | 1 |
| ,, to Mdlle. Marie de Guérin | | 5 |
| ,, to M. Maurice de Guérin | | 8 |
| ,, to the Same | | 10 |
| ,, to the Same | | 14 |
| ,, to Mdlle. Louise de Bayne | | 18 |
| ,, to Mdlle. Irène Compayre | | 23 |
| ,, to the Same | | 27 |
| ,, to Mdlle. Louise de Bayne | | 29 |
| ,, to the Same | | 33 |
| ,, to the Same | | 39 |
| ,, to the Same | | 42 |
| ,, to M. Maurice de Guérin | | 47 |
| ,, to the Same | | 51 |
| ,, to Mdlle. Antoinette de Boisset | | 53 |
| ,, to M. Maurice de Guérin | | 57 |
| ,, to Mdlle. Louise de Bayne | | 59 |
| ,, to the Same | | 63 |
| ,, to Mdlle. Irène Compayre | | 66 |
| ,, to Mdlle. Antoinette de Boisset | | 68 |
| ,, to M. Hippolyte de la Morvonnais | | 72 |
| ,, to Mdlle. Louise de Bayne | | 74 |
| ,, to the Same | | 78 |
| ,, to M. H. de la Morvonnais | | 80 |
| ,, to Mdlle. Louise de Bayne | | 84 |
| ,, to the Same | | 87 |
| ,, to the Same | | 90 |
| ,, to M. Limer | | 94 |
| ,, to Mdlle. Antoinette de Boisset | | 96 |
| ,, to M. Maurice de Guérin | | 98 |
| ,, to Mdlle. Antoinette de Boisset | | 101 |

## Contents.

| | PAGE |
|---|---|
| Letter to M. Hippolyte de la Morvonnais | 103 |
| ,, to Mdlle. Louise de Bayne | 107 |
| ,, to Mdlle. Antoinette de Boisset | 112 |
| ,, to the Same | 114 |
| ,, to Mdlle. Louise de Bayne | 117 |
| ,, to Mdlle. Irène Compayre | 122 |
| ,, to Mdlle. Antoinette de Boisset | 124 |
| ,, to Mdlle. Louise de Bayne | 125 |
| ,, to Mdlle. Antoinette de Boisset | 128 |
| ,, to Mdlle. Louise de Bayne | 129 |
| ,, to Madame la Baronne de Maistre | 132 |
| ,, to Mdlle. Antoinette de Boisset | 134 |
| ,, to Madame la Baronne de Maistre | 135 |
| ,, to the Same | 139 |
| ,, to the Same | 146 |
| ,, to Mdlle. Louise de Bayne | 152 |
| ,, to Madame la Baronne de Maistre | 154 |
| ,, to the Same | 158 |
| ,, to Mdlle. Irène Compayre | 163 |
| ,, to M. de Guérin | 165 |
| ,, to Madame la Baronne de Maistre | 168 |
| ,, to Mdlle. Louise de Bayne | 172 |
| ,, to Madame la Baronne de Maistre | 176 |
| ,, to Mdlle. Louise de Bayne | 180 |
| ,, to M. de Guérin | 187 |
| ,, to the Same | 190 |
| ,, to Madame la Baronne de Maistre | 197 |
| ,, to Madame de Sainte-Marie | 200 |
| ,, to Madame la Baronne de Maistre | 202 |
| ,, to Mdlle. Louise de Bayne | 204 |
| ,, to the Same | 208 |
| ,, to Mdlle. de Guérin | 214 |
| ,, to M. de Guérin | 218 |
| ,, to Mdlle. Louise de Bayne | 222 |
| ,, to M. de Guérin | 226 |
| ,, to Mdlle. Louise de Bayne | 229 |
| ,, to Count Xavier de Maistre | 233 |
| ,, to Madame de Ste. Marie | 234 |
| ,, to Mdlle. Louise de Bayne | 237 |

|   |   | PAGE |
|---|---|---|
| Letter to Madame la Baronne de Maistre | .. .. .. | 242 |
| ,, to Mdlle. Louise de Bayne .. .. | .. .. .. | 243 |
| ,, to Madame la Baronne de Maistre | .. .. .. | 246 |
| ,, to the Same .. .. .. .. .. | .. .. .. | 250 |
| ,, to the Prince de Hohenlohe.. .. | .. .. .. | 252 |
| ,, to Mdlle. Louise de Bayne .. .. | .. .. .. | 253 |
| ,, to Madame la Baronne de Maistre | .. .. .. | 257 |
| ,, to Mdlle. Louise de Bayne .. .. | .. .. .. | 258 |
| ,, to Mdlle. Antoinette de Boisset .. | .. .. .. | 261 |
| ,, to Madame la Baronne de Maistre | .. .. .. | 263 |
| ,, to Mdlle. Euphrasie Mathieu .. | .. .. .. | 267 |
| ,, to Mdlle. Louise de Bayne .. .. | .. .. .. | 268 |
| ,, to Mdlle. Antoinette de Boisset .. | .. .. .. | 272 |
| ,, to Madame la Baronne de Maistre | .. .. .. | 274 |
| ,, to Mdlle. Louise de Bayne .. .. | .. .. .. | 278 |
| ,, to the Same .. .. .. .. .. | .. .. .. | 281 |
| ,, to Madame la Baronne de Maistre | .. .. .. | 283 |
| ,, to the Same .. .. .. .. .. | .. .. .. | 287 |
| ,, to the Same .. .. .. .. .. | .. .. .. | 291 |
| ,, to the Same .. .. .. .. .. | .. .. .. | 292 |
| ,, to the Same .. .. .. .. .. | .. .. .. | 296 |
| ,, to the Same .. .. .. .. .. | .. .. .. | 298 |
| ,, to Mdlle. Irène Compayre .. .. | .. .. .. | 301 |
| ,, to Mdlle. Louise de Bayne .. .. | .. .. .. | 303 |
| ,, to Madame la Baronne de Maistre | .. .. .. | 307 |
| ,, to Mdlle. Antoinette de Boisset .. | .. .. .. | 311 |
| ,, to Madame la Baronne de Maistre | .. .. .. | 314 |
| ,, to M. le Baron Almaury de Maistre | .. .. .. | 317 |
| ,, to Madame de Sainte-Marie .. | .. .. .. | 319 |
| ,, to the Same .. .. .. .. .. | .. .. .. | 320 |
| ,, to Madame la Baronne de Maistre | .. .. .. | 323 |
| ,, to Mdlle. Louise de Bayne .. .. | .. .. .. | 324 |
| ,, to Madame la Baronne de Maistre | .. .. .. | 326 |
| ,, to M. Hippolyte de la Morvonnais | .. .. .. | 329 |
| ,, to the Same .. .. .. .. .. | .. .. .. | 332 |
| ,, to M. le Baron A. de Maistre .. | .. .. .. | 334 |
| ,, to Mdlle. Louise de Bayne .. .. | .. .. .. | 336 |
| ,, to Madame la Baronne de Maistre | .. .. .. | 338 |
| ,, to the Same .. .. .. .. .. | .. .. .. | 343 |

|   |   | PAGE |
|---|---|---|
| Letter to Madame la Baronne de Maistre | .. .. .. | 344 |
| „ to M. Hippolyte de la Morvonnais | .. .. .. | 345 |
| „ to Madame la Baronne de Maistre | .. .. .. | 348 |
| „ to M. H. de la Morvonnais | .. .. .. | 350 |
| „ to M. de Guérin | .. .. .. | 352 |
| „ to Mdlle. Marie de Guérin | .. .. .. | 356 |
| „ to M. H. de la Morvonnais | .. .. .. | 360 |
| „ to M. de Guérin | .. .. .. | 362 |
| „ to Mddle. Louise de Bayne | .. .. .. | 365 |
| „ to M. H. de la Morvonnais | .. .. .. | 370 |
| „ to M. de Guérin | .. .. .. | 373 |
| „ to Mdlle. Louise de Bayne | .. .. .. | 376 |
| „ to M. de Guérin | .. .. .. | 381 |
| „ to the Same | .. .. .. | 383 |
| „ to M. H. de la Morvonnais | .. .. .. | 386 |
| „ to Mdlle. Marie de Guérin | .. .. .. | 389 |
| „ to M. H. de la Morvonnais | .. .. .. | 390 |
| „ to Mdlle. Antoinette de Boisset | .. .. .. | 393 |
| „ to Mdlle. Louise de Bayne | .. .. .. | 395 |
| „ to M. H. de la Morvonnais | .. .. .. | 399 |
| „ to the Same | .. .. .. | 403 |
| „ to the Same | .. .. .. | 407 |
| „ to Madame d'Assier de Tanus | .. .. .. | 409 |
| „ to Mdlle. Antoinette de Boisset | .. .. .. | 411 |
| „ to M. Paul Quemper | .. .. .. | 413 |
| „ to the Same | .. .. .. | 415 |
| „ to M. H. de la Morvonnais | .. .. .. | 416 |
| „ to the Same | .. .. .. | 419 |
| „ to M. Paul Quemper | .. .. .. | 421 |
| „ to Mdlle. Antoinette de Boisset | .. .. .. | 423 |
| „ to the Same | .. .. .. | 425 |
| „ to M. de Guérin | .. .. .. | 427 |
| „ to the Same | .. .. .. | 430 |
| „ to the Same | .. .. .. | 437 |
| „ to the Same | .. .. .. | 441 |
| „ to Mdlle. Antoinette de Boisset | .. .. .. | 448 |
| „ to the Same | .. .. .. | 449 |
| „ to the Same | .. .. .. | 451 |

## *LETTERS OF*
# EUGÉNIE DE GUÉRIN

To Mdlle. Louise de Bayne, Château de Rayssac (Tarn).

Cayla, 12*th July*, 1831.

OU think me now very far away from you, my dear friend, and yet I have never left you. I am still in your room,—at the swing,—at the church; in short, you would see me constantly, if thought could be seen. Mine travels very nimbly; in less than a moment there it is on your mountains which it enjoys so much. It will end by taking root there. Really and truly, you'll come across me some day, planted among your woods. Meanwhile, here I am in those of Cayla, which also are far from distasteful to me. My journeys are all over, except those to Cahuzac; indeed, I could not take any which would not seem tedious after the one which afforded me so much amusement. Why is Rayssac so far off? Why are you

twelve leagues from me? Why should what one loves be so distant, and what one loves not, always too near? It is because nothing in the world goes quite as one would have it. Happiness and unhappiness, pain and pleasure, walk hand-in-hand. After the greeting comes the farewell; that sad farewell, which one has to say to everything: first of all to one's doll, then to one's eighteen years, then to this, then to that; but the saddest of all is the farewell of departure, especially to a kind, tender friend like you. My dear Louise, it cost me so much to leave you that I have half a mind not to see you again.

I went away very sadly after your last hand-clasp, turning my head round in your direction from time to time; but I could see nothing but the white walls of the castle, which soon vanished, then the trees, then the mountains, then everything. . . . . There I was at Villefranche, where at least I still had Fingal and Criquet:* the latter was very affectionate; he came and sat himself on my knee. I caressed him, gave him his supper, and, after a parting kiss, off he set, with a remembrance of me *on his neck* and in his heart, too, I believe. . . . .

I don't know why I have not told you before this that Maurice is here. I am the happiest person in the world just now. He came last Monday, just a week after I left Rayssac. We had been somewhat uneasy about him, but now we have him near us and always with us. However, he means to leave us, and that to go and see you. I say "Yes" and "No," when he talks of it to me, but

* A horse and dog belonging to Rayssac.

at last it will be "Yes," for I ought to prefer his pleasure to my own. As he is only just arrived, he will not be going off at once, and, besides, before then he has to see grandmamma, great-aunts, great-uncles, and second cousins. To-morrow is the arrival of the mail—after the traveller a most welcome event: a store of books, prose, verses, that one rifles as a thief does a strong box. I know there is a share of the treasure for me, and for Marie too. Just now Cayla is in high force: everything laughs, sings; even certain fowls, who, without knowing it, sing their death-song, To the spit, to the spit!

I found Albi in commotion as to the choice of a deputy. Nothing else was spoken of, not even by Madame——, who prefers discussing dress to politics; but in truth this subject comes home to the heart more than a bonnet. In Paris they turn it into a jest; they laugh at Philippe, but fear everything besides. Hence the deputy for —— does not attend the Chambers for fear of the windows, and waits to set out till the season when they will be kept closed—the month of November. . . . .

I have been here now six days without finding any messenger for Gaillac. At length the good muleteer of last year informs me that he sets off to-morrow, and instantly I take up my pen-cutter and the large paper you told me to use. Here I am in my little room, tête-à-tête with a pen, or rather with you, for a pen is only a conversation. Will you answer me soon? After the pleasure of seeing comes that of reading you, because it brings you back to sight; therefore turn yourself into note-paper until you can come and see me at Cayla in a more satisfactory way. I have informed Marie that you are to be with us this summer. Judge of her delight, she who has not seen you for more than a year. She calls out, "Come! come!" with all her might; nor is she the only one. Papa is not the last to congratulate himself on this delight, and you must receive for you and yours the homage and tender messages that he hopes soon to offer you in person, accompanied by Maurice. As to Marie, I don't know whether she will set out just yet, in spite of her desire to come and explore your mountains. Not, though, that she is afraid of the roads. I praised them as they deserved. I defend and shall defend them against all attacks whatever. In short, I shall puff them up to such a degree that the whole Cayla party will go to Rayssac with more pleasure than to Paris.

I got up the day before yesterday at six o'clock to make an expedition that was not so amusing as going to see you. I went off to M. Bories, and it was high time, after running about the world for two months. Accordingly, my soul was less satisfied than my heart, which you had used so well; but now it feels all right again, for it has what it requires. People may, if they like, say that I am fond of the world; but they are wrong. It is not there that I find happiness. I have told you so already. I must have something besides excitement, amusements, even a friend: I must have my God, and, as He is not to be found in the world, I should never enjoy myself there long. Adieu, dear Louise! you will tolerate these reflections of mine; I know that they do not displease you.

To MDLLE. MARIE DE GUÉRIN, Cayla.

*Rayssac, Tuesday, 5th September,* 1831.

Already a week that I am far, very far, from thee, my dear one; but I am so loved and welcomed that one would be consoled for having come from the ends of the earth. Louise and her sisters are most charming friends, combining much attention and care with an absence of all formality, which makes one perfectly at home with them. But for all that, I think daily of leaving, only I say nothing about it; they expect us to stay for some time. Louise said to me yesterday, "I feel as if we ought always to have you." "And my Cayla, do you suppose I could forget it?" I have been there very often since I came here. Who knows what Mimi may be about at this moment that I am writing to her? I wish she could see me in my little room, with a bookcase before me, and a mirror that I do not look into. I see nothing but my inkstand. The weather is charming; we shall take advantage of it to go and visit the invalid, who wishes to see me before she enters heaven. . . . .

Pulchérie is quite inclined to come to Gaillac, but she does not tell me when. Louise wishes it were to-morrow, and so do I. I should rejoice to see her at Cayla, and to return her a little of what she pours on me in such full measure—kindness, affection, all that the heart can give. We are always together, she and I: at dinner my place is beside her. Sitting or standing, 'tis like the right arm and the left; but we are far away at night. I don't sleep in that bed so convenient for chatting. I have been placed beside Maurice, in the most awful room in the Castle, in that bed of fears that I told thee of. It is there I sleep, and not without some fear. I do hear the wolves sometimes, but only under my windows. One of these last nights there was a terrific uproar; dogs and wolves were waging war, as is everywhere the case just now. M. de Frégeville told M. de Bayne yesterday that they have had regular fights at Montpellier every evening for a week past. Here they fight a little in the public house, but it's the wine that does it. I think our country is the best of all; neither opinions nor wine quarrel.

We are still fasting as to milk; all the cows are or have been sick. To-morrow the sixth is to be thrown to the wolves. Sheep, horses, pigs, all are affected. I am afraid of this murrain coming down to us. They say the cholera is at Toulouse. Very possibly; I am not afraid with my medal. They have no medals here; if I can get any at Albi I shall send them some.

I am going to breakfast, then to mass, this evening to take a walk, and then I shall relate my day to thee. Days pass here as sweetly as at Cayla. Our evenings are very lively, and are kept up till midnight. We have an encounter of wits, little battles with Maurice about Victor Hugo and Lucretia.* Leontine is his sharpest assailant: I call her the bee. Maurice is sometimes charming on the battle-field.

* Lucretia Maria Davidson, a young American poetess, who died in 1825, at the age of seventeen.

.... I am just come, my dear, from the church, whither we went, after our walk, to pray to the good God for the living and the dead. It is thither we always go to end the day, according to the custom of the mountaineers. The church is as full here in the evenings as at Andillac on a Sunday, and everybody prays with a truly delightful devotion; there are even simple women as well versed in contemplation as Fathers of the Church, who can repeat you any number of prayers without knowing how to read.

Paul expects me at Rondille; Lili,* too, is looking for me; but you will easily understand that I cannot go everywhere. I am too anxious to get back to my Cayla to find pleasure elsewhere. The poor Lili! If there were any way of getting to Albi from hence, I should be delighted to give her a few days; but 'tis impossible. The horses come for me here. It is cold enough to-day to numb one's fingers, which rather interferes with our outdoor enjoyments.

It is very reluctantly that I have refused the little goat: she is a darling. Louise had been feeding her with bread, and paying her a daily visit; now she has to be weaned from all these indulgences, since no longer destined to be ours. Adieu, my very dear one! I follow thee about in thought, and long to do so in reality. Now let me embrace Papa.

This, dear Papa, if you will allow it, is to serve as a reply to your letter. I shall tell you nothing fresh. I

* Mdlle. Louise Mathieu, of Albi, a cousin of Eugénie's, who died in 1838.

have given Mimi all my news, and her letter is for all, being long enough for everybody to take a share. Your part is that where I say how much I long to see you all again, which I repeat to make you thoroughly believe it. If I were to heed Louise, I should spend my life here, and I would heed her if you were here; but so far! so far! .... I mean to return soon. We often talk of you with Louise; she tells me she is very fond of you. As for me, I have no need to tell you so, but I greatly need to see you again.

Maurice is just now busy surveying the mountain with Charles and M. Carayon. They are all three good boys. Ours is not the richest, but he is the one who gives the most. Everything here has something of his, even the crickets.* One of his poems has been set to music by M. Carayon.

---

To M. Maurice de Guérin, Paris.

Cayla, 9th November, 1831.

How long time is when one is sad! Is it three years or three days since you went away, my dear Maurice? As for me, I really can't tell; all I know is that I am wearying to death. Positively this is the first moment I take any pleasure in since your departure, and this will be a very short one. Jules is in a hurry to leave us for Paris. And so, my dear, this word or two will

* See in the works of Maurice de Guérin some pretty lines addressed to the "Cricket of the Rayssac hearth."

follow you without your knowledge, as I have sometimes gone behind you very quietly to catch you unawares. But, good heaven! how far you are from us by this time! There you go on rolling, ever further and further away, and here have I to follow you without very well knowing what road I am taking. I am afraid of your being upset, and recommend you to the *little cross*. I have great confidence in its preserving you from every evil chance. Be as devout to it as you promised me, and I shall be at ease. I am over head and ears in household matters, but I left everything to take its chance that I might come and have a word with thee in thy little room, where I discover all sorts of memorials of thee, without counting thy waistcoat and shoes. If thou wert dead they would all turn to relics for me, but heaven preserve me from such devotion.

I shall go to Cahuzac on Monday, to see the fair and other things; the following Monday I depend upon having tidings of you, if indeed you did leave Toulouse the day before yesterday. Nothing has happened since Sunday that deserves to be recalled. Rain, mud, wind, and to-day sunshine—that is all. I was forgetting a fowl that Wolf slaughtered, which procured him some cuts of the whip that made him cry for mercy; I do believe he was calling upon you. The poor fellow had good reason to invoke his knight errant, for no one took his part. Trilby* kisses and licks your hand. As for me, I devour you. Good bye.

My influenza seems inclined to leave me, but does not

---

\* A favourite dog at Cayla.

leave the house; the herdsman has it as well as Maritorne. People are dying of it at Franseilles; this is indeed having death at our heels. But is it not always before us, behind us, everywhere in short? Yesterday, at Andillac, a little child went to heaven. If I were a little child I should like to follow it, but when one gets old, if one could help it, one would never die. Then it is that the threads that once attached us to earth become cables.

Papa sends thee 10 francs as his subscription to the 'European Review.' For me, I send thee nothing but a couple of hugs. I have no time to reply to my cousin to-day. Give her my love. Adieu.

---

To the Same.

Cayla, 24th *November*, 1831.

Here we are then, back again at letters, my dear Maurice. It is by no means what I would wish, but I content myself with them since I cannot have you. A charming prophetess has just been predicting that before long I shall be consoled for your absence. If she thinks I shall forget you she is a false prophet. What, then, can she mean? That you will return? But that return is so far off. That you will write to me? True, this consoles, but not quite. I have it, I have it; yes, you will write to me, but the letters will be printed, gilt, bound. There you are an author made rich by fame, and there I am in Paris. That is the very thing she meant to say; she knows what I wish, the venerable little witch, and she could not mean to foretell me misfortune. I accept the augury, which, besides, your letter has just confirmed. At length you are launched in your course, far, far from that Code which weighed you down like Mount Atlas. Papa is satisfied with your determination.

To-day we have seen M. Bories, who is going to subscribe with Papa to the 'Courrier de l'Europe.' I am longing to see thee in it. This will compensate us for 'L'Avenir,' but we shall make haste to take that again as soon as it reappears, for no one doubts that our pilgrim will soon return blessed and triumphant. It is a measure indeed which cannot fail to have happy results, be they what they may. If the Pope approve, 'L'Avenir' is thenceforth on a pinnacle; if he condemn, a thing impossible (they say), Lamennais' defeat will be a triumph for him as it was for Fénelon, for who can doubt that he will submit. The Gaillac Abbés who had given you some subscriptions are quite disconcerted; I suppose they have written to you. Let them have the 'Courrier de l'Europe.' If your articles should give you a right to send it to us as well, it would be no bad thing to do. At present it is I who am the reader; every evening we have readings aloud; I work, I read, I write to some one, and the day is gone. I was a good deal alone last week; Erembert* was at Lacage, and Papa here, there, and everywhere, as is his way, you know, in fine weather. We had spring for four days. The evenings were delicious, but I did not care

* Erembert de Guérin, elder brother of Maurice and Eugénie.

to go out to enjoy them all alone. I spent them in my own room, my elbows resting on the window, and my chin on my hands, and so I gazed and thought and regretted. Just think of my finding myself alone with Trilby, the only creature who came to smile at me, consequently the little dog got many a caress. Gazelle has some idea of taking to me, but it comes and goes like a caprice. I am fonder of her, however, than she knows, on account of the good milk she gives us.

My thoughts often go round the world in a second of time. If legs could follow them, you know very well where I should be. Indeed I often am beside your fire, blowing and raking and sending you a spark or two in case you should be too grave. I always fancy that your chimney corners are somewhat like ours, and that you recover your home feeling at my cousin's.* At least what you tell me of his wife makes me think so. Tell me if that sweet face has not the calm expression that I attribute to it, something in the style of Léontine.†

I have had a charming letter from ——; she speaks to me of Lucretia. That name she says will not soon escape her. "Whenever we are inclined to be dull Lucretia is there to restore our cheerfulness. I own that in the place of M. M. I should prefer to be an enthusiast about the living rather than the dead; but it shows us that he does not overlook merit." Then she speaks of your future,

---

\* M. Auguste Reynaud, Professor, and later Rector, at the Bourbon College, of whom mention is frequently made in Maurice de Guérin's correspondence.

† Mdlle. Léontine de Bayne, sister of Louise.

and that after praises that you would not treat more graciously than those of the Abbé, which is the reason I do not repeat them to you. She adds, "He will be happy." Take the words as you will; I leave it to you to comment on them, and above all to fulfil, for it depends in part upon *yourself* to be happy. Not indeed with a happiness that has no foothold on earth, which you would, I believe, like, but with the happiness made for man, that little portion of felicity which God gives him here below.

There is one part of your letter which has much edified me. It is well to say to each other—Let us pray, pray. Yes, I have prayed, poor little ant that I am; I have prayed very heartily for our pilgrims' prosperous journey. God grant that they may return content!

I have no incident to tell you of; only politics still keep stirring like the spinning-wheels in the village evenings; those women spin politics capitally. Poor Romiguières is in for a quota of ten francs; he or his asses. If all in France pay as much, that would go far to comfort him. We are expecting Charles next week with Armand. What do you wish me to send for you to Rayssac. But you ought to write to M. de Bayne. Console the poor man; that intelligence must have grieved him. Mimi has written to me; she remains till New Year's Day at Toulouse. I fancy that Jules has arrived; certainly he must open very wide eyes in that great Paris. My influenza has left me. This immense letter informs you that one of these days I shall write to my cousin; I should be very sorry that correspondence fell asleep.

They say the cholera is in England. I could almost wish it at Paris, to have you three coming here. Leave at once if it approaches; tell my cousin this from me, but I hope to see you here under better auspices.

---

TO THE SAME.

*22nd January*, 1832.

It is Sunday, the day of rest; accordingly the only noise I hear is that made by my pen on my paper. I am thinking of you; you are not so quiet in your great Paris, except in your own little room where you recover Cayla beautified. Yesterday, when I saw the great oak of *Téoulet*, covered with hoar-frost, I thought of Maurice's great fir. Nothing prettier than these trees in their winter dress, but long live that of summer all the same! When one has nothing to see but trees, one would rather have them green than white. For you who see so many things, a little snow goes for nothing; for us here 'tis a great event, was so especially when I used to make snowballs, but for some time back that has been a lost delight. Winter gives me none now, except the gentle warmth of the chimney corner; 'tis the pleasure of the old. What a distance between the doll and the tongs! And I've got to these last. Next will come spectacles, a stick, loss of teeth; sad new year's gifts these, for after all the years do bestow them; and hence, since time has left off bringing me anything sweet, I would gladly send packing this first day of the year like a bore who returns too often. As you say, it is strange that one should be so gay at this time. That children should is natural enough, they come in for *bonbons;* but we .... Even if I could some times give new year's gifts to my taste. .....

I have had one welcome gift at all events, your letter. None ever gave me more delight than this. Just when I was picturing you more than ever wandering and straying in the realm of the *void*, you inform me that, shut up in your own room, you are bending yourself to regular work; why, what an advance you have made in this, my dear friend! Frankly, I did not expect so rapid a conversion. May God maintain it! Did I not always tell you that will was power? You have willed, and you have been able, been able even to resume the Code. I am much pleased with you and your courage. Are not you well rewarded for your first effort by seeing its result? "I can now intrepidly encounter the day." These are the very words you have kept me waiting for so long, which I have preached about so often. Nothing has given me so much pain as to see you on such bad terms with life. You will find how far sweeter it is when one knows how to manage it. Order in your thoughts is for you the beginning of happiness; little by little everything will shape, harmonise, and arrange itself in your existence, you will resemble our clock, which strikes very well in fine weather. Long may it last, this fine weather that shines on you now; and when the *frost* of discouragement threatens to attack you, attack it as you have already done. He who can give one blow can give ten, can give a thousand. I can easily believe that those fits of depression which come over you at times must be terrible conflicts. If only I could cure or help you! .... Thomas à Kempis has one very true saying: *Often the fire burns, but its flame does not rise without smoke.* This is certain; there does not arise in us a single good thought, or good intention, which is not soon mingled with a little smoke, a little human weakness. But the good God blows upon it and it all goes away.

We have had some days of cold that made the little birds cry out. This, however, is less sad than to hear the poor cry; I can well believe that they spoil the pleasure of your fireside, but it is a pleasure to me to find that they do pain you. If ever I came to knock at your door, you would not, I see, close it against me. You would very often hear a *rat-tat* at that door if it were not so far off. For instance, I should forthwith have come to embrace you on seeing you so wise, studious, and retired. You make upon me the effect of one of the Fathers of the Church, meditating in your tranquil cell on the Bible and religious philosophy, though I doubt that any of the former were as comfortably lodged. Really it's a charming abode! I can understand your making pretty verses there, arranging the embers the while. I am sure there are verses everywhere about, on the tables, chairs, mantelpiece, and here I am without any! At least tell me what you are doing. Whereabouts is your drama? I should be delighted with that 'Peter the Hermit.' You wanted, I fancied, to present something to Lamartine; if you take my advice, you will. I am sure he would receive you like an angel from whom you requested kindness and encouragement.

I sent what you told me to Rayssac. No doubt of the 'Blessed Nicholas'* being welcome. Who does not love the 'Lives of the Saints'? I cannot give you the explanations you ask me for; how would you have me set about obtaining them? Only in a *tête-à-tête* could I ask anything of the kind; *never* in a letter, question and answer both would be too indiscreet. Meanwhile, content yourself, my dear, with the *chiar oscuro*. As for that, Louise has not written to me since the great long letter; I sent you in my last a few lines which ought to satisfy you. Charles made a great stir in this neighbourhood, especially in the city of *gossip:* 'twas for this, 'twas for that he had come to Cayla. I was asked about his age and his fortune. I could hear people saying at the low mass, "Too young for her;" and she was thinking the while, "What have you to do with it?" But they have to do with many things besides, from our clogs to our conscience, at that sagacious tribunal; they know everything, thoughts, words, actions, omissions, everything in short except how vexatious such curiosity is. I am for liberty of the press, but not for that of tongues. There should be a seizure made of some of these last about here.

Really you are leading the most charming life in the world. Our amusements are not much like yours. One of these past days, when it was exceedingly cold, Mimi

* Article on the 'Blessed Nicholas de Flue,' by Maurice de Guérin, in the 'European Review.'

and I went to take a walk in the woods and pay a visit to the crows; but though very well clothed and well hooded, the cold was too much for us, and fortunately we fell in with a fire made by some young shepherds, who very graciously gave us up the place of honour, a stone larger than the rest, in front of the fire. These children told us all they knew: one had just been eating some *fry*, the other had fresh eggs at home laid by a yellow hen; and from time to time they threw a few handfuls of *brouquilels*\* into the blaze with a look of such satisfaction that there is no king but would have said, "Why am I not one of you?" If I knew how to write verses I should sing the 'Shepherds' Fire.'

You would never guess what work I got for a New Year's gift; it was an author who did not, I believe, write to be read by women—accordingly I shall not read him —'tis Montaigne. Tell me if the 'Love of God,' by Count Stolberg, is a very expensive book. I should like to have it.

---

To MDLLE. LOUISE DE BAYNE.

*2nd January*, 1833.

What a New Year's gift I should have bestowed upon myself yesterday morning, my very dear one, if I could on rising have thrown my arms around your neck, wished you a happy new year, told you that I loved you at the

\* Little branches.

beginning and end of every year, and put up for you prayers without number! I should have been too happy. What a sweet New Year's Day for me who am dying to see you! I had hardly opened my eyes and made the sign of the cross on waking, when your image came to me on my pillow to tell me that you, too, were thinking of me at the same moment, and that, if we could not see each other, still our prayers and good wishes met on the way to heaven. Yes, my dear, I prayed for you first of all on waking, and then at mass, in the *memento* of the living, at that place where God permits our thoughts and our hearts to redescend for a moment to earth, to take up the wants of those we love. I rank you among my family; and so I asked the good God to bestow on you all that I wish for those I love best in the world: health, peace of heart, head, spirit,—and finally, whatever you require for your own happiness and that of all belonging to you.

Do you know that you, by your silence, are making me begin the New Year sadly? Not one word, not a sign of life! I begin to fear that winter has frozen up Rayssac. At first I accused the charcoal-makers, Gosse, every one but you; and now I know not what to think. I pray you write to me at once; take off this little icicle that your silence has laid upon my heart. If it be indolence which keeps you mute, surmount it; if forgetfulness, do not forget me, I have not deserved it. Perhaps you suppose that I have received some of your letters since I wrote last—not a single one, my dear. I ask; I institute a search. No one has seen anything. Who knows into what hands these dear tokens from my dear Louise may fall! "Poor letters of Louise! who can tell where you are imprisoned? How I regret to see you turned into rolls of paper for groceries, or food for rats! What a pity! Here am I losing all your sweet words. I shall never know what you were bringing from her heart to mine—that heart that sends me such pretty messages, tells me so much, and that has suddenly grown dumb. Come, charming messengers! it is now that I have need of you."

You see, my dear, I talk to the paper. I would implore everything—pen, inkstand, and those little fingers which play at being dead just now; will not you take pity on me? But, seriously, dear Louise, I am really anxious: are you in bed, or from home? I do not believe in your forgetfulness, but you might be ill. I think of your teeth, your ears that made you suffer so much, and I am sad. To believe you ill and weary, as you must be of this dull winter season, afflicts, torments me.

The first sunny day I set out for Gaillac; that is decided. I must go and have the Toulouse gown made; I would much rather come and give you a hug. How glad, happy, enchanted I am! I have just read one of your letters. Thanks, dear friend, for the pleasure you have given me, for your tenderness, your love for me. My hand still trembles with the delight of having broken the seal; but this little thrill of joy only speeds it the faster. I wish I could send you on the wing the whole swarm of pretty thoughts your pretty letter has occasioned me. Just now I saw everything black; now all is rose-coloured. You have revived me, set me up. Your recollection of me has had the effect of sunshine when one is benumbed. I do not, however, the less regret your stray letters, especially as they are full of many things, it seems; but I don't despair of getting them as soon as I can send some one to rummage Gosse's drawers, in which assuredly they are now sleeping.

I am much obliged to you, my dear, for the pitcher of water, the black bread, and the cavern. My heart is not yet sufficiently penitent to lead me, like the Magdalen, into the desert to weep for my sins. If you think I need it, pray for this grace to be given me; I promise to follow its leading, and to come and be the hermit of the grotto, provided you sometimes come to see me there, and promise, on your part, to guard yourself against the wolves of the world as I against those of the desert. Do not let us jest, my dear: recluse souls are far safer than we in the world with the *roaring lion going about us!* I think that St. Paul means by this the demon who tempts us in such various ways, who drags us so far, so far from heaven that we come to lose sight of it, and *God, who is good, so gracious, so perfect, to be always our last thought.* What an inversion, my dear Louise, to give the lowest place in our heart to Him who ought to occupy the highest! to go over at once to the enemy, and forsake the Friend, the Father, the Brother, the Husband; for—

> "Under these names so dear,
> Lord, thou to us draw'st near,"

as a poet says.

Will you not think it rather droll that I should so often mount the pulpit, my dear friend? If I grow tedious, say so; but I love you too much not to tell you what you want to make you happy: it is piety. With that the more, you would have many sorrows the less; not, indeed, that one grows insensible, but resigned. If depressed, one prays; if one regrets the world, if one's mind wanders off in the track of balls and amusements, one checks it by reflecting that this is not the way that leads to heaven. Do you know that we really are very blind, very senseless, very stupid to occupy ourselves merely with this world, to take root here below, and to forget that other life, that glorious kingdom? We were talking over this on Sunday with a gentleman, full indeed of cleverness and *dormant* good feeling, but who pleads guilty to not acting up to his belief. These reflections occurred to him *à propos* of a bit of the hair shirt of Julie de Saint-Fons, which his wife had had given to her. He said to us, while looking at the relic, "The world at the sight of a thing like that would call the devout mad; but 'tis we who are mad not to be devout." Don't you think so too?

I should have set off, but for my African cousin,* who has returned on a visit to our part of the country. I am not sorry to be detained; the pleasure of hearing and questioning him will more than console me. Maurice is

* M. Philibert de Roquefeuil, of the Isle of France.

happy as in Paradise in his La Chenaie solitude. All his time is filled by study or prayer. For the rest, he is leading the most easy life: a good breakfast, an excellent dinner seasoned by a running fire of jests and witticisms chiefly originating with M. de Lamennais. It is thus his genius escapes when he is not at work; from being sublime he becomes charming. There is no end to the liveliest and raciest sallies on his part; and M. Gerbert, too, is pretty skilful in *maligning*. You are not the only one. I, too, am fond of the midnight mass, but not quite in your fashion. The reason is, that I am a long way off *eight years of age*. My dear child, when will you leave off being a child? Adieu! I shall love you neither more nor less when you do, since I love you now with all my heart. I tenderly embrace your sisters while offering them my New Year wishes and those of Marie.

---

To MDLLE. IRÈNE COMPAYRE, Lisle-du-Tarn.

*29th April*, 1833.

Again a relapse, dear friend! I was on the point of accusing you of forgetfulness, and asking whether you had left your whole heart at Castelnaudary. But your kind letter, this moment arrived, has scattered all the troop of dark thoughts which were flitting across my heart like wicked gnomes. "I will write no more to Eugénie: the correspondence tires, bores me. What can she have to tell me there in her woods? Accordingly, she draws everything from her heart, and after the one word 'love' there is nothing at all in her letters. I shall leave off answering her; I am sick of that repetition." . . . . That's where I had got to, my dear, when your tender strain arrived. Thanks, and forgive me! I am very penitent; here is the proof: I love you more than ever.

But, then, why do you go and play the dumb? I am so fond of a speaking friendship that I should like always to hear you. However, it is neither coldness nor forgetfulness, nor being tired of me—that is a settled point—'tis only a little slumber that overtakes your heart every now and then, and leads to your saying charming things when it wakes up again.

You tell me nothing about your health. I see there has been some disturbance in that particular amongst my friends at Lisle, and I always fear for yours, which is none of the strongest. But the journey to Castelnaudary will have ensured you a provision of health and happiness. I see you have spent your time there very agreeably, and that everything in that neighbourhood pleases you. I can understand your friend making everything delightful to you, she herself is so delightful! I take great interest in her well-doing and that of her family. What do they call the little stranger? Not *Yves*, I hope : a pretty thing should have a pretty name. Poor Augustine must be very sad at seeing M. de Gélis ill and being herself unable to go to her sister and her little angel, who must be so pretty in all those embroideries she worked, and would take such pleasure in seeing him wear. Tell that dear, good Augustine that I do pity her, and will, with all my heart, say one of those *Paters* she is so fond of, in order that the good God may cure her Papa, and soon grant her the pleasure of embracing her little nephew.

Are there any tidings of M. Henri? We were told that he was in India. A distant return that to look to! How many things we have in the distance, and always what most we desire! But for the thought of Providence, one would say that the world went all wrong; but it is rather we who do not see right. We complain, we get frightened, just as though God were not there. Never let us forget that it is He himself, and not man, who guides us, else there would indeed be reason to despair, and to set out, like Columbus, in search of a new world.

We have got the newspapers again, and they tell us no more than you about our poor Princess. My God! when shall we see her away from there? I tremble lest she should only leave to go to heaven. For a long while back the Bourbons die martyrs. I daily repeat the prayer that Antoinette sent me, and think it very beautiful, especially the psalm. Let us go on praying and hoping: it is the only thing left to us.

I wrote last night to Mdlle. Lisette, and announced the approaching journey of M. Bories to Lisle. I have since heard that he is gone to see his mother, who is seriously ill. I much fear he will have the sorrow of losing her: she is very old. We spoke of you a great deal on Thursday; the Cahuzac clergy were dining here. M. Bories regrets that you should be angry; he will come and see you, and, to punish you, will tell you nothing.

Are you afraid of that? Thank heaven, my dear, the time is not come to put in practice the excellent advice you give me. The canons of Saint Flour no longer distress me,* and, in return for the alarm they caused me, I wish them a happy and long life, like that of Methuselah, that they may do so no more. By the way, I have to scold you. I don't remember now what it was I told you on that head in my last letter, but it was repeated to me, before M. Bories, by M. ——, who had already hawked it about in all the presbyteries of the canton. He never would tell me from whom he had it at Lisle. It was not from you; but you read my letter to a friend, and she passed it on to another, and so from mouth to mouth it has found its way here. I do entreat you, my dear, not to make my letters public property: I should be sadly taken in. Your former *Father of Secrets* promised me he would scold you for betraying my confidence. I implore you not to do it again. Don't read out my communications in open conclave as though they were newspapers. They require to be read in a little corner of their own—if rather dark, so much the better—into which neither brothers nor neighbours, male or female, are ever to intrude.

Adieu, my dear! I embrace you, by way of punishment. Do not prevent me from telling you that I love you. My remembrances to your sister; and, as for you, take as best you may this packet of *bitter-sweet* that your friend sends you.

* See the following letter.

To the Same.

*28th July*, 1833.

Your little epistle, my dear friend, has given me the greatest pleasure. I see you are always good and loving, and remember to write to me even while undergoing an examination. I observe with joy that the soul does not make you neglect the heart, and that you find time for everything. What a thing it is to know how to employ it well!

For the rest, be sure, my dear, that the time you give to friendship is not lost, and that it will even count as regards heaven. The minutes you devote to me are so many alms, which enrich me with kindnesses and a thousand excellent things. Your dissertation on pride, for instance, impressed me like a sermon. Go on; mount the pulpit, play the Guyon; perhaps you will at length convert me to humility. At present, however, I am so far from it that you will have to preach a long time. I am so blind, say what you will, I cannot see that I have constantly to defend myself from the demon of vanity. Where would you have him perch, unless it were on our oak-trees? I find nothing that can harbour him. I know, indeed, that he has a trick of thrusting himself in everywhere, but I also see that in examining your conscience you lay rather too much stress on this capital sin. I don't think so much about it or dread it as you do.

What are you doing in the town at this season? I thought you were long since at Convers. The air of the fields is so sweet, and does so much good, why not go and inhale it? I do, indeed, pity those who have not in summer got a little *nest under the leaves*. One is so happy in it. Long live the country! If we had the church nearer at hand I should consider our woods Paradise. But, if one likes to think it so, this little Sunday pilgrimage is but another charm; it makes a variety from other days. One meets Sunday-dressed figures on the way; children who have grown during the week; one receives *adisias* from every side; all which amuses and pleases. Very often my sister and I spend the Sunday with Françoise,* the most gracious person you can possibly see. We talk of Lisle and Cahuzac; she, who knows all the sisters of the presbytery, has always some holy anecdote or other to tell us of.

I am truly sorry for that poor Antoinette, so often ailing. That little frame is so delicate it seems as though the air must injure it. I have had no tidings of her since those you gave. You must have disturbed her very pleasantly the other day, since she told me such pretty things afterwards. I know I would give something to be often disturbed the same way. Just now, for instance, I would throw my pen a hundred feet off, and jump into your arms! I own that in that case a little pride might sprout in me, I should have such charming thoughts on seeing you! But even then it would occasion me no scruple, friendship would wash all out.

Do you know what is occupying me? five ducklings that have just been hatched and a lame chicken. I take

---

* Mdlle. Françoise Limer, sister of the Andillac Curé.

pity on whatever suffers, and make much of the poor little creatures; one can limp about now, and will soon get as far as the spit.

The canonry no longer alarms us. Monseigneur de Saint-Flour has chosen a quite young grand-vicar, who will not give up his stall for a long time to come. So much the better for us, for Cahuzac, and the whole country. There is no one who would not have felt the greatest regret at seeing M. Bories leave. Adieu, dear friend! my sister goes halves in my thoughts and my affections. Adieu! Love her who loves you.

---

To MDLLE. LOUISE DE BAYNE.

*Festival of St. Louis, 25th August, 1833.*

The Sainted King made me think of you very early this morning, dear Louise, and after having prayed to him on your behalf, I come to wish you a happy anniversary. How rejoiced I should be if you could have heard me and received my nosegay, accompanied by a kiss on each cheek! Instead of this bit of paper that I am sending you, I should have gathered all your prettiest mountain-flowers, and should have come, at the break of day, to wake you in the midst of fragrance and fondness. How sweet that would have been, and what a beautiful morning this must be at Rayssac! Dear mountains, when shall I see you? Dear friend, when shall I be beside you? Do not ask me the question, I know nothing about it; one can't do all one would, as you very well know.

The church bell is ringing, and my spirit saddens at the knell of a young girl for whom the whole parish is in tears. That poor Angélique was only eighteen, and there she is dead, in spite of her youth, her health, her freshness. One would have given her a hundred years of life but a fortnight ago. How quickly Death comes! It is enough to make us meditate upon our fragile existence. My God! it holds to so little, and we hold to it so much! To see how we act and think, one would say that we believed ourselves rooted in life for centuries like the oaks. This poor child was unable to confess, having lost the power of speaking and hearing. They could only administer extreme unction, which she received with perfect consciousness but great regret at dying. When she saw the preparations for her last moments, she took to crying and wailing so sadly that M. the Curé himself sobbed. The poor man was heartbroken, especially at being unable to make her hear a single word of consolation. She was a good creature, however. Poor young girl! my heart is full of her. I saw her on Sunday, and did not think it was for the last time. Who knows where her spirit is now? One must be so pure to go to heaven! But the good God is full of mercy—above all, for the simple, ignorant souls who serve him as well as they know. It is towards those who have received instruction, grace, assistance, that He must show himself severe. We see what we ought to do, and do it not; without actually departing from duty, we allow ourselves to be led away by a thousand thoughts and cares, which preoccupy the mind and divert it from God and the great idea of salvation. As Lamennais says, there is always something pressing that we cannot postpone; and under this pretext, without any fixed intention, merely through the stress of the occupations we have made for ourselves, we neglect piety, devotional reading, prayer, the indispensable duties of religion; and this life glides away, full of projects, cares, anxieties, in oblivion of the *one thing needful*.

You utter a great truth when you say that over and above the affections of this world the heart requires something spiritual. I feel, without being very well able to say why this is, there are certain things of such an intimate nature that they cannot be externally produced, but every one is conscious of them. The Mother Abbess who came to see you would have been better than any other able to tell you what that spiritual love is of which the heart has need, and why she left the world. How much I should have liked to see and hear her! There is nothing I am so fond of as these veiled figures, these mystical souls, all made up of devotion and love of God. Do not you feel a longing to follow her to the Convent? Those black robes have a sort of magnetism about them which attracts you I think. I wish much I could see that mountain Convent. We had been told that the Superior was a remarkable woman both in mind and appearance. Do people imagine that there are no charms behind the grating? You assure me of the reverse too much to allow me to doubt it; but, indeed, I never doubted it. I once dined with Madame Duterrail, who gave me when very young the highest idea of the conventual intellect.

I know nothing of Gabrielle since I wrote to her more than a fortnight ago. Marie will probably go and see her soon; I shall then be alone, and shall come and find you in the little room, not being able to do so in any other way. I did not tell Henriette that I should not go to you, only that as yet it was impossible, because so long as our farming operations last we can't take a servant away. It was only the day before yesterday that we finished our threshing; now they are beating aniseed, and there are always a thousand things to occupy our people. Soon all will be finished. It is through no want of will that I am not already on the way. If you knew, my dear, the pleasure, the happiness I find in being with you, you would pity, instead of being angry with me.

We are expecting tidings from Brittany with great impatience, some day I will tell you why. We have neither newspapers nor news of any kind, and the world wags without our knowing how. Have you heard anything of the Duchess? It is strange that since her arrival one should be just where one was as far as she is concerned. When will this be cleared up? We live in a time of strange occurrences.

Adieu, dear friend! I had not intended to stop so soon, but Erembert is just setting out for Cordes, where he will meet with an opportunity of sending to Albi; and I must

---

* Well known in the south as having gathered together at Toulouse, under the rule of the blessed Jeanne de Lestonnac, the nuns dispersed by the first Revolution, and having founded several convents.

not lose it, I find so few. Adieu, very dear and loved one! may Saint Louis protect you, and take you with him to heaven! I have prayed much to him both for you and France, that has such need of saints. I do not forget your sisters; assure them of our remembrance.

---

To the Same.

*23rd December*, 1833.

I write to you, dear Louise, to the sound of the *Nadalet*, to the merry peal of bells, announcing the sweetest festival of the year. It is, indeed, very beautiful, this midnight celebration, this memorial of the manger, the angels, the shepherds, of Mary and the infant Jesus, of so many mysteries of love accomplished in this marvellous night. I shall go to the midnight mass, not in the hope of a pie, coffee, and such a pleasant dish as your nocturnal cavalier; nothing of the kind is to be found at Cahuzac, where I only enjoy celestial pleasures, such as one experiences in praying to the good God, hearing beautiful sermons, gentle lessons, and, in a quiet corner of the church, giving oneself up to rapturous emotion. Happy moments, when one no longer belongs to earth, when one lets heart, soul, mind, wing their way to heaven! Oh, how much better this than the amusements of a party! Do you believe that Emilie* would change her moments of ecstacy for all the delights of the world?

* Mdlle. Emilie Vialar, granddaughter of Doctor Portal, Court Physician, foundress of the Sisterhood of Saint Joseph in Africa.

Papa came from Gaillac the day before yesterday, bringing your letter to Marie. Thanks in her name and mine; for I have my share in whatever comes to her, especially of this kind. This dear recovered letter completes the series of five that I have received since your change of office. This has been a fortunate thing for us, for me at least, to whom all your kind thoughts arrive one after the other, like a flight of birds, into their nest. It is because they know their home is here.

*St. John's Day.*

I left you rather suddenly the other day, for I know not what occupation; but this I know, it must have been pressing, since it caused me to break off our pleasant chat, which Saint John sees renewed to-day. He is one of Papa's patron saints, and, by way of a festival, I mean to write to you.

This morning at sunrise we were in the Andillac road, on our way to hear the Mass of the Holy Evangelist for our holy Papa; I think I may safely call him so, and say to myself that both Louise and I shall have a father in heaven. Do you remember that saying of M. Guyon's, " He will go straight as a taper to heaven " ? That taper made a great impression upon me, and I look upon it as a bull of canonisation. Yesterday M. Bories said, in speaking of M. de Bayne, " He is a man whose faith is firm as a rock, I am not surprised that he should say the Pope is right." We were speaking of M. de Lamennais, and M. de Bayne came next, like one page after the other. We are, like him, entirely upon the side of Rome.

All the world is questioning us as if we knew what was doing and to be done, and most certainly all the world is equally wise, the newspapers having given publicity to these affairs. I was at Madame de C——'s one evening when all this was warmly discussed, in consequence of an article in the 'Gazette.' No sooner had it been read than one heard on all sides, "What will M. de Bayne say now?"—"Gentlemen, he will say whatever Rome says."—"What will your brother do?—where is he?" I knew nothing about it then, nor do I now, and I find this uncertainty no small distress. All we do know is that he is no longer at La Chênaie; he wrote to us from the house of M. de La Morvonnais, one of his Bréton friends, that he should be setting out soon either for Paris or Cayla. Since then I take every rider that I see for Maurice, and my heart begins beating, but not entirely with pleasure. You can perfectly understand this, dear friend, and how grieved I should be to embrace a *heretic*. God preserve me from seeing, or even thinking this! But young men are so easily seduced by whatever is brilliant and novel; and then, how escape the powerful attractive influence of M. de Lamennais when one sees and hears him? May God deign to open his eyes, and give him the virtues the rebellious angel lacked—humility and obedience.

I left you with that poor brother in the musical night.\* Actually that thought occurred to me in church, and, in spite of myself, I kept picturing Louise and her eccentric companion; but however, my dear, you were the one who most disturbed me, and you may without any excess

---

\* The nocturnal cavalier of the early part of the letter.

of vanity accept the preference, and believe that my mind is not silly enough to dwell upon that thistle, for instance, when it can have a rose. And besides, it is you I straightway select out of a hundred thousand charming things, as I run at once to your letters amongst a hundred thousand writings. You should see when one is brought me amidst a packet of others. I leave the packet and seek out a corner to read and re-read, then I pass on to the indifferent, to the lukewarm at most.

Marie writes to us pretty often, sometimes every week; I am fond of her little notes, all full of news and things in general; but the last were very dismal, telling of three or four most sudden deaths, that of poor Madame D—— the most distressing of all. Those two little children, that poor heartbroken widower, fill me with pity. She died of inflammation of the brain, after the joyous christening of a fine boy. My God! how short the duration of the joys of this world! A poor beggar-woman died of the same malady, leaving two children, and a husband who swallowed poison very devoutly, making, he said, the sign of the cross, as if about to take his soup. It was perhaps that, which changed the poison in some way, for it did not kill him, but afterwards he went and threw himhimself into the water at Fédiès to drown his widowed anguish. That widower ought to have a place given him in the dictionary of illustrious men. He would be a good model for husbands.

You ask me for news from the four corners of the globe, as though I were in relations with the whole human race; what news can you get from a poor recluse who does not inquire about the world, who hardly likes to hear of it, and, with the exception of the affairs of her family and her friends, takes no interest in any, no more than in the bird that passes, or the water that runs by? I shall seem to you very ice; yet I am not cold, not indifferent either, still less forgetful; only ask me if I love you, if I think of you, if I forget Rayssac, its kind inhabitants, its rocks; why even Criquet has his place in my thoughts! There can be nothing associated with you but I love it warmly, and take infinitely more interest in it than in politics, war, journals, news of the world, and gossip of drawing-rooms. If in the relations of one family to another, and in society, there only reigned a little more charity, or even a little indulgence, one might enjoy it, and listen with pleasure to what gets said; but people are so malicious, so caustic; one flays the other with so much skill, that all the pleasure of meeting and conversing is spoilt by this intolerable ill-nature. What a tiresome fault it is! Accordingly, I detest it more and more, and avoid nothing so much as passing any one under review, for fear of that pleasure of criticism, so easy, so attractive, so racy, and so cruel. Witticisms are fire-arms, that make a noise and give pain; let us beware of them, my dear, and use loving weapons alone; those are mine, the only ones I like, and which do no one harm. I must be bent upon amusing you, my dear hermit, to go on chattering thus, putting down whatever comes under my pen; but we have long been upon easy terms, and with you I make no effort of any kind.

What do you do with your long evenings? I should

better know if you were in the world. You read, I suppose, as we do. In the country it is with books one converses, makes for oneself a society of dead and living, which returns each evening at the same hour with the fascination of new minds and new faces. I am very fond of this variety in every page; just now we are with the English, admirably painted by Dr. Lingard. History is to my thinking the most interesting and instructive of all reading, because it makes us reflect so much on this world and the other, and leads thought up from men to God who governs them.

Since I have returned from Gaillac I know nothing of Lisle; Irène has not written to me for an age. She is idle like myself, I suppose, and I excuse her. A pen is sometimes a very heavy thing, which you would not find out from this of mine that trots over the paper at such length. The fact is, that it fancies itself on the way to the mountain, and Heaven knows if it be not prompt and light when it sets off for your country. My dear Louise, good bye; tell me of the midnight mass, and everything you do. It is thus that hermits used sometimes to write from their cells, and send each other news of the Desert, just adding a few edifying words to sanctify the act. But at this moment I have nothing very holy to say to you; in thought I am yours only; if I look up to the sky, I see it dull and rainy. I have a touch of influenza; the will of God be done!

To the Same.

Albi, 15*th March*, 1834.

I find myself alone for a moment, and in order to spend it pleasantly come to join you, dear Louise, in the little study. And yet I am not really alone there. Together with your image a charming child is with me, the sweet pretty little Marie, who follows me everywhere, playing with her doll at this very time by my side, but so quietly that I have to turn round to make sure of her being there. I have just been arranging a *relic* for her—four or five flowers placed between a bit of glass and of paper. How happy one is at that age! She was radiant with her relic. Now that I have pleased Marie, I please myself, and am as happy as she in looking at a paper all filled with relics of friendship which came to me the other day from you. But 'tis a short-lived joy, for you write to me no longer; fairs, markets, mountaineers, all these pass and bring me nothing from you. Neither do I get a word from Cayla, and so find myself in a famine of news which depresses me, and I lose all the pleasure I might have had with these kind relatives in thinking of those I do not see. Why am I not written to? I have only had one letter from Marie since I am here. No doubt there is one on the way, but oh! that it would arrive! I long to read, to know what they are doing, and how they are. Perhaps they on their part are waiting in the same way, for I have been unfortunate in my despatches; a large packet that I thought had reached its destination a week ago, came back to me the day before yesterday. Judge whether I was not properly disappointed, I, who thought I had Cayla news, to find nothing but my own handwriting!

You know that I am nearer to you here, dear Louise, waiting for some neighbourly tokens, as for a festival. Why then do I not hear from you? Will you come and speak a word to me during my retreat? I promised myself so much pleasure in my visit, were it only that I should be able to chat with you from a less distance. Let us then chat, dear Louise, look for and resume that pen that tells me so many sweet things, so many things that I cannot dispense with. It is like the evening sermons; whenever they fail me I find the time long—my soul as empty as a supperless stomach. This is what will be my fate to-day, a day of rest for the pulpit; but I shall go to the chapel to hear another lecture, the recollections of which will fill the rest of the hours.

Here we have only men who come in in the evening. I shall not try to tell you what they say. I listen to them very little; I knit my stockings, it is my only task in the absence of books, or anything more absorbing.

The time I spend here is one of rest; God grant that I may turn it to profit, and gather for heaven while I have not to trouble myself about earth. It will certainly be my own fault if I be not enriched, if I do not come away the holier for this jubilee. Instructions, prayers, humiliations, rain down constantly and from all sides upon my soul. What happiness if this could always last, if once having entered a church one need never leave it again! Willingly could I settle myself in a niche beside the statues that surround the grand choir.\* It is really a great delight to pray in these great houses of God, where it seems that devotion grows greater. Here everything disposes to religious thought: the sight of the walls, the pavement, the pious worshippers; in short, my dear, one feels as though one's soul were at home here, and breathed her native air, which is not that of the world, whatever may be said. The latter, at least, does not give it life.

M. Roques† still goes on conflicting with the world and its vices; but for the last week we shall have a course of morality, in which will be something to suit us all. I am longing for this, for until now his discourses have been better adapted for men than for us. One day he preached on education, and was generally approved by all the right-minded; the following day on marriage, less successfully, to my thinking; 'tis a delicate subject, difficult to treat, and requiring to be dealt with otherwise than extempore—and M. Roques always extemporises. This proves he has a great deal of talent; one would say he was born in the pulpit, he is so perfectly easy and natural and graceful there. On Sunday we shall have M. Calmels for the evening, and we shall also hear him to-morrow at mass, as well as the Abbé de Rivières. I take great interest in seeing this friend of Maurice's in the pulpit, but shall not do so without some feeling of envy and regret. Adieu, my dear; Marie is getting up, she wants to go to the fire, I must follow her. Till to-morrow!

\* Of the Albi Cathedral.
† Professor of Philosophy at the Albi Seminary, and a very distinguished preacher.

The morrow has turned out happily; news, parcels, letters for me from all, from everywhere. How sweet these joys are, my friend! I have spent the whole day in thanks, tender thoughts, and writing. Marie and Papa are well, and have each told me so. Maurice, too, sends me good news. God be praised! here is one beautiful evening; here is happiness for one day, for who knows what may befall us on the morrow?

*17th.*—More happiness, dear Louise; one of your letters, a great budget, came to greet my waking. The sweet morning! the worthy man of the mountain, who thought of me rather than of his breakfast! Thanks, my dear; thanks for everything, for your loving words, your farina, your seeds. They shall set out this evening to Cayla to tell them there how good and kind you all are. Neither shall I, you may be sure, consider my happiness complete if I cannot jump into your arms from here. After the holy joys of the jubilee, the sweet enjoyments of friendship will set me longing a good deal. To be so near and not to see you, to return without coming to embrace you, is an idea that pains me. Will you have me?

---

TO THE SAME.

Albi, *March*, 1834.

It was a great pleasure last night on coming in to find your letter, dear friend. I read you beside Lili's chimney corner, fast, very fast, because I am always in a hurry to read you, and next because I was expected to supper at Emilie's. I told her on entering that I had you in my bag, and that there were many messages for her from you and the Countess, which were all very cordially received. Emilie truly loves you; she told me she would much like to have you here, and certainly she is not the only one. Who, indeed, does not want you? You will say to me, "Come, and we will believe you," but 'tis not so easy. How can I make up my mind to leave Lili, this poor invalid, always alone with her pains? She gets out of spirits whenever I go away from her, and hence I hardly do so at all, except to go to church. Charity before all, and the care of the sick is a charity. Be ill, and I shall soon come. But no, keep well, and let us wait till we can meet. Let us leave it to Providence to order events as we wish. I desire nothing better than to see you; I shall not raise obstacles, but one must not want what is impossible. Whether I stay or go I shall always be deeply touched by your affection for me, your longing to embrace me, which would make me set off like a shot if . . . *If* and *but*, life's great impediments! Dear friend, you, too, are well acquainted with some of these amidst your rocks. But there you are, with Pulchérie, and I am at ease. She is your good angel, listen to her, follow her example, and you will not *often* require anything else. I don't say *never*, because there are times when more than a sister, more than a friend is needed; the heart has wants, desires, that God alone satisfies. Love God . . . . 'Tis a pity that I must leave you, just when we were in full talk. But I shall soon return.

It is past ten o'clock, my time for sleep; but my pen is under my hand, your image in my heart; both the one and the other prompt: Good night, Louise. I yearned to say just this one word. Now I am going to think of the good God, for at night everything should sleep but the thought of heaven. To-morrow I shall tell you about sermons. We shall hear Abbé Roques. He is still my favourite preacher, not but what the others are excellent too. M. Caminade gave us a very good, familiar discourse. I was longing to hear him preach in a louder voice. But I won't go on. Till to-morrow!

I shall now inform you that I have just left the chapel of St. Joseph, much satisfied, much impressed with the gentle and pious teaching of M. Caminade. He is an internal man, what one calls a man of prayer. Sure and experienced guides those who commune much with God. What happiness for me to find some one to teach me the love of God! I feel as though, indeed, I were learning it, as though my holy father were imbuing me with the fervour and charity of which he is himself so full. It was only to-day that I told him who I was, because a proper opportunity for doing so presented itself, else we were indulging in the *incognito*. You wanted to know to whom I addressed myself; but why do you say I made a mystery of it? Mysterious towards you! It was only that it did not occur to me when writing to you.

Did not you, too, think that I went to Bon-Sauveur with conventual intentions? My dear friend, you know whether I can leave my father. At all events, I beg you not to speak of this: to myself as much as you will, and even to your sister, but to no one besides. I don't want to scatter my idea of a vocation about the world. One might be happy in that convent, life is peaceful there. It is only the lunatics who would alarm me. They are not shown to any of the outside world. I should prefer the care of the dumb, but you must enter there without a will, the *me* is left at the door. I saw the Superior of the hospital again—a good, strong intellect, spite of her eighty years. I thought her charming, the good, holy Mother.

· Who should you think I have just seen and embraced at the hospital? A sister I love, and have not seen for fifteen years—sister Clémentine d'Yversen. She was passing through on her way to Paris, and sent word to Emilie that she could give her an hour. Off we ran to the parlour, where were the Mother and M. Calmels in conference, but they left us with our friend. What a pleasure to see her, to give a kiss under that hood! She is the same as ever, lively, witty, and good. Maurice perplexed her greatly. She wanted to know what became of him after the dispersion of La Chênaie. I reassured her.

M. Roques has been speaking admirably to us on spiritual blindness, and the means of curing it. These means are meditation, reflections on the truths of salvation, and our final destiny. "Go to the grave, meditate on what it encloses; but push on further, follow the soul into eternity. Behold it before God, between heaven and hell. Realise the flames that devour sinners. Ask yourselves if you are not of the number of those ambitious, those proud ones, those misers, those unbelievers, those cowardly Christians that God condemns." A stirring preacher, Abbé Roques. Finally he concluded by a meditation on the words, "If any man will be saved, let him take up his cross and follow me," and in its course unfolded the great truth of self-abnegation, and of the necessity of sufferings. The whole discourse lasted for nearly two hours, but the time does not seem long when spent in listening to those who speak to us of God. I am sorry that this course of teaching is over.

I communicated the tidings of M. Cuq to those who felt interested in the good missionary. He had been reported dead. God spares him to save some soul. Here are well-filled, well-employed lives for you. M. d'Aussac has set off for foreign missions; three of his sisters are in the hospitals. This is what may be called a holy family. The bells of St. Salvy, which are very wailing, are ringing just now for a lady who died almost suddenly, leaving a daughter surrounded with children, ill and unhappy. Every one is pitying both mother and daughter. There is not a week, not a day, that does not bring one some intelligence that saddens and reminds of the other world. But these reminders are useful, without them we should forget eternity. I am surrounded in every way with means of edification, fed upon lectures and sermons. What a good Lent I have had! Poor Marie is less well off at Andillac. She contents herself with the pastor's simple instructions, which, indeed, are very excellent; but you will feel that one must needs have something very different here. My little cousin Euphrasie is much touched by the Countess's remembrance, and begs her to accept hers. The little girl has a good heart, a very good one; she loves her little brothers, and caresses them in a delightful way. She is my companion by night and day. We sleep together, under the holy keeping of an image of the Virgin, a vessel of holy water, and a rosary, the cross of which Euphrasie kisses vehemently on getting into bed. With all this you can easily imagine that useless words and other temptations are kept at bay. We fall asleep. Lili is expecting me; you will consent to my going to embrace her; I have not seen her to-day.

---

To M. MAURICE DE GUÉRIN, at M. Vacher's, The Park.
(Eure-et-Loire.)

Cayla, 15*th July*, 1834.

Here are two welcome letters that have come to us; thine, my dear Maurice, and one from Félicité, telling us of the situation offered thee at Juilly. You will not, I hope, say no, unless it be for reasons to us unknown. What could be more desirable as you now stand, than a situation where you will be able to wait for something to turn up without other outlay than a little will and determination? for will is needed, I should think, to play the master, wherever it may be. Thus, one after the other, all your faculties will be brought into play, and when the opportunity comes, each will be ready for its work, and reply, Here I am.

I like what you tell me of the family and country life

you are leading with your friend. I remember that he used to write from time to time while we had you, and that he seemed devoted to you, and now he proves to us that he really was so. Tell him from me how I rejoice in the signal service he is rendering you, and what gratitude I feel for his cordial affection. Has he a mother living? has he sisters? As I know you like to be reminded of us sometimes, I ask whether M. Vacher has sisters who make much of him, who fondle brothers and poultry as we do at Cayla.

Yesterday I witnessed the death of one of my delights, my pets, murdered by a step-mother. I covered it up with sugar and wine, but it died nevertheless, and the poor little one is at present in the deep well, the great charnel-house of hens and dead creatures. With the exception of the poultry-yard, I have no live stock this year—no birds'-nests nor sparrows. In taking care of these little fledgelings one gets fond of them; then they die, and one regrets them. One has troubles enough without that, and 'tis a loss of time besides; and time is so precious that I become more and more miserly about it, and only afford reluctantly a few moments to mere amusement, though really I don't know what that is, for everything turns to the useful with me, even the pleasure of writing to thee.

My correspondence continues as brisk as ever. Long letters to the mountain, little ones to Gaillac, but often to Lisle as well. My beautiful Antoinette cannot forget me, and sends me graceful notes, charming gems of the heart. I owe her an answer, as well as to many others.

Yesterday I had seven letters to write; my quiet little room is a very post-office. You know how comfortable one is in it. At this moment I hear the grasshoppers chirping, and every now and then the song of a nightingale who has his nest down among the junipers. This side of Cayla is rather spoiled by the fall of the great oak and great cherry-tree which the wind blew down in the winter, but this is nothing when one sees the Sept-Fonts wood laid low—our dear avenue without shade, our seats overturned, half broken, it pains me to look at, and I go there now only to meditate. Where shall I be, where shall we be, when those trees have grown up again? Others will go and wander beneath their shade, and watch, as we have done, the sweep of winds that are to lay them low. In all time there will be storms upon the earth.

I am reading Châteaubriand's 'Etudes.' After Lamartine, he is my favourite poet; sometimes, even, I have a fancy to tell him so. Perhaps I shall do so and send it you. I am busy now for my friend *up there*,* and, by way of giving her a pleasant surprise, I should like my poem to come before her, as it were accidentally, in the 'Revue Européenne.' Her father takes it in, and Louise lately told me she should always look for my appearance there. I should be very much pleased if the piece I send you could find a place. M. Cazalé will not refuse you, if women's poetry be admitted into his journal. I have been told it is, and come to offer my flower. But it must bear no name. I only wish to be recognised by

* Allusion to the Rayssac mountain.

Louise, who will require no signature to find me out. Oh, how it would delight me! I am going to work at it, for 'tis not finished; then I shall come back to tell you all Papa wishes you to know.

There now, it's done; my piece is completed, but not as I should like it to be; there's something wanted at the end, but I leave a blank, not to delay sending off this letter; you might think us too long in your debt, and I should be sorry to make you say all we do when *you* are dilatory. Auguste must be charmed with this little boy who is born to him. We thought you would be godfather. Now this is Papa talking, or making me talk. . . . . Adieu, dear friend; I recommend my poetry to you. If you cannot get it inserted, tell me, and I shall send it in manuscript. Eran is at Albi; Papa and Mimi embrace you as I do, with all their heart.

On the subject of poetry, I have long had an idea that I am going to impart to you. Have you not observed that while we are inundated with poems nothing gets written for children? and yet their little minds have their wants, and their little hearts their enjoyments. How many pretty things there are to say to them! It seems to me that poetry of this character is a thing lacking amongst us, and would be welcomed. I have the inspiration; what do you think of that? Am I to get rid of my ideas by stifling them, or allowing them free scope? I do not know why I have them; may God enlighten me! Answer me on this head, and tell me whether I need fear loss of time, whether my 'Infantines' would succeed. Then, no more indecision, I set to work at once; otherwise I would rather make stockings all my life long than useless verses. When one thinks of the account we shall have to render to God of all our actions, all our hours, one may well be careful as to the use made of them. Life is so short to gain Heaven in, that each lost moment deserves tears.

I have a sorrow of conscience or heart. That holy priest of whom I told you in my jubilary travels is leaving the diocese. I regret him the more that he had permitted me to write to him, and that I hoped much from this spiritual correspondence. Do not let us speak of it. Do you remember me in your prayers? We ought to pray as well as love. You have both the one and the other from me. Adieu.

---

To the Same.

*13th September,* 1834.

Raymond sets out in a month, and is to come and take our parcels to thee, my dear Maurice. I shall hardly give him anything beside the little manuscript book\* in which I mean to write every day till your friend's departure. It will only be a letter in thirty pages more or less, according to events and the current of ideas, for sometimes many things occur both in the soul and in the house, and at other times nothing at all.

This week, for instance, Cayla has been roused out of its habitual calm by the arrival of our cousins De

\* This book was unfortunately not to be found.

Thézac and De Bellerive, who are come in sporting trim to amuse themselves and frighten the game. They are all tall young fellows by this time, which makes me *think*—I who saw them born. My God, how fast we grow!

They went away yesterday, our sportsmen, after such brilliant exploits, such killing and killing that the whole country smells of powder like a battle-field. Here we are quiet again; nothing stirs at this moment save my pen on the paper and a fly that buzzes in my room. There is something so sweetly agreeable in this calm that I would fain enjoy it ever, and fall asleep in it as on a bed of rest. Positively I must shake myself to get away. I am too comfortable in my little room. I must leave it.

*14th.*—It is Sunday, the day of long walks at Cayla. Accordingly, at sunrise, we, Mimi and I, were on the heights of Saint-Pierre on our way to the early mass at Cahuzac. Here I am returned and thinking of the grand sermon of Father Bories. He is still our Massillon, preaching better than any one else, and moralising to perfection. It is not his fault if his hearers be not already high in heaven. Instruction, exhortation, fortifying counsels, nothing is wanting to me, and yet I am still prostrate on the earth, not even having strength to change my position. I do not know why it is thus with me, nor whence this singular languor comes over my soul, which should be so light, should spring Godwards as easily as a bird on to a branch, for I know of nothing which keeps me back or attaches me to the world. Neither should the past have any more power to enchain me. Hardly has it left one memory too many on my conscience; apart from which my life is much like that of a child. You know me, my dear Maurice, but you have not been aware of this, you never suspected that I was sometimes sad to tears from pangs of conscience without knowing why or being able to cure myself of them. To-day I am happy, because I have been to the Communion; I notice with admiration how powerful a remedy it proves, and that, according to the expression of St. François de Sales, I feel that I have Jesus Christ in my heart, my mind, my spirit, in all my being. May this calm endure! Then everything is in health, soul and body; and poetry, too, comes back to me. It is only in times of peace that I *sing*. Do you understand this, dear friend?

---

To MDLLE. ANTOINETTE DE BOISSET, at Lisle-d'Albi.

*November*, 1834.

Your sentence is pronounced, my dear Antoinette, but do not be alarmed, it is not a very rigorous one. How be severe with you, my fair suppliant, when you come and tell me a hundred tender things, and then throw your arms round my neck as though leaving the case to the discretion of my friendship? With such a criminal, justice resigns at once and lets the heart decide. Thus, then, it becomes the judge, and your cause is gained. A two months' silence, apparent forgetfulness, indifference, everything that cried against you, is hushed; I only hear what you are telling me now. Thanks, my dear friend, thanks, a thousand times, for this charming return of remembrance, this pretty waking up of friendship, which has given me so much pleasure in my solitude. Did not you know that I was alone, and that nothing passed by but a few crows, my only diversion? Happily you have come to me at last, and I lay upon your conscience those sweetest wanderings of thought you have occasioned me in prayer, for I was going to my *chapel* when your letter was given to me, and you certainly followed me there.

I pity you most sincerely for having lost your Elix. I quite understand how painful this separation must have been, and how many regrets so amiable a child must occasion you all, but especially you who seemed to me his favourite sister. Have you heard from him; and how does he get on with his new master and his seminary life? Poor little fellow! Does he wear a cassock? I should like to look at him; never could the Church have a prettier figure. You must be very impatient to see him again. I admire Madame de Boisset's courage in consenting to the sacrifice thus early, but God who has made a mother's heart so tender makes it also very strong. A sister's is like it, is it not?

I have often felt this, and hope to repeat the experience if I live a year, for Maurice has just written me word that he will come in the month of August. I am already counting, and the months seem long; but meanwhile the days glide away, and *that* day will come at length. After so many events, you will understand what pleasure it must be to see the poor exile again: for is it not indeed an exile for young men to be separated from their family, from home, where one is so happy? What place in the world can be a substitute for home? I know none; it is true that I have not extended myself far, and that a mole-hill seems to me a mountain; but it's all the same, the little teaches us what the great must be. I am content with the happiness of home; and have enjoyed it to my heart's content for a whole year during which I have hardly stirred hence, but just now I am without Marie. What a blank she leaves! God forbid that it should be for ever! At table, in the drawing-room, the kitchen, my own room, the Cahuzac road, everywhere I miss her. She is at Gaillac with our cousins, where they treat her in a manner calculated to make her stay there long.

You ask me about my chickens: I am still fond of them, and prove it by leaving you a while to go and give them their supper. They have all good appetites, have my dear little chicks, but one came up with a broken leg. The poor thing moved my pity—there it is in the infirmary till it gets well, that is, in the kitchen, where I shall pay it as many visits as a doctor. You will laugh at me, but I am fond of living creatures—dogs, poultry, pigeons—of all animals except those that are big and fat, and in no way appeal to the heart.

You want to know my life, dear Antoinette. It is always the same, much taken up with a thousand household nothings, sometimes in making soup. We have got a cook of sixteen years old; the old one has left us, and is going to take to herself a master to beat her, I much fear; but that is her affair, ours is to prepare our dinner. I am rather fond of doing so, the kitchen chimney-corner and the fragrance of the saucepans have a charm of their own. However that may be, I like them, especially when I have little Peter for a turnspit. He is a rather pretty child, who amuses me by the questions he puts. One evening when I was hearing him his Catechism he stopped me short to ask me whether the soul was immortal, and, soon after, what a philosopher was, and when I replied that it was some one wise and learned, " Then, Mademoiselle, you are a philosopher." This was said in such droll innocent good faith that my Catechist gravity was upset for the evening; I thought I should have died of laughing. What gave him that philosophical conception of me was his seeing me open a large book and my knowing the Catechism by heart.

Such are my winter evenings and their amusements, very innocent ones doubtless, and having their pleasing side. After dinner I generally go and pay a visit to new-born lambs, tell them they are pretty, and bid them grow as fast as they can; but then I see all this alone, and that deprives it of half its value; every pleasure should be shared. At the head of all I place the pleasures I derive from the letters of friends; I prefer them even to lambs, but I enjoy them more rarely. One would say that Antoinette especially wants to accustom me to waiting, but my heart is too impatient. This is not a scolding, 'tis a complaint that I make just as I leave you, in order that out of compassion you may return the sooner.

To M. Maurice de Guérin, Paris.

1834.

An unexpected courier on his way to Albi reminds me of our deputy, who you tell us will willingly take charge of our letters. This will be a short one, an abridgment, a nothing that I write in galloping haste while waiting for Délern, our messenger. Papa came in breathless from Pausadou to announce the opportunity, and here are our pens set going, Mimi one side, I the other. She is replying to thy letter of the day before yesterday, and I merely mean to add a word or two to mine of Friday. The time is short; I should like to write to Louise by the same messenger, which will make me rob thee of a few minutes. You will not be angry at that, and besides, what could I tell thee to-day that I have not told thee a hundred times? I get tedious, I repeat, I am like old people, going over the same ground in the evening that I did in the morning.

But here is something new, a reproach; don't be frightened, 'tis rather a complaint. I wanted to tell thee that thy letter to Mimi would have given her much more pleasure if it had been somewhat longer and did not need the addition of a thousand things that are always wanting in thy letters. Is it thy fault, or that of thy man's heart? Ours, methinks, is more skilled in matters of affection, does not wait to be asked for kind words and all one likes to see in a friendly correspondence. These poor brothers, we spoil them, we are too fond of them; we are so fond of them, that it seems an impossibility to them to feel the same for us. But I intend to correct myself, and, instead of the long epistles I used to write thee, thou shalt have nothing but abridgments. This is a resolution taken till you write to me according to my fancy. Adieu, therefore, to the little journal: of what use is it? It does not make you write to me at greater length. Nothing for nothing. I am never to know a word about your life, because, say you, you would be carried on so far that I should get tired of following you. Where could you go then, were it to the ends of the earth, that I should not arrive there with you? It is nothing but a pretext, the excuse of idleness, or of a little frosty heart.

Now you will begin to be angry and to complain, but why then do you write so briefly? But for this letter to Mimi I should tell you much prettier things, sweeter at least, for I have not much bitterness in my soul, and already my mood softens. This poor Maurice, who loves us no doubt, what do I require of him, what would I have? Instead of thanking him for all he is now doing I am sending him a scolding. That is not right. There, then, I say no more; let us embrace and all is over.

How rich you are again, my friend, with your eighteen hundred francs! God be praised, and blessed be thy friends and that good M. Buquet. Be very sure that Papa no longer forms hasty judgments about them, and that we are all gratitude for what they have done for thee. Has thy dear Lefebvre anything to do with thy good fortune? You know how much I liked that friend. And those in Brittany, are we never to hear any more of them? Pray send me a word or two on that head, and do not omit La Chênaie if you know anything about it. Do you suppose that I forget it? Oh, no! but I never think of the fallen angel without a feeling at the heart that I cannot express. Tell us what he is doing. Here they say that he *grumbles* against Rome in his solitude, and has just published his 'Philosophy;' but, however, our papers have said nothing of this. True, however, we only see the poor little 'Gazette de Languedoc,' which gives nothing but mere gossip. Here is Délem. Adieu, my dear friend; I love you always, and have only time to assure Félicité and her family of all my affection.

---

To Mdlle. Louise de Bayne, Rayssac.

*2nd January*, 1835.

Do not look upon what I wrote to you on Sunday as a letter, my dear Louise. It was a mere chance word or two given to a person who came from Albi to go back at once. But whether long or short, I snatch the pleasure of writing whenever I can, I do not say whenever I will, —that would be often, every moment, always, but life cannot get spent in enjoyment; a thousand things parcel it out; one has not too much time for housekeeping, walks, stockings, the distaff, a little reading, prayer, sometimes writing. But I write little, the least possible, except to you, dear friend. To love you and to tell you so ranks among my occupations; there you are classed with all sorts of things, for who knows all that I do and think in one day? One has so much time for thought in the country! However occupied one may be, 'tis with nothing that engrosses the mind, which works away on its own account like a mill-wheel. Let us try to make it turn to some purpose, give it good grain to grind, it yields us what we intrust to it; let our memory be filled with beautiful things, and our thoughts will be beautiful. Imagination takes the hue of what it dwells on.

I left you there the day before yesterday, my dear friend, to give luncheon to a woman who had come to my room to wish me a happy new year. After having thanked her, and talked, and chattered about *time flying*, she made me a curtsy, and I came back to think of you. But I could not write, a thousand things kept me away from my room. Yesterday I passed the morning in grease, opening and cutting up our geese with Marie. In the evening we went to Cahuzac, and on our return were occupied with reading a long and very kind letter from Brittany. It was full of tenderness and affection, too much so perhaps for a stranger; but I am none the less grateful; one is always pleased to be loved, above all, gratuitously. Madame de La Morvonnais has been long ill, which has prevented her writing to me. She tells me of M. de Lamennais, whom she has been to see; "Never," she writes, "did he seem more cheerful or more agreeable." He took them all through the walks his disciples had made for him through the woods, and beside the ponds; each tree, each blade of grass was the subject of some lofty thought or some memory. He also insisted on showing them the spot chosen for his tomb beside the little chapel. "Seeing him so fragile," she says, "one trembled at the idea that a trifle might lay him in the place he pointed out so cheerfully." He is there alone with one of his pupils who has not forsaken him, occupied entirely with his great work on philosophy, which is to be published in two years, a work from which great good is hoped. "God grant it!" This is the only reflection added by this visitor of La Chênaie.

I could have wished her to have told me something different, and that she should have found the poor wanderer in less mirthful mood. My God! to have the thunders of the Church on one's head, and yet to smile, and say, "I was never happier!" This pains one, pains one much. We shall never see him return. And yet all his friends are abandoning him: there is M. de Montalembert, who has just given in his adhesion to the Encyclical. I have one anxiety on this head, I am afraid Maurice's eyes are not yet opened. It would indeed be unfortunate if with all his good qualities he ran his head into error. The errors of the intellect are fatal, still more dangerous than those of the heart. May God preserve us from all and keep us in the right road! There are a thousand ways of erring, a thousand occasions of falling, which should keep us on our guard, for alas! we are so weak! A mere nothing sways us like a blade of grass. Poor human heart! always falling on one side or other: now 'tis sadness, now joy, now the world, now solitude; everything has its dangers, and Christian life is spent in alarms.

Am I wrong to look upon it in this light? Tell me, my dear, you have every right over my soul. Do not you consider it too fearful? I am told so, and I found it out when I thought you no longer loved me because I did not sufficiently know how to make myself loved. But that's over, let us leave our old sorrows to rest. I am going to take a turn in the kitchen.

Sunday is a day of dispersion, and I am often left guardian during the morning, after my return from the early mass to which I often go. To-day it was to write to you that I got up by candlelight, being anxious to profit by an opportunity of sending to Albi this afternoon. When the mass was over, I came as fast as ever I could to tell you of my affection. So it was on Sunday, only I was in too great a hurry to say much. Still 'twas happiness to me, short though it was, to meet with an opportunity—a very rare thing just now.

Adieu, my dear! I must leave you, always too soon. Twelve is striking, they are returning from mass, dinner must be got ready, my letter leaves after it. I shall write to you at greater length for the fair. To-day good bye; an embrace as my new year's gift to the two hermits. I did not forget you in my new year's prayers. Few words and many thoughts, this is all I give you.

## To the Same.

*9th February,* 1835.

We are at Cahuzac, besieged by rain, and, while waiting for the horses to arrive, I seat myself at the desk of a notary to write to you so as to send you a remembrance by M. Bories, who sets out to-morrow for Albi. The good Father sent for me yesterday to give me a parcel, it was your letter. This dear friend, how she loves me! That was what I read on the address, and my heart responded with infinite tenderness, while I held your letter on my knees, and chatted with M. Bories. I spent a delightful hour with him, but once in my aunt's great dark room my sadness returned, and I began weeping again for a dear friend of Maurice's, who is just dead. I shall never write more to that kind affectionate Madame de La Morvonnais, of whom I spoke to you the other day. Even then she was dying, and my letter will reach her tomb to-day or to-morrow.

Her poor husband is heartbroken, but, being profoundly religious, he bears his anguish with resignation and offers his sacrifice to God. Nothing but religion can enable him to support a sad desolate life, disenchanted of all its former charms. There he is all alone with his little Marie, who is only two years old. Maurice writes me these sad tidings out of an aching heart, telling me that this death turns all his thoughts to that other world where one after another all our affections go. My God! how can one cling to life when one sees it depart so rapidly? This young woman was taken away out of the midst of a family gathering, while she was chatting and laughing as people do when they are happy. She was so, beloved by her husband and every one who knew her.

My dear Louise, I am really afflicted, and look with tears at those few letters she wrote me so cordially. Farewell to tidings of Brittany, La Chênaie, and so many things that I took pleasure in hearing of. How I wish I had never begun a correspondence that death has so soon broken! But what is there it does not break? Do we not know that little by little everything leaves, everything escapes us, except eternal affection? M. Bories was telling us this very eloquently yesterday in his sermon upon perseverance addressed to the children about to attend their first Communion. The ceremony was as beautiful as it could be at Cahuzac, where everything except the Curé is small. I do not tell you of my emotions during the ceremony, 'twas something too intimate, too heavenly to be expressed. My dear friend, I thought of you, that too was heavenly; I prayed God to make you happy; to give you more and more love for Him, to preserve you to my friendship. With you, Louise, I can console myself for all my griefs. In your letters, your affection, your heart, I find all I need in all the situations of life. Thanks then, and ever more thanks, for these proofs of your remembrance. I am just going out of the office for a minute or two to repeat the Angelus.

I resume by the kitchen fire; the inkstand in a niche for matches, and Azor, my aunt's pet, at my feet. This would amuse me if I were not in so sad a mood. Without ever having seen her, I now see that poor dead friend everywhere. 'Tis that I had her in my heart, with all her goodness, tenderness, affection for me.

I shall fill my page with regrets, and I have sweeter things to say when I think of your friendship, amply sufficient as it is to console me for all others that come to an end. Together with this mournful letter came another, also from Brittany in the first instance, but only sent there on its way to me from the Isle of France. It was from my cousin De Roquefeuil, who writes me the most interesting details from his corner of the world. I wish I could read it to you, I should be sure to give you a pleasant half-hour in listening to it. You shall see it if I come.

Here is my inkstand wanted. When I have everything of my own about me in the little room, I shall spend more time in telling you that I love you.

I look upon you as very wise, very resigned in your solitude with Léontine. Take me in between you, at the fireside, under the limes, wherever you may go, for everywhere I follow you. My very tender regards to the traveller and to your companion. Marie embraces you, and I repeat that all my heart is in yours. Good bye, I am going to carry my letter to the parsonage. A shower has detained me, but I have no more paper.

To MDLLE. IRÈNE COMPAYRE.

*Saturday,* 14*th February,* 1835.

Only see, dear Irène, how different our days are! On Saturday a funeral letter came to me written at the very same hour as the rose-coloured letter I have just been reading. I admire how God sends consolation to succeed tears. Here I am, less sad, now that you have laid your affection on my heart; 'tis a very soothing balm for which I am full of gratitude because it has done me good. Your friendship and that of Antoinette, who also has written to me, have made me for a moment forget that I have a friend less on earth; I feel that with your affection I might dispense with all others, but I do not the less weep for what has just ended. No, it is not ended; the soul must depart with its affections, and my poor Marie must love me in heaven as she did on earth. This hope which immortalises our feelings is very sweet. Oh how the heart that would fain love always, rests in it! Accordingly it is to satisfy this need that God wills we should love Him, for He is the only friend we do not see die, and neither do we lose those that we love in Him. This is what makes me hope for a happy reunion in Paradise, where I shall have you, my dear Irène, and very near me too.

If I have not spoken to you of this friend who has just died, 'tis because you did not know her, and she lived very far away. She was attacked by brain fever in the midst of a cheerful conversation with a circle of friends and relatives, without even being aware of her danger.

She was hardly twenty-six; and leaves a heartbroken husband, and a little girl who is only two. The poor child not long ago sent me a kiss in one of her mother's letters; all these recollections are sad, and yet I like them, and go over them one by one. I do not know what it is that makes what death has consecrated dearer than ever. My dear friend, forgive this mournful strain that I fall into to-day in writing to you; I let myself run on and have no disguises with you.

I approve your charity which preserved you from a hasty judgment when you saw M. Limer arrive empty-handed. Any one else would have called me idle, and scolded me as I sometimes have you, dear friend. In this you teach me a lesson of indulgence which I shall remember with many others that I owe to your friendship; not, indeed, that I mean to allow myself to be guilty, this would be false humility; I did not know of our Pastor's journey, else I should have written to you, as well as to the angel. Truly that Antoinette is as you say a heavenly being, and to me to see her at church was like a vision of Paradise. I recall, too, as a very happy memory, the chapel companion with whom I used sometimes to tell my beads. 'Tis two years ago, yet it seems to me yesterday, so present is it to my heart, and so fast, too, do the days glide away.

Your carnival enjoyments are charming; they would be mine exactly, for I am not fonder than you of those whirlwinds of company that sweep the soul off no one knows where. Our evenings too pass very quietly, in reading, and caressing Trilby, our little pet; when one has no other diversion one takes to the distaff, and the little whirr of the spindle amuses one; in the country, my dear, one grows clever in devising pastimes.

To-day we have mud, rain, cold north-east wind, a winter day that prevents the pilgrimage you wot of. You see, my dear friend, that my zeal *does not brave everything*, not even a little rain. If you knew me better you would form a very different judgment of one whom so small a thing keeps back! Do not be afraid of my catching cold in our wet roads, where I never walk but from necessity when God wills I should, and then my health is under the care of his providence. And, moreover, I do not think one should lay such stress upon health as to become its slave, or to provide for the body's comfort at the expense of the soul. Decidedly, my dear, I quite approve your theology; even M. Bories refers to it.

---

To Mdlle. Antoinette de Boisset.

*14th February*, 1835.

I have just been writing to Irène, and with my pen still tinged with friendship I resolve to tell you, too, my dear Antoinette, that I love you and thank you for your most affectionate and sweet letter which reached me this morning. It gave me much pleasure, first of all because I delight in news of you, and next because it did me good, being as I am in such affliction about the death of a friend suddenly snatched from us. We lost her by one of those lightning strokes, the very possibility of which we always refuse to believe in for those we love, as though our affection consecrated the heads on which it rested and could avert death from them. Alas! how often it does the very reverse! God permits this, to detach us from all beside Himself, and to teach us that happiness has no abiding-place here below. This poor friend had just written to me; she was cheerful, told me of her plans, was occupied with the future as the young and happy are. When I think of this, and of my letter finding her in her coffin, I shed many tears. Even if she had had time to prepare for death! but it came so suddenly, so unexpectedly! It was in the midst of a lively conversation, in a party of friends and relatives, that this poor young woman was seized with brain fever, which carried her off in two days without her being aware hardly that she was dying. I ask you, my dear Antoinette, for a prayer for her soul; regrets are not enough before God. Every one can weep, but we do not all know how to pray, and therefore one appeals to those holy souls who can make themselves heard of God. Pray then, my dear friend, for my friend.

I was thinking of you just as I got your letter, and wanted to write to send you messages, dated last August, which have just arrived from the Isle of France. The good cousin tells us all sorts of kind things. These are for all of you: "Do not forget to remember me to the De Boissets; knowing them as you do, you can judge how much attached to them I am. If I were with you, I should make you go oftener to Lisle, where I had such pleasure in accompanying you once." Then he goes on to mention a hundred pleasant recollections which have followed him from your drawing-rooms to his island. Poor man! he has great need that some cheerful memories should divert him from his anxieties; there he is reduced to poverty by the expenses of his journey, and the sad state of the colony; 'tis a lost country in every respect.

M. de Roquefeuil and all his family desire nothing so much as to get away from it, but they have less hope of this than ever. It is in the month of February that the negroes begin to enjoy their liberty and will show us what free men are. I thought I should please you, my dear Antoinette, by this sample of the letter of our cousin who loves you. I wish I could read it to you; you would not find it tedious though long, you would find both charm and feeling there. This poor cousin is all heart; there is a tender "Memento" for the Canoness as well. Have you any tidings of her? Here no one knows whether she is in this world or the next.

Would one not say I was forgetting you in this review of the world? Not a word yet about yourself, and yet I have a great deal to say, and cause, too, to be angry. This surprises you; but why do you begin by scolding me, my dear, without my knowing why? If I said any harm of my own letters I am not aware of it; and besides, have I not a right to run them down without your charity taking offence and constituting itself their champion? However, I willingly submit to your authority, and receive your sentence whatever it be, even if it consign me to prison; only do not banish me, that is all I ask; I want to preserve the hope of seeing you again.

It will not, however, be this carnival, as you are kind enough to wish. We shall probably spend it at home in our accustomed pleasures; amidst which I count that of the distaff of which you revived the idea. Since your letter came I have spun two spindlefuls, and really I found, as you do, that 'tis impossible for time to hang heavy while one is spinning. As to that, 'tis an old pleasure, that you have awakened, with which I was familiar at the age of six, when I indulged in it at the expense of a canvas door in which I made a hole to extract its stuffing.

Have you taken the journey to Albi? What say you of the forge and the terrifying *Saut de Sabo?* No doubt Mdlle. Laure will only go to Gascony in fine weather; I should not advise her to travel in winter; the wet roads are dangerous, except for *invulnerables* like you. Since when have you so presumed upon health? I think Irène says the same thing, but do not neglect yourself on that account; spare your strength that you may always be able to feel well. No doubt you will soon have news of Elix; is he already learning Latin? Adieu! I show great dependence upon your friendship in sending you this packet of words and bad paper; but I have no other, and then you have told me you are not hard to please; to-day I am going to put this to the proof. My love to your sister and your friends. Adieu, dear Antoinette.

P.S.—You acquit yourself so well of the commissions intrusted to you that I am going to trouble you further with my remembrances to Mdlle. de Sainte Colombe, to whom I am much attached. Say so to her, I beg, you who say everything so well. Again adieu! As last word, let me embrace you.

---

To M. HIPPOLYTE DE LA MORVONNAIS, Val de l'Arguenon.

*17th February,* 1835.

How my last letter must have wrung your heart! This one will not console you. I write you nothing but tears; but I want to weep with you, leaving it to God to comfort and be Himself everything to you, since He has taken everything away. Each day I pray to Him for you, I ask Him to pour on your wound the heavenly balm that alone can do it any good. What can we do for afflicted friends? When Jesus was sorrowful unto death, an angel appeared, comforting him. May that same angel support and strengthen you, for your cup is bitter indeed!

God has willed it: His will be done! This sublime expression is yours, in the anguish of your sacrifice; it is mine, too; I repeat it weeping! How many tears I shed in thinking of you, of your little Marie, of her mother who loved me! How dear to me her friendship was, and how deeply the tokens of it that I received touched my heart! Nothing can efface them any more than the memory of her. I shall always recollect her, and that her sweet spirit bent down to me to love me. How much I loved her, too, and what a delight I took in our correspondence!

O my God! and must all this be at an end? Must there be no longer any relations between her soul and mine, and all those who were dear to her? This cannot be, for heaven is the abode of love and immortal affection. Thus then our dear one loves us as she did on earth; she hears our prayers, she sees our tears, and communicates to us something of Paradise. There is no such great distance between her and us. A little time separates us from those who depart—a time of tears, a time of sadness and solitude; but, that over, we go to rejoin them and to enjoy with them the society of the blessed. Oh, how sweetly the heart rests in this immortal hope! how it hushes its sobs to listen to the voice that says, "I am in heaven!"

You have doubtless heard this voice which tells you that your beloved Marie is happy, that her soul has been transported out of her pure bosom to that of God. This is the only thing that can calm your regrets and give you strength to endure a withered, broken, devastated life. Will you continue at Val? What must that solitude be to you now that she who filled it with the charms of her heart, her mind, her whole personality, has carried these all away with her! How I pity you! how many tears I give you! I weep over your little child. How I should like to take her on my knees and rock her as her mother did! She would get almost as fond of me, and then I should return her those kisses that the poor child once sent me in a letter, every word of which will be for me a regretful memory. I shall carefully preserve that letter as the last token of a precious friendship, the last utterance of a soul about to leave me.

What a heartrending surprise it was when Maurice announced this loss; I was so far from dreaming of it! But this is to trench too much on sorrowful recollections: let us confine ourselves to prayer. I could not help sending you some evidence of my grief and that of my family. The blow that has fallen upon you has echoed in our hearts, and plunged Cayla into mourning as well as Val, for Cayla belongs to you, as you once told me under happier circumstances; and thus encouraged, we would fain hope to see you here. You would be received as a brother, and perhaps our friendship, our beautiful sky, our soft air, would do your sorrow good.

Adieu, Monsieur! receive the assurance of my pure affection and of all the sentiments that I entertained for your other self.

---

To MDLLE. LOUISE DE BAYNE.

*30th March,* 1835.

In order not to lose an opportunity of writing to you, I take advantage of a half-hour afforded me by a flour-dealer from the direction of Albi, who will carry this as soon as he can to Gosse, for I fear to overwhelm M. Mathieu, to whom so lately as last Monday I sent a letter from Cahuzac, where we were. My dear friend, 'tis not you that I fear to tire out, but our post-offices.

Be that as it may, however, let us go on writing, 'tis a case in which charity begins at home.

To write to you I break off in the midst of a letter of condolence to that poor M. Morvonnais—a sad letter to plan and indite. What can be said to console under such grief? One feels that human speech is inadequate; hence I address it to heaven. It is a comfort to be able, in such cases, to employ religious consolations with a hope of being listened to. The man of the world hears, indeed, but does not understand you, for the language of piety is not to be learned all at once, and it is piety that is needed then; what is called religious sentiment is too vague, penetrates the soul too little to be able to comfort it.

My dear friend, see how different days are! On Saturday I was reading a rose-coloured letter, full of gaiety and details of festivals, written on the very same day and hour as the funeral letter of which I told you. There you have life strewn alike with tears and pleasures.

The cheerful letter was from Lisle, from our amiable Antoinette, and there was another from Irène, who has written to me twice without my replying. This zeal on the part of good Irène touches me. Really, people are too fond of me; I should not know what to do with so much affection, if ever affection could be burdensome. But I do not think it can: my heart feels only too comfortable in the midst of so many pretty nets that surround it, only I fear that it will cost me too great an effort to part with them when the time for parting comes. The sweeter our ties the more we must cling to them, and we ought, if possible, to be free at the moment of leaving earth for heaven. You alone, Louise, are enough to make me wish to live always. Let us both try, you to be less loveable, I to love you less: that is, let us do the impossible.

The young dinner-party at Madame Combes' must have been charming. It was a pretty gathering of attractions, Pulchérie at their head. I know Mdlle. Gaujon, and used to see her sometimes during my last year's stay at Albi. She is one of those I should like to see more of; I delighted in her lively, intelligent expression, her sweet speaking eyes. Without being beautiful, I admired her more than the beautiful R——, who wants grace in her beauty, though for the rest gentle as an angel—a quality still more beautiful than grace. I rub out the name, not knowing into whose hands this letter may fall; when one writes, prudence should always hold the pen. Let me take the occasion of paying you a compliment, for you have made great advances in this virtue; your letters might almost be seen without any risk, they contain nothing but what is pretty, what pleases all the world.

If I were less hurried I would transcribe for you some portion of M. de Roquefeuil's letter, which would give you an interest in his part of the world. He speaks besides of Abbé Delmont, who still makes himself revered at Bourbon, and of Abbé de Solages, who died on his mission to Madagascar—poisoned, it is supposed. What men these are who go and get killed for the salvation of a few savages! This alone should make us fervent—we who have so little to do—in at least saving our own souls, since we have only ourselves to save. I don't know, my dear friend, whether you may not find me too much given to preaching, after the manner of your *capettes*, who are always scolding people. It is not, however, that I scold; 'tis that my thoughts naturally betake themselves to the serious side of things, and I let them have their way.

How do you stand with Alex? It is possible that I may see her soon. My father means to go to Caylux, and wishes to take me with him. It will be a week's excursion. I shall not see without some degree of pleasure a good old Chevalier of that part of the country, who was very fond of me ten years ago. They will have it he is fond of me still, and so too am I rather fond of him, despite of time, for I am so through gratitude and veneration for his fourscore years. Adieu, my friend! I think that Marie tells you the news of the world, I confine myself to that of the heart. What would you like me to say to Alex, if I see her? I embrace Léontine and the traveller, however far off she may be. My respects, too, to M. de Bayne. Adieu! the sacks are filled. That pretty Criquet! has he ever dined upon your hand, like Trilby on fried brains off mine? It was to soften his tongue, and afterwards give you a kiss with it.

TO THE SAME.

*18th July*, 1835.

When I wrote to you the day before yesterday how little I thought of the sad event that has just taken place! I had not seen my grandmother for three days, and believed her to be better; but on Thursday I found her very much weaker, so much so that she could hardly breathe or say a word to us. My aunt, Marie, and I held a consultation, and determined to speak to her about confession. She had no objection to it, but put us off till the morrow. My God! who is there that does not depend upon life? Hers was on the point of dying out. We took leave of her by pressing her hand. That was the last time. At nine o'clock that evening she had fainting fits. The doctor announced danger, and pressed M. the Abbé to administer the last Sacraments. You know that M. the Curé is absent: this absence is unfortunate for us under more than one respect. At last she confessed, received the Viaticum, Extreme Unction, and the Last Indulgence, and all was over.

There she is before God, that grandmother we had! Thus one after another we vanish from earth—a small misfortune, if we all meet in heaven again to form one family there. I think of my mother who preceded us all sixteen years ago. My poor mother, who loved us so fondly, when shall we go and rejoin her? I wish it might be soon. What have we to expect in this world? Sorrows, tears, tombs. But oh, my God! how holy, how pure one must be to enter heaven! When this thought occurs, we no longer want to die, because of the need of expiation we recognise in ourselves, and so we remain bound to life like the criminal to his chain. The misfortune is that one goes on sinning, and that in growing older one grows no better. The *Imitation* tells us so: " A long life does not always avail to correct us." Rather the reverse. How sad to retrograde in the way to heaven! All other advancement is indifferent to me; but here I would have wings, would outstrip everything, at least my faults, at least one of them. This is no easy matter; one can get rid of a limb sooner than of one's cherished imperfections.

My mother was a perfect woman: accordingly, I believe her among the blessed. Besides, she suffered so much, and with such resignation! I cannot recall a single complaint, but still see that always calm and smiling face that then I could not comprehend. I used to say to myself that she did not seem in pain, and that no doubt it was nothing serious, that she would not die as they said; and how great my mistake, poor child that I was!

My grandmother was nearly eighty years of age. That long life had its full share of evil days. My dear friend, let us pray that she may be happy now. I give her all my prayers. To-day my father, Marie, Erembert— the whole household, in short—are at Cahuzac, and accompany that poor mother. I think of all that is going on; I hear hymns, prayers; I am a coffin. They would not take me with them: I had depended upon being alone and doing what I liked with myself, but

Hippolyte de Thézac arrived, so there was talk to be carried on and a dinner to be got ready without any assistance for poor me. Finally, we dined tête-à-tête at one o'clock, I being servant and mistress both. When the servant had done her work, the mistress went to sleep. I was tired, overdone, heavy, only fit to throw myself upon the bed; I left it to write to you. The letter that M. de Bayne must have received was not enough for me, I wanted to write to you as well. I tell you my joys and sorrows; all that crosses my heart reaches you.

You see very well that I cannot come to see you. But for this I was, as it seemed, to have set out next week. A sad result of the sad event; it will not be the only one, but for me it is none of the least.

---

To M. H. DE LA MORVONNAIS, Val de l'Arguenon, near Plancoët (Côtes du Nord).

Cayla, 28*th July*, 1835.

Did you imagine, Monsieur, that I should not write to you any more? O how mistaken you would have been! It was your journey to Paris, and, after that, other obstacles, which prevented my speaking to you earlier of Marie. But we will speak of her to-day; yes, let us speak of her, always of her; let her be always betwixt us. It is for her sake I write to you : first of all, because I love her and find it sweet to recall her memory; and then, because it seems to me that she is glad you should sometimes hear terms of expression that *vividly recall her*. I come, then, to remind you of that sacred resemblance so sweet to myself when it strikes you. How I bless God for having bestowed it upon me, and thus enabled me to do you some good! This shall be my mission with regard to you, and with what delight shall I fulfil it!

Do not say that there is any merit or act of profound charity in this acceptation. My heart goes out quite naturally towards those who weep, and I am happy as an angel when I can console. You tell me that your life will no longer have any bright side, that I can elicit nothing from you but sadness. I know this; but can that estrange me—I, who loved the Marie you weep? Ah! yes; let us weep over her; lean on me the while, if you will. To me it is not painful to receive tears: not that my heart is strong, as you believe, only it is Christian, and finds at the foot of the cross enough to enable it to support its own sorrows and those of others. Marie did the same . . . . let us seek to imitate the saints. You will teach this to your daughter beside the cross on that grave whither you often lead her. Poor little one! how I should like to see her, to accompany her in that pilgrimage to that tomb beside the sea, and under the pines, to pray, to weep there, to take her on my knees and speak to her of heaven and of her mother. This would be a joy to me: you know that there are melancholy ones.

Will you bring me your little girl? O do bring her to me, since I cannot come to Brittany. I want to see her, to enjoy her intelligence, her caresses, all her infantine charms. Bring her to me; I want to enjoy this sweet little creature, who belongs to me because I love and because God gave me her mother. Do you consent to the adoption, and to my giving your child a maternal affection, as it were? Her mother loved me, I love her; this love will only have changed heart. Tell me of her progress in every way, and if she still speaks of going to join her mother. Poor child! 'tis when she is older that she will especially feel this desire. Once more to see her mother is the sweet thought which remains to the orphan till heaven opens at last. But that time is, perhaps, distant for your Marie, and till then who knows? . . . . . Jesus himself only entered upon his rest after having followed the long way to Calvary. All we Christians, great and small, walk in his train, each bearing his cross. Yours is very heavy: I cannot contemplate it except while praying for you. It seems to me my prayer helps you. Nor is this an excess of faith, since God tells us that prayer is so powerful; and besides, I can understand nothing so well as prayer. For me to pray means to believe, to love, to hope. Therefore I pray for you, your child, and Marie, at the Angelus of every evening; 'tis the hour when I think of the dead, ever more and more numerous as they become.

   I have not told you that I am again in mourning, that I have lost my grandmother. She left us ten days ago, and went away to join almost her whole family. My father is the only survivor of all her children. There she is now happy with the others in heaven. O how blessed we Christians are, we cannot lose each other! We weep over our departed, but we hope; we weep, but we look up to heaven. My family commission me to inform you of this sad event, as well as to express their desire that you should visit Cayla. Come here to console the afflicted; come here to pray with us. Yes; let us all, relations and friends, pray for our mother. Let us pray: it is now our best form of tenderness, the true tenderness of Christians.

How did the Val strike you on your return? As a tomb, no doubt; and there you are settled in it for ever! And your brothers come and visit you in that mournful Thebaid! Maurice goes on writing to you: what do you think of his soul? It strikes me as depressed, without any misfortune to make it so. It is a vague depression, a sickly condition that enervates the soul, enfeebles it, and at length kills, if it do not struggle against its disease; but it requires help in this, and I tell Maurice to apply for it to God like a good and pious Christian. He is religious, and yet complains! Oh, if he could but pray! If I only knew that he did so! Tell him that no one is religious without prayer; no, nor happy either; tell him so, you to whom he listens so readily. Tell him what you do, tell him what consoles you who have so wept. Let him join himself to you. Let us look up, all we who feel the anguish of life and the bitterness of tears. See, the heavens are so near us we only need to lift our eyes to see them. Blessed be God, who has thus surrounded us with hope and brought our happiness within our view!

Adieu! Monsieur. I embrace your little daughter, and pray you ever to believe me the tender and faithful friend of her mother.

---

To MDLLE. LOUISE DE BAYNE.

*30th July,* 1835.

I wanted to write to you the day before yesterday; I wanted to write to you yesterday, my very dear one, but visitors took up all my time, and it was only in thought that I could think of you. I like, you know, to think in speech. What is it you are going to see? I have no idea. I am tempted to write, and keep this paper; it might be put over a pot of jam or mend some broken panes: it would then be useful. But in that case you would not know that I love you. Oh, yes, you do know it. But you would not read my affection of the day: I mean the tenderness flowing from the heart to this paper, that conveys it to you like a small canal. Let it reach you then, reach you as soon as possible. I am impatient of postal delays now, I should like to find a bird.

Do you know that I have some cause for being impatient? first, about this letter I am writing, and then to know the state of things in Paris. Yesterday a passer-by told me that there had been explosions, deaths, dreadful disturbances there. We know nothing about it, but my father, who saw the despatch at Cahuzac, assures us it is true. Therefore here we are again in anxiety. What a misfortune to have brothers, friends, on that volcano of a

Paris! And we know nothing of Maurice, and the postman does not come. He ought to have been here, and the whole of to-day I am expecting him. I wrote last night to Marie, who will, I fancy, be rather better informed of the events of the day. The world might go to pieces without our knowing anything about it here. It is over-much calm at such a period; there are circumstances in which repose does harm.

They say there are many families thrown into mourning in Paris. God grant that we may not have any one to weep! The mourning we are in already is quite enough. In connexion with this let me tell you, my friend, how sensible I am of the tender interest you show for me and for each one of us. Your sweet sympathy—the sweetest I have received—did me good like a balm from heaven. 'Tis that your words do flow thence as well as your true and beautiful tenderness; the beautiful and the true come from God. Thus your friendship is a celestial gift to me, and so is the kind little letter now before me. I can see in it that you are sad on my account, that you have prayed for me, that you are prompt to feel, to weep, to console me. I see in it . . . . Oh! what is there that I do not see? Your whole image, in short, as in a little mirror.

My poor grandmother was old, and her long life had been much chequered; her eyes had shed many tears. But do not let us speak of it. God had, no doubt, permitted it. Let us pray for her: 'tis our best consolation, our best tenderness. Of what use is all besides? I assure you, my own friend, that all that passes seems to me so much vapour; even the affections of our heart, what are they unless we carry them into heaven, unless we raise them up to God? They, too, die. We must love each other, not for this world but the next, where we are to abide; otherwise 'twould be like two travellers attaching themselves to each other just to cross a road. Not worth the while, indeed! My dear Louise, do you not think as I? Oh, yes! I should indeed have valued the gentle teaching of Father Bories, who knows so well how to soothe and strengthen me; but God has deprived me of him, and chosen to leave me, as it were, to myself. I have had full experience of my weakness, my nothingness. My God, what a reed this poor soul of mine! Do not think me overwhelmed with sorrow; it is not that; I am not so sensitive as you suppose; besides, death does not prostrate me, 'tis so natural. We ought to be far more overwhelmed by sin than death. I fear that M. Bories will not be back for the Assumption, and I who love the Festivals of the Virgin shall be much disappointed not to keep this one.

Emilie Vialar and three sisters were to set out last Tuesday to Toulon, on their way to Algeria. There is a beautiful instance of devotedness! Many people call her mad, but almost all the saints have been mad in the eyes of the world. This establishment may do immense good in those countries where Christian charity is as yet unknown. These sisters will take care of the poor, the wounded, will shelter the newborn children that are cast out like dogs. 'Tis M. Augustin who told my father this. He has had the house got ready; when they arrive, the sisters will only have to set to work. The little Rieunier took lessons in dressing wounds from M. Rigal, who himself provided all the apparatus necessary for broken legs and arms.

Adieu! Embrace Léontine and the Countess, whom I see beside you. How happy you are! How did she find the mountain on her return? I know one who would consider it very beautiful. I have a thousand things to say from my father and Marie for you all and for you only.

---

To the Same.

*Cahuzac, 2nd September,* 1835.

Here I am, dear friend, before a little lamp, leaning on a little table, beside the room my grandmother has just left, and thinking of you. Oh, how useful this sweet thought is in somewhat calming the agitation of heart and mind that harasses me! I do not tell you what causes it; you can infer it from the place whence I write to you. Never has any letter that set out hence been like the one I am much inclined to write now; but I restrain myself, and my heart's tendency shall not this time drag me along whither I ought not to go. I bend over to your side: or rather, I am passive in the matter, for it is a natural inclination that costs me little effort. Oh, how happy I am in you, dear Louise!

You will ask me what I am doing at Cahuzac? I overlook the meals of the workmen who are repairing the house, and as cook I have a good old maid, whom I have no trouble in watching. When all is done I work, sew, read, think. Oh! I think much at the sight of that *empty* bed amid these rooms, all in disorder as when one is dislodging. But I must leave you to go and see my aunt. Good night!

I have just come from mass, and return to my little room and to you. It is nine o'clock; the morning passes quickly in church, and I rather enjoy it. Here is a visitor.

It was an Andillac woman married here and my next-door neighbour. I have others who also come to see me, and would like much to see me settle among them. But it is very well for a week and no more, this life of separation, which I do not at all object to, because of its novelty and the small pleasurable excitement that some arrival from Cayla daily gives me. My father generally comes over every afternoon; you cannot think how much pleasure I find in embracing and receiving him *in my own house.* Then I bid him good-bye with sorrow, and fall to thinking gloomily of what a longer separation would prove. I had Marie this morning, and have just accompanied her to the bridge; she will return on Saturday, and Sunday I shall rejoin my family. Delightful return!

This makes me enter into the happiness you have had in seeing Pulchérie again, that dear absentee, so wanted and called for the last nine months by all who cherish her, especially by you. Accordingly, you appear radiant: your letter is one expression of joy. Louise, how well you can love! Love me, and tell it me at some little length, now that you have thoroughly heard and seen and caressed your sister.

Thanks for the letter that shows me your happiness: it does me good to think of it. Those little clouds that sometimes cross your spirit sadden me, as your joys rejoice. But let me always see and know all your moods. Fill the pockets of your mountaineers with those thick packets that I love. It would be a blessing if one of them came to me to-day when I need something loving and loveable to revive me. I have the church at the door; I have Fénélon that I read a little of. This does me good, but it is not enough to keep me calm. Mdlle. d'H—— comes every other day to edify me. She arrives early in church, confesses, and receives the Communion with an angelic look that enchants and disheartens me. How I envy her her soul, and how beautiful to see a young girl of seventeen instruct us in piety! The brothers, too, are little saints; the eldest, who has just been admitted to his first Communion, hears two masses on Sunday and communicates at the first. Is it not very edifying? I was told yesterday that Father T—— was dead. This is possible: he received the Sacraments on Monday, poor man! He returned long since to religious sentiments that much console his family. What but this one hope remains to us, my God, in the long farewell of death? Without the thought of another world I should not comprehend this.

You are free now from the fear of cholera. God be praised! We began to tremble for Rayssac. But you did not mean to leave it; you were bent on dying of the disorder while nursing the sufferers. That was beautiful in the sight of God, but sad for me who should have wept you so bitterly, my dear defunct! Blessed are the dead! you would have been in heaven. With that holy thought, adieu! Adieu! I love you with all my heart, and your sisters also.

---

To the Same.

*May*, 1836.

I arrived a week ago from Gaillac, where I made a halt, after my Lisle retreat. You will look upon me as a great wanderer, my dear Louise, you who live so retired, are such a recluse in your mountains. I am not like you in this respect. Though a solitary, I often leave my desert; I rush into the world, while you no longer appear there. Have we, then, different vocations, and can it be that God, who often inspires us with the same thoughts, bids me to go and you to stay? I know not how it is in your case, but, for my part, I assure you that missions have an irresistible attraction for my spirit, and that I needs must go where I can hear God spoken of.

Antoinette had written, and engaged me to spend with her the week of privileges and instruction that was to precede the planting of the Cross. That was a festive invitation indeed; accordingly I accepted, accordingly I heard Father Gondelin again, accordingly I am one of the congregation by him established, accordingly I have

Saint Agatha de Gelis for President, Augustine for Secretary, Antoinette for Prioress. In short, a thousand spiritual advantages make me bless my pilgrimage to Lisle.

I greatly value, too, the acquaintances I made with persons who know you, and, above all, with a saint who likes me, who loves you, who has conquered and charmed all the "salons" of Lisle by her piety and her wit; who is neither young nor beautiful, but infinitely loveable and good, and unsophisticated—at that you recognise Mdlle. de Gais. I admire the way in which our acquaintance was made at a party where she heard my name: "Does Mademoiselle chance to be the friend of Louise?" As I did not say no to this, came such attentions, compliments, kindnesses, obliging ways; the saint would have ended by spoiling me; each time we met, all this began over again, beginning by speaking of you; the sweet subject led me far, and I enjoyed returning to it so much that I dogged the steps of Mdlle. de Gais; I should like to have had her always with me, I could have put her into my pocket. In short, we love each other, we have even discovered that we are cousins, and said a thousand tender things on that head. If you write to her be sure to tell her that her Cayla cousin preserves the recollection of her very sacredly, and would rejoice to see her again. But there are some of these meetings which never recur in life. It needed a retreat, a Father Gondelin, to bring each of us out of the desert, to come across the other for a moment, that must last us till Paradise perhaps.

I should not, dear friend, like our meeting to be put

off so long; I should be very sad. Whatever charm I may find in a new acquaintance, I always return to the old, to Louise, my earliest friend; it seems to me that I have loved you for a hundred years; so strong, so rooted is my affection, I compare it to an oak, while other affections are reeds.

Shall I tell you everybody I saw in that world of Lisle? These details amuse you, I hope. Oh! I have seen an angel, really an angel in name and face, Angèle de Saint Géry. I was told of her piety, being so admirable and so admired that the holy man cited it from the pulpit. There I also saw Madame ———, full of intellect, oh, yes, full of it to the very tips of her fingers; it is even said that she was once alarmingly clever, but Father Gondelin has changed her, and softened the over-pungency of her wit. If you could hear her speak of the missionary, how fervently, how tenderly she paints him! You see Father Gondelin on her lips, so completely does she reflect his eloquence. Picture to yourself that she goes from one end of Toulouse to the other to hear him say mass. There is enthusiasm; never would my admiration for the first orator in the world take me so far—to hear his prayers, that is to say—for otherwise I would betake myself to the Antipodes to hear a Guyon, a Deguerry, or even a less degree of eloquence.

Apropos of preachers, I admire our own Curé. His style is simple, connected, precise, and touching; our peasants are enchanted, and quite proud of him. Let us hope he may do good. But I shall always regret Françoise, the good and pretty sister of M. Limer.

Since she is gone we find the priest's house empty, and Andillac dull. Accordingly we only stay for church, whereas we used to spend the Sunday there with infinite pleasure. Françoise was gay and witty, and knew how to amuse us by a variety of little stories connected with churches, chapels, and village-life, which she related to perfection. There she is now in your mountains. I should regret her less were she near you; you would like her, she is a charming "dévote." Since her exile she has written to us regretting Andillac. Her letter enclosed a mountain prayer; I answered her, but sent back no prayer; we have not got any here to give.

Cahuzac is still as it was; that shows you there are no changes that affect our consciences. I tell you of this, knowing the interest you take in such a change. Tell me, too, something of your fears on the same head, for I, on my part, are much occupied about your soul. I should not like to see it orphaned, though on one side you might be better suited with a nearer substitute. M. Amalric is much too far off; 'tis like a doctor who only arrives when the illness is over.

Are you keeping the month of Mary? This devotion is spreading a great deal; and, in fact, how beautiful and cheering it is! What can be sweeter than to pray amidst flowers, and to feel one's soul rise with their perfume before God? Marie and I shall celebrate our month of Mary in the little room before an image of the Holy Virgin and some flowers. We are told that by so doing one may participate in the privileges of the month of Mary when far from a church. There are three hundred days of indulgence for every day; this is not a thing to be neglected. My God! we have such need of indulgence! Adieu, my dear, you will be indulgent to this gossip; I am going to look after my ducks.

I had meant to go on with my chat, but here is a person going to Noailles, and I give him my letter that it may reach Albi to-night. Adieu! I am very sorry to leave you, I could say so much more. When Madame Mathieu sets out you shall have the weekly packet.

---

To M. LIMER, Curé at Angles.

SIR,— *25th June*, 1836.

First of all, how much I thank you for having kindly given us tidings of Françoise; her foot made us uneasy, and I was very anxious to know what had become of it; I was almost afraid of her losing it on the way, and it was not a little sad to think that Françoise would only limp in future, and could no longer cross the mountains to come and see us. I am, therefore, enchanted with your good news, being able to hope that the poor foot will yet make its way in the direction of Cayla.

This does really delight me; but I *have a grudge against you*, Sir, who are the cause of this injury to the foot, and of many others that you have pitilessly inflicted upon us; as, for instance, the depriving us of Françoise. Never shall I forgive you your conspiracies, which you call slight ingratitude, and which are nothing less than high treason.

Accordingly I am inclined to inflict the penalty upon you; but I remember what is due to the Church, and, then, is it not our duty to forgive? You see that charity disarms me, and so effectually that I feel disposed to come and sign a treaty of peace at your house whenever I set out for the mountains. We have arranged this, Françoise and I, but I know not when it can take place.

Papa is encumbered with workmen, and will not be able for some time to accompany me to Rayssac, whence I shall make my descent upon you. This was our plan, but who can control events? The departure of M. Bories is a very sad one for this country and for ourselves; every one regrets him; I mean all worthy people, the other kind always rejoice at the departure of a priest. Last night new follies were sung to the Curé of Vieux. It was the parting song of the conscripts of his parish. You, Sir, have not any of these demons in your mountains. Hence, we ought not to complain of good souls who leave us to go away with the saints; people only like their own country; nevertheless you must not forsake us quite, but afford us at least a remembrance in heart and prayers. Permit my sister and myself to embrace Françoise on this paper, and to remind her of all her promises. M. d'Andillac will also be pleased to receive the affectionate regards of all of us. Nothing new in his old parish.

To MDLLE. ANTOINETTE DE BOISSET, Lisle.

*2nd September*, 1836.

I am just come from the mountains, from Louise, whom I had not seen for four years. You may imagine the charm, the happiness of those three weeks, and the regrets of the present time, my dear Antoinette. No longer to see each other, to be so far away, to converse only in letters, is sad for friends who would like to spend life together. Pity me, you who are so kind, who can understand friendship and the pain of separation. I remember how the departure of your dear Blanche saddened you this spring. Since then you have had many other griefs of the kind, in which I have sympathised with all my heart, without telling you so, because I, too, was going away. I wanted to wait till my return to reply to your kind words, and tell you of all the pretty things I had seen. I am yours, then, after the first family embrace; let us talk, talk of the mountains; I am sure that country will please you; you love what is amiable and holy.

But to form any idea of that pious district, so different from its neighbours of the plain, one must have seen it. What faith, what knowledge, what devotion in church! To turn the head round during the service is so rare an occurrence, that it is denounced from the pulpit as a profanation. The holy anger of the Curé at this peccadillo very much edified me; it testified to the habitual solemnity of demeanour; and, in truth, these people are like praying statues, so motionless do they remain before God, so dead to all impressions of the senses. How we need such model Christians in our district! I do not speak of Lisle, where people are so wise, where there are sisters who instruct the children, pious souls who edify others, congregationalists who disseminate good books, and pray for the righteous and for sinners. Grace abounds at Lisle, and the good God has blessed you; but we, without aid, with very few examples, and who have lost our great luminary, M. Bories, oh, how much we are to be pitied! What good right we have to the prayers of happier souls! Therefore do you, filled with grace as you are, and your sisters of the congregation, pray for us poor sinners; scatter prayers among us, as you do pious books amongst others.

I should like to know what books you have received. I could wish there were some to suit all minds, that those who just know how to read, as well as the better instructed, might be able to find in our library whatever their piety required. I know that one must not be too particular, and that everything that treats of God is good; but, nevertheless, I remember the pietism of which Father Gondelin spoke to us. What can you tell me of that holy man, and of M. Verès? I should like to know if the latter is at Toulouse or in heaven. Not though that I am ready to go and find him, wherever it be, especially not on high! In the mountains I learnt more than ever how one needs to prepare oneself for heaven.

How happy I was there in every way! The church two steps off; a most tender Father, who had taken an affection for my soul. The worthy man! If it were not so very interior a matter, and rather long to tell, I should relate one instance of his kindness to my conscience. In short, I was spoiled there; everything amused me; the excursions up and down by hill and dale with Louise and *Don Quixote*,* mounted on *Pierre-à-feu*, his courser; then the luncheons of goat's milk, barley bread, *fromajou*, which awaited us in the cottages around. How pleasant all that was! Nothing can be more courteous, more civil, than these mountain men and women, even down to the little children, who get up almost out of their cradles to curtsy to you. I do not speak of Louise, or of her unspeakably kind and amiable family; it is, indeed, happiness to see and know them intimately.

Adieu, dear Antoinette! What of the health of Laure and Augustine just now? All those who suffer interest me. I believe you to be well, but I do not love you the less. Yes, believe me always all your own.

---

To M. MAURICE DE GUÉRIN, Paris.

*St. Eugène's Day, 6th September,* 1836.

About a week ago I was coming down very sadly from the mountains, thinking of Louise, my heart full of her friendship, and regrets at our separation. How much it costs us to leave a friend when one has found such happiness in being together! Adieu is a word which makes

* The same as the *Nocturnal Cavalier* of a former letter.

one weep, which kills. Fénélon is very right in saying that friendship, which constitutes the great delight of life, inflicts inexpressible pain as well. We felt this, Louise and I. 'Tis that at bottom the sweetest things of life have their bitterness; I learn, I experience this ever more and more. What is to be done? One must become resigned, adapt oneself quietly to the current of the world which flows on so diversely.

My friend, I thought of you everywhere while among the mountains: under the limes, in the little drawing-room, in the gallery, where they gave me some of your letters to read; those dear letters that M. de Bayne preserves with other precious documents. I think that you would please him much by sending him more from time to time, and giving him some account of what goes on in the literary world. The worthy man is particularly attached to you. The name M. Maurice must be in his heart, he has it so often on his lips. His affection ought to please you; it pleases me I know, and, so much the more, that I share some of it, probably as being your sister. Indeed, I do not know why M. de Bayne should treat me with such special favour, but he used to come and converse, and tell me about his great authors and great thoughts; we opened every kind of book together—history, philosophy, legends, poetry. His evening conversations were quite a course of literature, for it was in the evening we talked, he in his arm-chair, back turned to the window, I on the great sofa in the Countess's special corner, Léontine at the other end, Louise on a chair as near me as possible, and Criquet at her feet or on her knees. You would also have seen the round table with books, pamphlets, journals, stockings, heaped round a chandelier, and underneath it the shade into which the cricket used to venture. All is just as it was four years ago, minus you. Louise is not in the least changed. She has the same look of youth, the same gaiety, the same eye of fire. What a glance it is! I wish it had fallen upon Raphael; what would he not have made of it? As for me, I have in my soul a charming picture of it, and a faithful one.

I was cut short there by the arrival of Miou, my pupil, a gentle, pretty little girl, and a stupid, according to Papa, who does not like her slowness, which makes him judge my poor "protégée" rather severely. A hail-storm came down yesterday, to put an end to our grapes. It was pitiful to see the poor broken vines, that had promised such an abundant vintage. We had not calculated on less than seventy barrels: so much for calculating on anything in this world!

To-morrow we expect the Raynauds, great and small. Papa longs exceedingly to embrace Auguste, and his wife and children. I was the first to have that pleasure on my way to Albi. Judge of the delight, and how soon acquaintance was made with Félicité. The look of old friends that we had from the very first, surprised all who were not aware that we were already known to each other in heart. I find our cousin kind, simple, friendly; very fond of you, which makes me not a little fond of her. We talked of you. "Tell me of Maurice; what is he doing, does he think of us, will he come at last?" and other questions, which I shall repeat some of these days more at leisure. It rains, unfortunately, which will prevent our going out and seating ourselves under some oak-tree well adapted for telling secrets.

If only we had you, what happiness! Do not let us think of it, since to do so merely occasions regrets. But, however, recollect that I will, that we positively will, have you next year; therefore arrange your plans accordingly, or tell us that you do not choose to come. I see nothing but the "*Agrégation*" to detain you, but in the course of a year you have plenty of time for preparation. Prepare yourself, then, in time; present yourself without hesitation; a little courage, come; the courageous are the successful. Think of the pleasure you will give us, the pleasure Papa will feel, that dear father who loves thee so much that we should be jealous had we not each our own share of affection. A father's heart is infinite.

---

TO MDLLE. ANTOINETTE DE BOISSET.

*29th September*, 1836.

How I pity you, my poor Antoinette! How overwhelming I consider the blow which has just fallen upon you and your whole family! I see you heartbroken, weeping, needing consolation, and I, who would fain offer it you, can do nothing, no, nothing but associate myself with your affliction by acutely sharing in it. I feel my insufficiency, and that of all human compassion, in such a sorrow. Our support comes from above, as you once told me on a similar occasion. I love to recall these words, and the tender friendship that prompted them. To me it was something heavenly, which makes me ask God to-day to grant me the favour of returning you the good you did me then. But, once more, what can I do, my dear friend, except mourn with you, and pray God to give you the resignation and the strength of which you have such need in the sorrow He sends you now?—a very bitter, very profound sorrow to you—I enter into and share it both as friend and sister. It is so sad to lose a brother!

But it is God's will that, sooner or later, we should be separated the one from the other, and that in these separations our heart should attach itself more strongly to Him, and turn entirely towards the place whither those we miss are gone. The death of our loved ones teaches us to detach ourselves from life, and all that goes on in this poor land of exile, and to have no other than heavenly hopes. It is when we are sorrowful that we feel the need of Heaven; accordingly God promises it to those that mourn, and calls them blessed because they shall be comforted. Oh! fortifying promise! How powerfully it helps us to bear our cross, heavy though it be! Heaven is held out, but we must gain it by suffering, and, like Jesus Christ, arrive at glory by the long path of Calvary. You, my dear friend, who have so often and so piously followed the way of the cross, have learned resignation there, and strength in the afflictions of life.

In this affliction that God sends you now I depend firmly upon your courage and your religious feelings, but I am anxious about your health, and that of your dear Laure, so delicate, and so shaken by a blow like this. Hence I shall long much for a word to set me at ease both about you and Mdlle. Laure, and I expect it from your friendship.

---

To M. Hippolyte de La Morvonnais.

*Cayla, 2nd February, 1837.*

It is two years to-day since a letter from Maurice informed me of the death of your dear Marie, a death of which I thought on waking, and would solemnise the anniversary by writing to you. I do not think I can spend the day better than in speaking to you of her, of your daughter, of heaven, where she is, and whence she watches over all she loved. Marie prays for us, is occupied with our happiness,—yours especially,—as if she were still on earth, and even more, for she loves us far better in heaven. Hence I hope much for your soul; it will benefit, by graces obtained for us by the saints, those friends that we have with God,—I mean those interior aids that console and sustain the soul in its weakness, and which are so necessary to you, as I observe from your letters; nor is it without pain that I still find you so inconsolably sad. And yet you know that faith gives us hope, and that a Christian is not allowed to sorrow as those who know not God, for, for thy faithful people, Lord, to die is not to lose life, but to pass to a better.

Let us then console ourselves by reflecting that those

who leave us are happier than we. The blessed dead say to us, Weep not, rather follow the way which will bring you where we are; one gets here by loving God, serving Him with all one's heart, through the mourning, the separations, griefs, depressions, tears, that fill up the whole of life. Heaven is at the end; we must pass through trials as the soldier does, without fainting or dismay, across battle-fields, to glory.

How I wish I could see you attain to that strength which comes from God, and is to be found in prayer, pious reading, in the practice of religious duties so consoling and so sweet. Why do not all the afflicted know how to have recourse to them? Why cannot they discover that treasury whence all good things needed by the soul so abundantly flow! My God, how little we know how to profit by thy gifts! I know more than one of the afflicted who is lost for want of seeking consolation where it is to be found. 'T is not in study, nor in the contemplation of nature, not in man, nor in anything created, that the soul can find consolation; but in God, in God alone, in his Word, in the divine Scriptures, in a faithful and believing life. Ah, Monsieur, who is there that kneeling down with his heart full of tears does not rise comforted?

You have experienced this, no doubt; it is not for me to teach you these truths, but I love to speak of them, because there is an infinite charm in these heavenly communings, because they naturally flow from my heart when I think that God has authorised me to console you. What else, indeed, could I say? I know nothing besides, I have learned nothing from the world, both it and its language are alike strange to me. I only know the language of piety; you would find me dumb if you did not understand it, but you will do so, I see, since you speak of prayers; only tell me, why do you add that your soul is deteriorating more and more? Those words distress me; they are the expression of a sick faith, of a heart estranged from God. It would be sad indeed to see you fall away thus, you whose trials have placed you so high and near to Jesus on Calvary. Accordingly, I looked on you as one of the elect, one of those of whom Jesus Christ declares, "Blessed are they that mourn." You suffer so much: do not lose the fruit of suffering. Look up, like Stephen, at the open heaven. Have faith, hope! Let your soul soar, and it will not deteriorate; let us leave the earth, that soils, that tarnishes us, poor swans:

> "For how retain the spotless white that was our heav'nly dower,
>   Amidst the mire and clay, the dust that flies around
> And lights on all things here below, yes, even on the flower!
>   Oh fear, then, fear a stain contracted from the ground:
>     Virgins, doves, the Lord's possession,
>     Little children, flakes of snow,
>     Poets, priests, a pure procession,
>     Thro' a world corrupt that go,
> Pass as a ray of light thro' vapours dank and low!
>
> "Let us not dare to linger on this globe of clay;
>   Oh, whosoe'er we be, still let us lift our eyes
> Where the sun lights with everlasting day
>   The home of men and angels in the skies.
>
> What has the world, alas! to offer us in store?
> What is the earth, my God? a grave immense—no more!
> Within which buried ages, monarchs, nations rest,
> And oh! how many of the loved, once folded to our breast:
> Pass we then, pass we on, like those who thro' a churchyard tread;
> Pass we on, shedding tears and prayers o'er our beloved dead."

Yes, let us pray. I would repeat it in a thousand forms, because prayer is what you need, because, as well as poetry, it consoles poor poets in their sorrow. Make trial of God after poetry, and you will feel yourself better, and your soul will no more go on deteriorating. Your soul to deteriorate! what a misfortune! I pray God to preserve you from it; what a grief to Marie if she were to see you! Be what she has seen you—after God, the natural guardian of the child she has left you, of your dear little girl, for whose sake alone your soul should keep itself pure.

Forgive me; I believe that you are still good; it is I who go too far, who have been too ready to take alarm at an expression imperfectly understood; no, you are not deteriorating, but you weep too much, you do not, perhaps, believe enough. I merely throw out ideas which proceed from a great fear and great love for your soul. What would not I do for its salvation, for that of all men, those brothers redeemed by the blood of Jesus Christ? This is, indeed, to speak to you as a sister, but you have given me that title, and I use it to express myself freely, to thank you with all my heart for what you say so kindly and graciously of me and mine. In the name of all, I ask you to come and see us, and to bring us Marie; we long to caress her and hold her on our knees. Be good enough to embrace her for me, dear little thing. Will you also convey our remembrances to your sister Adèle, and tell her how her fear of me made me laugh? let her be reassured and pleased to consider me within reach, in order that I may embrace her very tenderly.

As you say, Maurice is changed for better and for worse; in growing stronger his character has lost some of its tenderness; he is no longer the same brother who loved me like a child, and innocently told me everything. He is silent and reserved now; why, God only knows. It pains me, but I, too, am silent. Must we not resign ourselves to everything? What good would complaining do? I wait to see him. But, indeed, I am not sure if I have rightly understood what you say of him, or many other parts of your letter, not being very well able to read your handwriting. Could you make it a little plainer? I wish you could, because of the pleasure I take in reading you.

Adieu! forgive me all my plain speaking, and always believe in my devoted friendship.

P.S.—I long that every obstacle to the publication of 'Wordsworth' should be removed. My father and my whole family enjoin me to offer you their affectionate remembrance.

---

To Mdlle. Louise de Bayne.

Albi, *Tuesday, 4th April,* 1837.

Cholet arrived just as I was going to church, bringing me your sad letter, which I read close to the gate of Sainte Cécile. This will tell you, dear friend, that I took you with me before God, that I prayed Him to enable you to support with resignation these heart griefs, these losses, these deaths, which are constantly falling upon us. Such is life, full of separations and tears. 'Tis sad, very sad to nature, but faith consoles, the soul knows that when the earthly house of its tabernacle is dissolved, it has one that is eternal in the heavens. This passage of the 'Preface to the Dead' is sublime, and more consolatory than all we can say to console ourselves for the loss of those we love. Human language is very cold, very powerless; 'tis only a mournful sound, like that of the tolling bell. Let us go into the presence of God if we would have what really comforts and fortifies. I have observed that pious people, even the most simple and ignorant, can find admirable things to say on such occasions. Jeannette, who was alone with the dying Madame de Faramond, exhorted her like a missionary. 'Tis that they are inspired by love and piety. Let us love God, and we shall know how to speak of Him.

That poor ——— died without any other sacrament than that of extreme unction, so rapidly did death come at last; not but what he had been very ill, but no one was alarmed by a complaint in the foot, when all of a sudden the pain mounted to the leg, then higher and higher through all the body. M. the Curé, who was dining in town, was sent for in all haste, and had only time to give him extreme unction. I have these details from Madame de Tonnac, and told you them in the letter I burnt, together with a thousand things that I shall not repeat; they were nothings, words that fall from the pen and leave no memory behind.

We might laugh a little over these conversations in

ashes, but this is not the time for it; the heart is only disposed to sadness in the midst of the dead and dying; mine especially, which so regrets that good, amiable, pious Laure, whose death I have just heard of. Poor Antoinette, poor mother! how afflicted the whole family must be, they loved their dear Laure so much!* She was their joy, the treasure, the consolation of them all. Intelligence, sweetness, piety, tender and thoughtful affectionateness endeared her to everybody. Not a year has yet passed since I saw her in her home, and admired her good qualities, her cheerfulness in suffering, her angelic piety. It cost her nothing to do or to endure what was painful. Always God's will and that of others! All Lisle must mourn her. It was influenza that carried her off in a few days; nor is it surprising in the state she was that her fragile frame should succumb to the least shock. I must write to Antoinette, and you can imagine how much I dread it; as you say, one trembles to renew anguish by touching upon it. And yet friendship must needs lay tears on these heart wounds. One thinks of God and heaven, and piety makes such tears very sweet. Nevertheless, this letter is hard to write; if you were near, I should say to you, Help me—I should appeal to my good angel. Always I had a foreboding that it would fall to me to console Antoinette for her sister's death. Dear friend, may God spare me this office of consoler, which is so heartrending, so very painful!

Poor world! thus it is one leaves it; now on this

* Mdlle. Laure de Boisset, who died the 30th of March in this year.

side, now on that, we see those we know go away from our midst. Before long one finds oneself alone, isolated amongst the new comers, like leaves of a former year still clinging to the tree when those of spring arrive. One often sees this on oak-trees. 'Tis sad, and many a time has made me reflect in our woods. Everything may be turned to profit by the soul, everything lifts thought on high; the good God wills and approves that all should have reference to Himself, and a dead leaf may utilise apparently purposeless walks.

Yesterday, on getting up, I saw two swallows skimming the steeple of Saint Salvy. These little heralds of the spring are delightful; one thinks of fine days, of flowers, fruits, grapes, of friends that one will go and see, a whole series of smiling images come flying round with the swallows. Euphrasie laughed a good deal, and almost ridiculed my burst of joy, when I opened the window; a child such as she is does not know at what she is laughing, nor all that I saw at once—Cayla, Papa, Marie, the mountains, Louise, my dear friend. This well deserved a cry of joy.

Yes, I shall come to see, to embrace, to listen to you, to do all that we did last year, What happiness, dear friend! Be sure I shall not deprive myself of it, nor afflict you by a refusal. As to delay, I cannot avoid that; forgive it; my poor father is too impatient to see me; Marie is almost in tears, and says, "You will go and see Louise later." What would you have me do? I shall go and return. This is what my father and your friend prefers. Above all, do not go and imagine that Papa opposes my journey, he was the first to propose it to me. He speaks of it in every letter. Yesterday, again, he says, " I long very much to see you; but for your good friend's sake I consent to spare you as long as you like, because there is nothing I would not do for her." How happy I am! This dear father thinks he is doing great things in sending you his daughter; he knows well that you love her.

You see, dear friends—for I love you all, and my fond words are addressed to you equally—one must not have a divided heart if one would be happy anywhere, were it even in heaven. In my Rayssac paradise I should just now be thinking a great deal of Cayla; therefore give me a little more time, I entreat you; do not be angry with me if I refuse to embrace you at present, 'tis but to hold you longer by and bye. Therefore it is settled to our mutual satisfaction, is it not? I have but to occupy myself with my commissions, and my return, which will be on Monday next. I am going away much made of, much spoiled —that is the right word—by friends and relations. The good Mathieus and Emilie load me with kindness; dear cousins, how grateful I am for their kind reception, and then for so many benefits to my soul as well! I am going away nourished with sermons, means of edification, all sorts of holy things.

If Cholet had not told me that the charcoal-burners set off at eleven, I should dwell at length on the ceremony at Bon Sauveur, a beautiful, touching sight, which makes one admire, indeed, but also makes one weep. No help for it when, after the vows, the young professed stretches herself out beneath the funeral pall to the sound of the requiem for the dead; but how loveable religion is! While every one is weeping, two children cover this celestial tomb with flowers: and after a little time—like that we shall pass in the grave—the pall is gradually folded back, and reveals the radiant saint, who rises to the chant of the Te Deum, and, led by the Mother Superior, goes round to give a kiss to each of the sisters. This overcomes, then electrifies. Neither the world nor anything in it is worth what passes under that flower-covered funeral pall. They say that whatever the nun asks from God at that moment is granted her. One prayed to die—she died. Do you know what I should ask? that you might become a saint. M. ———, the almoner, gave us a sweet and pious discourse. But adieu!

---

TO MDLLE. ANTOINETTE DE BOISSET.

*Albi, 11th April,* 1837.

May God console you, my poor Antoinette; may He sustain, may He succour you! Your sorrow is beyond your strength, beyond all that can be said to you. Accordingly, I say nothing. I can only write tears, and how overwhelmed I am by the loss you have just had. What a thunderbolt! but God strikes us when He wills, as He wills, and in the dearest places. He is a Father; He knows why He afflicts us, and takes from us those we love. Let us enter into His views, let faith help us in these sacrifices impossible to nature; let us look up to heaven, where go those that leave us, where we shall join them for ever, after a short separation. We all pass rapidly on earth; happy they who, like your dear sister, take with them a pious, holy life, a life of suffering and resignation, so conformed to Jesus crucified. 'Tis to such souls as these that he says at the moment of his death, "Come unto me." Your Laure is in heaven, dear Antoinette, everything leads us to hope it. She was so pious, so angelic, and the good God is so good! He has promised heaven to those who suffer, to those who give a cup of water in his name; He has surely rewarded her whose life was all made up of suffering and of charity. This consoles, consoles greatly; a Christian cannot sorrow as those that have no hope. Let us weep, but be resigned; weep, but see the heavens opened. It is Fénélon who says this to afflicted ones like you, and I repeat his words which I find soothing. My dear friend, I feel that I can do nothing, that all my friendship and all human things are powerless in such sorrow; but I turn to God, I pray to Him for you, for your poor brother, for all of you, mourners that you are. I pray also for our departed saint, almost invoking her the while.

Adieu! I dare not continue and touch longer upon your grief. Who knows what you are doing, or what becomes of your health? How I pity you, how I share your tears! I am writing to you from Albi; when you are able write to me at Cayla.

More than ever entirely yours, dear Antoinette.

To the Same.

Cayla, 19*th April*, 1837.

I write to you again, my dear Antoinette, to reply to your letter that I found here, and to express to you once more how much I feel for your sorrow. It is great, very great! It is one of those blows that can only be supported by God's help; but He does not fail you, He is there sustaining your broken heart, giving you those strengthening and consoling thoughts of heaven that I find in your letter. My dear friend, how much touched I am by the believing sentiments that prevail in your heart, all torn though it be! I bless God for them, and pray Him very fervently to continue them to you, to increase them in proportion as you more and more keenly feel your loss.

Your dear sister leaves a blank that you will find greater every day. 'Tis ever so with these dear ones who leave us, and whom nothing can replace. "She was necessary to your happiness, she was the joy of the family." Touching words that make me weep, that will lead me as long as I live to pity you for so sad a separation. To lose a sister, to see her no more, live with her no more, my poor friend, oh! I can well believe you are desolate.

But say, say ever, "We shall meet again in heaven, and there nothing will come to separate us. Oh, joy of an eternal reunion! how that *always* consoles for an instant of separation. What calm and strength the Christian soul finds therein! You, especially, who may truly say to yourself that your Laure is in heaven. Do not grudge her to the angels, she makes their happiness as on earth she made yours; a holy soul is the joy of heaven. She leaves you very sad, but from the bosom of God she says to you, "Do not weep, I am happy, and I will send you many consolations." Believe this, you will owe much grace to her; she prays for her family, protects, and will be to you all that St. Francis d'Hiéronimo was to her, everything encourages us to hope it; you are the sister of a saint,—her pure life, her holy death, assure you of it, and cause you, as you say, only to weep for yourself.

I am very grateful to you for having written to me in such a sorrow; 'tis a proof of friendship for which I daily thank you by love and prayers—I who owe you both by so many titles. I showed your letter to Marie, who shares in all my feelings for you, and I am expressly bid to say so, both by her and my father. We pray you to accept the expression of our sympathy for each and all, beginning with M. and Madame de Boisset. What a daughter they have lost! My God! must their heart indeed be thus often and intimately wrung? How admirable your parents are in their faith and resignation! How happy one is to have Christian parents! Oh, how true it is, my poor Antoinette, that God blesses you, and gives you everything in them!

I should not leave you so soon, but that I fear to weary you. Tell me if you would like longer letters, you shall have them. I love to console those that mourn, but very often people like to weep alone. Let me again thank you for having written to me, and given me details respecting this holy death. They edify me, and make me love God the more, that I too may die with this calm, this joy of the saints. Indeed, what is there for them to fear? Hence St. Theresa said at her death, "Why should I dread to die? I am going to fall into the arms of Him whom I have loved above all." Our Laure felt the same. This makes one long for Divine love, long to be very very pious. 'Tis on the cross that we become so, that we learn with Jesus Christ all that pertains to salvation. Oh yes! the cross, the cross! Courage, you who carry it; from Calvary we go to heaven. Dear friend, how happy you are to the eyes of faith. You only need strength; nature gives way, sinks, but even Jesus fell thrice on the road to Calvary. I pray him to be your support.

Tell me of your health, of your mother, of Mdlle. Blanche, you all interest me. I remember that when I was with you a year ago you were all so good to me. The congregation was then forming, and I am indebted to an angel for having been admitted into it. This will remain in the heart all life through, and beyond it.

Adieu! my dear Antoinette, be very sure of my attachment. Assure your sisters, too, of my affection for them. Rousou\* has prayed, the holy girl that she is, and will again.

What is Irène doing, and your cousin De Gélis? No doubt they will not leave you; were we less distant, you would have another friend by your side. I came back last night from Albi, where I was also with an afflicted one, my poor cousin Mathieu, infirm and ill for a year past. O! this world is indeed a vale of tears.

\* Rose la Marguillière of the 'Journal.'

To MDLLE. LOUISE DE BAYNE.

Was ever such ill luck, dear friend! Two opportunities this very day, without my being able to write to you; and after having bewailed myself thereupon through a whole page, I find I have gone and written upon the back of a game called *Game of Wolf.* Vile wolf, that eats up my letter! It was folded like a sheet of paper, so that I wrote on in perfect security till on turning the page I discovered my stupidity. Always some accident is happening to my letters. You will accuse me of carelessness, I deserve it; I treat my own paper rather cavalierly, but assuredly not so yours, none of that has ever fallen into the fire. The moment I get hold of it I lock it up in my desk, but first of all in my heart. Thus I preserve you from the Wolf. 'Tis a game of our pastor's which we are to have pasted on a board, so I shall have to show it with my writing. This would annoy me if there were any secrets, but there is nothing to see but affection; so much the better, let all certify themselves of my love for you. The pastor has some acquaintance with you, and will not wonder at my tender strain; and then you know he is conversant with my heart, or at least my conscience, which makes me less reluctant to show him my thoughts.

My friend, I was thanking you in that lost page for your two letters and the seed, and so many other things for which I thank you again and again. I have had the seed sown; the kind words, too, shall be cast not to the winds, but into good ground, into that heart that fondly loves you.

We want to go and see ——, Marie and I, provided the weather settles, for one cannot very well go any distance in this rain and cold wind, it is just like winter. To-day our labourers are shivering in the fields; perhaps you have snow, I feared so this morning on seeing thick clouds pass your way, and thought to myself, "Poor Louise!" I know you are not fond of the white prison that the snow builds up for you in those mountains. It is not cheerful But patience! spring will be here by and bye, May will end by smiling upon us. The approach of fine days and verdure is very tardy! 'tis melancholy to see the nightingale singing beneath dead leaves; our woods are dry and bare as in January; 'tis a calamitous time for all, especially for those poor who are without bread and employment; crowds of them are passing by from all directions; not long ago there came a woman from Castres. Happy the full purses, this is the moment for emptying them!

Mdlle. de Villeneuve must be a great help at Castres. I know her costume, there is one singular thing about it, her head-dress; she has adopted, I am told, the *Cascoul* of the mountains. It seems that the head-piece is the most difficult point to adjust in the religious attire. M. Charles, who often goes to Castres, must know if there be any truth in this story of the *Cascoul*. I picture to myself La Mathane in convent costume! I think I also heard of Mdlle. de G—— entering at Mdlle. de Villeneuve's. All these instances of devotion are beautiful, and make me very hopeful as to religion in France. Whatever may be said, faith will always abide; if it goes down on one side it rises on the other, like a divine balance.

Send me the rule of St. Jerome, pray. I know his letters, they are much to my taste. That M. Fournier was leading you to perfection at high speed. Do you know that one could soon attain to it, by following the plan that he traced out for you in play? In truth, visitors, news, excursions, useless conversations, frivolous reading, all those things that he suppressed, would set the heart free and leave room for God. If He be not more within us, 'tis that our soul is encumbered with a thousand earthly things. You will consider me severe, but I am on M. Fournier's side. Those good priests are very understanding as to the inner life, that life that makes saints.

I used sometimes to see —— at my cousin Mathieu's; her visits amused us; she is intelligent, very pious, and a thorough *Bretonne*. What vivacity to be sure! She has rather a longing to return to Brittany. It is indeed quite a country to see, especially when one was born there. It is a long time since M. de La Morvonnais has written to us; he is just the man to bury himself more and more in his sorrow and his Val till he dies there of isolation and gloom. Those Bretons do nothing like other people; they are in fact a race apart, strange characters, alas! only too many among them! May God take pity on such and change them! Many prayers go up for this, and many tears get shed. M. Gerlich has showered them over those sad pages in which he opposes his friend with all the force and tenderness of his heart. You have seen this in the 'Chronique.'

Who told you that we were building a chapel at the castle? Would it were so! but we are a long way off it as yet. We can only do what is indispensable; accordingly we still turn the little room into a chapel. This May we have embellished it with a rather pretty statue of the Virgin, and some flowers on the table which serves as an altar. You see that we are keeping the month of Mary. At Albi I bought for the purpose a little book sent for by M. Cuq, 'New Month of Mary,' by Abbé Le Guillou; a little book I exceedingly like, sweet and fragrant as May itself, all full of flowers and devotion. Any one who got it thoroughly worked into his heart would be well pleasing to God and the admiration of angels. To resemble Mary! what could there be more holy and beautiful than this? This 'Month of Mary' contains the virtues and the life of the blessed Virgin, together with instances of her special protection and of the love certain souls have felt for her. Do read it, 'tis something heavenly.

One must needs allow that piety bestows many sweet things upon us; if the world knew this it would be jealous, poor world which lives upon so much that is bitter! I defy the delights of a Carnival to equal those of the month of Mary; only ask a dancer and a devout soul; methinks I see two before me, one of whom says, "My happiness passes away;" the other, "Mine does not." Upon which I leave you, embracing you very fervently to show you that I love you. That does not pass away either, it is not a worldly happiness; oh, no! rather a divine one, thus to love one another tenderly and piously.

My father wishes me to add his affectionate homage as a postscript. You and he have got on confidential terms, I think. You talk of secrets that you will keep for him; do you mean from me, to whom you tell so many?

If I find another sheet we will go on chattering.

Here is paper enough to detain me a little longer with you, dear Louise. What shall I tell you now? My short bulletin is soon ended when once I turn to facts. My desert gives one little to say or think, unless one lays one's heart open; there is plenty then to be said, and this it is which makes up our correspondence and is the charm of it for both. O! the pleasure of seeing and hearing each other intimately, 'tis what friendship loves!

One word about the world; we are not yet quite dead to it; what goes on there sometimes interests us. . . .

I know nothing more. Oh, yes, I am wrong, another great piece of news for you; the arrival of M. Vialar, the African, with an Arab prince! To any one who knows how to see events in men, there is something very significant in this arrival of a son of Gaillac from Africa, and of an African at Gaillac. Providence, who orders everything, has not, we may be sure, brought the Arab out of his desert for nothing. Emilie remains on at Algiers.

Now this time everything is really said, except that I love your sisters and you.

I should much like to have gone to Saliès, but I think I told you that bad weather or the influenza prevented me. All my Mentors were ill, and I could not go alone.

What is the typhus doing? I earnestly implore it not to attack you; don't let the doctor have to feel your pulse. Here we are wonderfully well, but surrounded by the epidemic, and people are dying of it.

---

To MDLLE. IRÈNE COMPAYRE, Lisle.

*25th May,* 1837.

Antoinette tells me that you complain of my silence, my dear Irène, which is telling me that you are very kind, and I very negligent towards a friend I love; for do not suppose that I have forgotten you during this long period of silence. There are occasions when the heart speaks without being even heard. I have silently told you many a thing, but knowing that you were still suffering I refrained from writing, lest my letters should fatigue you. At such times manuscript is wearisome, the aching head only wants to rest; but since you summon me, here I am; I never say No to friendship, to yours for instance which is so good and kind about me. I wish I were near enough to reply to it otherwise than by a few written words. We should often meet if I were at Lisle, but with fifteen miles between us 'tis only possible to see each other in heart and thought.

In this manner I often come to join you. I have seen you very sad, very much bereaved by the death of that dear Louise, and I have truly shared your regret. Who is there indeed that has not regretted that good and holy and loveable friend that the good God has taken from us? But she is in Heaven; this thought comes to soften our regrets and lift the heart higher than this poor earth, where everything passes away. Our soul detaches itself from it more easily when it sees those it loves depart. One whom we miss changes the world completely; no longer any charm, no longer any happiness here, and then we think of heaven. Thus it is that affliction leads to God. Let us bless Him for having ordered our griefs as means of salvation; this is making us like Jesus Christ, who only entered heaven through suffering. It seems to me, dear friend, that these believing views soften and make everything endurable. What becomes of those who do not hold them—what remains to them? They are very unhappy, and deeply to be pitied. That holy family de Boisset is admirably resigned; together with their broken hearts one sees in them a wondrous spiritual strength which sustains them under the cross.

It is time that I should say something of another afflicted one, of you, my dear, who are so severely tried in every way. Tell me when you can how your health really is, that delicate health, so roughly treated by shocks like these. Mine is good, but I am sad; we have had bad news from Paris. My brother is ill, sufficiently ill for his doctor to send him to his native air. It seems that the cold of Paris, influenza, and over-work, have undermined his health. Poor child—what happiness for us to see him! But God wills that this happiness should be a very sad one. I do not exactly know when to expect him; he is to halt at a friend's house to break the fatigue of the journey. I tell you this knowing the interest you take in me; and, besides, you ask for our news,—there you have it, such as it is. Pray for me and for the invalid.

---

To MDLLE. ANTOINETTE DE BOISSET.

*5th June,* 1837.

I am very happy to-day, my dear Antoinette, now that I am at ease about my brother. He has just written to us: his health is recovering, that dear health which has so terrified us the last fortnight. I have not told you of it, but we have had our poor Maurice very ill in Paris, so far away from us; it was indeed sad. Fortunately we have excellent relations there who took the greatest care of him; and thus rest and the hope of returning to us helped on his recovery. It was the influenza and overwork that gave us this alarm about his chest; the physicians he has consulted declare that there is no danger. May God grant it, and be gracious enough to preserve me from seeing my family in mourning!

We have had nothing but a threat, and that is enough to make one unhappy: I feel more keenly than ever for those who actually experience these terrible losses. Over and over again I have thought of you, dear friend, of your afflictions coming in such rapid succession, of those two most painful losses! Poor Antoinette, how much to be pitied, how stricken you seem to me! but at the same time I bless God for the strength I observe in you, for his grace in sustaining you under the cross. Without this heavenly aid you must have succumbed, you must have died of grief. Do not make any effort to conceal it from me; rather open your heart, weep, speak of all that most closely concerns you; this does good and relieves the soul; God permits us this relief, and after the consolations of faith grants us those of friendship. Nothing on earth is sweeter, and our divine Saviour seems to point us to this in choosing to have at the foot of his cross the disciple whom he loved.

I shall not tell you how precious are these tokens of friendship that you send me, and above all the holy image. I have too long delayed thanking you; to-day I do so with all my heart, by this expression of a pious gratitude, for to me this image is a sacred thing, a relic of you and the one who is in heaven. Here are reasons that may well make it precious to me.

---

To MDLLE. LOUISE DE BAYNE.

*21st July*, 1837.

Erembert has just told me that he had a fancy to go to the fair at Albi, a charming fancy which inspires me with that of writing to you. You know, dear friend, this is one I often have; on the slightest provocation, the passage of whatever passes, I have something ready to send, 'tis so sweet, so natural to send you loving words. It costs me no effort to draw them from my heart, or rather they spring from it spontaneously and flow like water on the paper. Were I writing to any one else the page would be different, though indeed I hardly write to any one whom I do not love; but affections differ, and I do believe that the one I feel for you is like no other.

Mdlle. Lisette,* my old friend, has written me word of the marriage of one of her nieces; a good match, but which took me by surprise; believing, as I did, that Clotilde had devoted herself to heaven. But as to that, so much the better that pious women should marry; it is they who make good wives, good mothers, far better than the worldly ones, who enter into that state without having any idea of duty; hence God knows what sort of household! This very modest wedding has made little sensation; only friends have taken a cordial interest in it, and you know that Mdlle. Lisette is much beloved.

Antoinette has not written to me since; and, besides, her letters only treat of sacred subjects; of the congregation, sermons, indulgences,—then of her sister, whom she cannot forget, and Antoinette is a soul quite out of this world; when I have read a letter from her something seems to draw me heavenward: she is a saint.

Our pastor brought me last week two letters of yours, one long, the other short. I have already answered them, but thanks once more; one is never tired of thanking you for so many tender, loving words, for the rarities, and novelties, and sweetnesses your heart sends me. Dear Louise, go on writing to me; the more you write, the more I want to read. It is heart-greediness, satisfy it; this kind is not one of the seven deadly sins.

* Mdlle. de Sainte-Colombe, cousin and friend of E. de Guérin.

Oh, it is so sweet to write to each other, and so lawful, when we only say what is good. Let us write on; I don't think that we are burdening our consciences.

What would Father Pernet say about it were we to consult him? "My father, two friends, separated by a great distance, wish to know whether it is permissible to write often to each other, to write tenderly, and a great, great deal, to write interminably in short. Their correspondence is a blending of all sorts of different things: God and the world, neighbours, convents, parties, kings, people, authors, preachers, missionaries, are all to be found in it; you, my father, might chance to meet with yourself sometimes. What do you think of such letters? They contain no backbiting of our neighbours; they speak well of missionaries. Oh! there is no harm in them; but to speak of the world, its pleasures, its gay doings, to depict a whirlwind that sweeps us away, is not this dangerous, my father?" "Very dangerous, very reprehensible; the pen resembles Christian lips, that should only utter words of edification. Rodriguez cites a monk who after a long interval received letters from his family, which he threw unread into the fire, for fear of some temptation, some regretful memory of the world. Admirable act, which shows us how much saints dread the world, and what strength God gives them to break with it." To burn letters without reading them! that amazes the heart, the poor human heart, mine, for instance, that could never bring itself to it. To throw letters from Louise into the fire without reading them! impossible! but then—I am not a nun.

To Mdlle. Antoinette de Boisset.

*September*, 1837.

What do I not owe you, dear Antoinette, for your letter with its pretty details, for the images, the indulgences, for so many kind and sacred things that you have sent me! This dear packet gave me much pleasure; I wanted to thank you for it at once, and I only do so very tardily. But I am entirely taken up with our invalid, which will be reason enough for you, who know what it is to be a sick-nurse, and who are so indulgent besides. So here I am, quite at ease on that head, and ready to tell you, according to your request, all that is giving me pleasure and pain just now.

The pleasure will soon be told; 'tis generally the shortest of life's chapters; nay, sometimes it is totally absent, as at present is my case. One sorrow spoils everything to me—that of seeing Maurice ill. How I can pity you, now, my dear friend, you who have had this grief so often and so long! It is my turn now: crosses pass round from one to the other; happy they who bear them as they ought. I hope that the good God does not deny this grace to me. It is very sad to see a person suffering and thinning under one's eyes, without being able to remedy it. Oh! how it makes one feel the very little we can be to each other. Of what use is the most intense affection? I ask myself this question a hundred times by the side of my poor brother whom I would so fain cure. Nothing does him good; fever and cough run their course, and make terrible ravages in the poor face: he is hardly recognisable. I fear I know not what; a thousand heartbreaking thoughts come into my head. Dear friend, how I wish that the good God would cure him for us! I now recommend him to your prayers, and to those of the congregation who will have the charity to interest themselves in this poor invalid. 'Tis for a friend of their sister; tell these good souls that, and how we form only one family before God. I shall be very grateful to them, and to you also, my dear Antoinette.

Your journey is delightful; I followed you to Viviers, to the pool, to Gaïx, to Castres, everywhere in short; I stop to return Mdlle. Coralie's gracious remembrance. She is a charming person, one of those who please from the very first. I wish that another retreat, or something else, might bring us together again. When will it be? There are things and persons one never sees twice. I hope for something better with regard to yourself, but I am sure I know not when. Here I am till Maurice recovers. Louise claims me, and I had promised her another autumnal visit, but our projects fall like dead leaves.

---

To Mdlle. Louise de Bayne.

*6th October*, 1837.

At length I am able to write to you. For some time past a leisure moment has been for me a rare thing, one of those moments that one can dispose of as one likes. It required a Sunday to give me one; 'tis the day of rest, rest from gowns, capes, caps, and a thousand other smart things, that our ladies are making up for us. We still have our Indians. Caroline* does not get at all tired of us, and often says that she should prefer the country to Paris. But this is all very well to say in summer, when th sun shines, and the roads are bordered with flowers. To-day, that one had to put on clogs and pick one's way through the mud to go to mass, out of doors was less charming. Is it not true, Louise, that the country is little attractive just now?

Dear friend, I am much afraid of your being out of spirits, especially if you have lost the Countess, whose departure leaves so great a blank to you all. In your last letter you told me that she was gone to Lastours; that visit may be a long one; Madame de Lastours will want to keep your sister, who is so amiable, kind, and comforting. Were I afflicted I should wish for her. Oh! what an excellent thing a Christian friend is when one weeps.

We are very happy for the moment here at Cayla: our invalid recovered,† the leg getting right again, perfect friends, music, singing, laughing, a look of joy on every face; it is all so bright that I am continually dreading something or other; one must not trust too much to happiness.

It is true that from time to time comes a passing cloud, some sorrowful tiding or sudden death, like that of our

---

\* Mdlle. Caroline de Gervain, whom Maurice de Guérin married a little later, had come to Cayla with her aunts. See 'Journal,' p. 183.
† M. de Guérin the elder.

cousin at Toulouse. She, poor girl, is gone to enjoy her reward. Her life was full of good works.

We also regret another friend, and a good one; worthy Lisette de Sainte-Colombe, with whom I used to stay at Lisle. Thus our acquaintances depart; this last is deeply regretted by young people, as well as by her own cotemporaries; she knew how to make herself beloved by all. Poor Lisette! how can I realise no longer finding her in that old house, beside that poor, infirm sister, who had seen nothing but her for more than thirty years? She is the one who deserves to be pitied, but I do not imagine that she can long survive such a shock. Yet Antoinette tells me that Mdlle. Poulotte sustains this loss with wonderful courage. 'T is that God sustains her now, as He has sustained her during sixty years of trial. . . .

There I stopped eight days ago, having thrown my letter into a travelling-box which stopped on the way, and I at Cayla. At last here I am, in spite of wind and rain, at my Gaillac cousin's; and only see how unfortunate! they are to set out this morning for Montels. It disappoints me to remain only a few hours with these kind friends that I have not seen for eighteen months. So many things have detained me at Cayla this summer! Our Indians are also leaving us; just now I am going to join them, and take the road to Albi, which these ladies wish to see,—that is to say, the cathedral. Oh! my dear, what a life of agitation mine has been for a month! But let me rapidly pass on to the pleasure I had in meeting M. Charles at my cousin's yesterday evening, and reading your dear letter.

Adieu! I am stealing a moment from the good God to write to you in, for I have abridged my prayers. I will not have M. Charles go back to you without some token from your neglectful friend, who, however, loves you very much. A thousand kind messages to your sister.

*8th October, six o'clock in the morning.*

---

To MADAME LA BARONNE DE MAISTRE.

Gaillac, *4th December*, 1837.

MADAME,—Your letter has just come to me from Cayla. I hasten to reply, and yet I shall have kept you waiting long, which distresses me. Happily I have good news to send. Maurice is going on well, very well; he has taken a new lease of life, and visibly proves the fallacy of medical decrees. This makes me very happy, very grateful to the friends who have taken so much interest in him,—to you, Madame,—to God above all, who has restored me my brother, who will, I trust, preserve him to me.

Since this wonderful recovery I have great faith in prayer, I delight in it. Oh! prayer is so good, so beneficial, so sweet to these poor women's hearts of ours! it was all I had when my brother was so ill. We need superhuman consolation when made to suffer by the objects of our love; in God alone is love without tears, and of eternal duration.

I would that all the world knew this, that the sick, the

afflicted, that all sufferers whatever, went to draw from the great fountain of comfort—they would be much less to be pitied. I tell this to Maurice, who also needs something from heaven. What happiness, Madame, if you were to bring back my brother to religious principles, to win over a beautiful soul from the world and lead it to God! This task would be a noble one, and well worthy of you. What a reward it would entitle you to, and how I should bless you! Try; your words have so much influence over him. I recognise, as you do, all my brother's fine qualities, and feel myself in perfect sympathy with those who appreciate them. I should dearly love one who helped him to make these qualities promote his happiness in this world and the next.

This is saying enough about him, I think, to calm your anxiety; I have still to express my gratitude for your lively interest, and to recommend your own health to your care, in the name of your relations, nay, in God's name, who loves you, and wills that you should live to love Him in return. May I venture to take any part in this recommendation? No doubt I may, since you have told me that you love me, and that I wish you nothing but good.

Adieu, Madame; be assured of my affection and gratitude, and permit me to conclude by embracing your charming Valentine.

To MDLLE. ANTOINETTE DE BOISSET.

*25th January,* 1838.

Maurice is on the point of going away. I want to give him your book, dear Antoinette, but I have hardly time to tell you how much I thank you for this pious reading. At the moment of a departure, a leave-taking, perhaps for very long, you can understand how heart and time both are taken up. I have filled that trunk as though it were a coffin that was just about to set out. But this is too strong an expression, for I do hope and trust I shall again see the dear trunk that I am so fond of unpacking. Your commissions will get executed rather late; the cold has detained Maurice a fortnight, but the day after his arrival he will go and see sister Clementine and will give her your packet.

And now a word of thanks for your letter and the images. Come, I see you still approve of me, which pleases me much. I shall always endeavour to deserve these images and the title of good congregationist that you give me. It will be well if I do not owe it to your indulgence; but be that as it may, I congratulate myself thereupon, and say Thank you.

A few days after your letter we had one announcing the death of Madame de Tholosany, and we have even been told that her poor sister followed her the same day. Let us hope that they are in heaven. We have a destructive epidemic around us here, a sore throat which attacks women and kills them. M. Rigal has been, we are told, at Vaour, for a fortnight past, in order to examine this new cholera. 'Tis singular that it should only fall upon us. Are we the most wicked? Who knows! I never doubt the existence of sin in either half of the human race. But there is enough to depreciate the joys of this world, in these diseases, these deaths, these leave-takings, too. Adieu, my dear friend! Father Geramb thoroughly understands how small a thing is life and all under heaven. His is a detached spirit indeed!

Always all your own.

---

To Madame la Baronne de Maistre.

Albi, 12*th March*, 1838.

Just as it happened the time before, there I was at Gaillac and your letter at Cayla. I am sorry for this delay, and write to you at once; I will write every day, since my letters do you good; 'tis so sweet to do good, especially to a soul like yours. God knows what happiness I take in it, how much I delight in your correspondence, and in being called *your friend!* Give me that name and I give you no other; believe me, my dear Marie, 'tis worth more to the heart than ceremony; let us by all means throw that aside as you say and do.

Oh yes, the date of your letter made me tremble, so much do I fear, dear friend, that the air of Paris should do you harm. It cannot indeed be healthy, since I have seen so many return from it ill, and you are about to re-enter the scene of your sufferings, to re-encounter the cause of your heart-attacks and all those deplorable derangements of health! I would much rather know you were in the country, far, far from the world. But you promise me to take great care of yourself, to avoid all emotion, all excitement; to refuse all that might do you harm or change your tastes. I don't know how it is that the world personifies itself in my thought as a being that you have loved, a loveable but dangerous being, with whom one cannot be free from danger. See what mischief it has done, see the state of your health, the state, too, of your soul, as suffering as the body. Alas! what disturbance, what discomfort, what a distaste for everything!

"Alas!" once exclaimed a saint in this condition, "what a weight of sadness the world has made up for me, what bitterness it bequeaths us on leaving!" All those it has seduced say the same from the moment that God enlightens them.

This light is a grace, and a very great one; it visits you, dear friend, and you are about to profit by it; you must open heart and soul to receive it from all sides, just as one throws wide every window in a house to let the sun stream in. How soon you will be a quite altered person, more tranquil and more happy! I long to see you so! You will come to it, be sure; you are not far from a Christian life. 'Tis not the being lost *in God's love* and *living only in heaven*, as you imagine about me. This sublime piety is not my condition, nor is it what God requires from a poor weak creature, hardly able to lift herself from earth. Our duties are not so lofty; God places them within the reach of men, not of angels. Which of us is there who cannot pray, give alms, comfort others, take care of parents, bring up children? which of us cannot struggle with his inclinations, overcome his tastes, cease to do evil, learn to do well? Is there anything in this that transcends human powers? And this is Christian life, the love of God, which is nothing more than the fulfilment of our every duty.

Oh! if people were but acquainted with piety, they would not fear it so much, or give it so unattractive a character; 'tis the balm of life, and perhaps in the world it is believed to consist of bitterness, harshness, uncouthness; but, take my word for it, nothing is more gentle, more yielding, more loving than a pious soul. I know some who suffer all, forgive all, love all, who are capable of whatever is great, noble, generous, who would be the admiration of the world if only the world knew them. This is what I observed while very young, and it filled me with love and veneration for that religion which rendered men so perfect, made them such kind and gentle creatures. I have had instances of this under my own eyes; I have seen my mother; and each recollection of her, of her resignation and courage in misfortunes and suffering, engraves more and more deeply in my heart that religious sentiment from whence proceeded her strength.

Think, dear Marie, whether it be not a special grace that God has granted me to have been thus early instructed and preserved. Then I have seen but little of the world since. Had I seen much of it, it would have seduced me like any other, no doubt; thus my *four talents* may easily be reduced to one, a state of preservation, for the which, however, I owe deep thankfulness to God, since thus resembling somewhat the Gospel vine with a hedge about it. How good you are to think me indulgent, and to wonder that I should descend into my own conscience to find excuses for the errors of others. Is not this what charity teaches us, what ought to be the reciprocal practice of Christians? A hermit, called to pass judgment upon one of his brothers, came forward with a basket of sand on his back, and when asked what he meant to do with that burden, "I am carrying my faults behind me," he replied. Admirable reply! so soon as we have to do with the faults and weaknesses of others, each should remember his own basket of sand.

The state of your health grieves me much. Oh! had I been one of those friends who came to see you during the Carnival I should not have left you for a ball. That is the way of the world, which knows not how to give up a pleasure; 'tis sad to contemplate and to experience.

There is one part of your letter which wrung my feelings; 'tis where you speak of gaiety, pleasure, parties, with a dead heart, and then add, "If I am to die young, if I am not to know you in this life. . . ."* Oh! do not speak thus; you will recover I hope, we shall see each other. It is probable that I shall come to Paris: Maurice wants me, and many reasons draw me thither.

* Mme. de Maistre and Mdlle. de Guérin had not yet met.

Adieu! I am very glad that you have a habit of prayer; that sweet fruit of the spirit. Each morning we are together before God and the Blessed Virgin; believe that you will get good from it. I have intrusted Maurice with a pious keepsake for you; a book\* that I beg of you to read. You will find charm and consolation therein. Believe me, my dear Marie, wholly yours; do not leave me too long in suspense; remember that your health makes me anxious.

---

### To the Same.

Thanks, my kind Marie, thanks for the good news you send me of the invalid.† I believe you, I am at rest on that head, but about you, you, I am very far from being so. In bed for a fortnight past, always in a suffering and precarious state! My God! when will you recover? when will you prove to me that my letters do you good, as you say? I believe they avail you very little, that I can do nothing more to relieve you; friendship does not suffice you, you need a more powerful remedy. In the name of Heaven, turn for help towards God, I implore you to do this; believe me when I tell you that health, life, happiness, are there. If I knew of anything better I would impart it, for I love you, my dear sufferer, and wish you nothing but good.

\* The 'Introduction to a Devout Life,' by St. François de Sales.
† Maurice de Guérin, again ill in Paris.

Nevertheless I hurt you sometimes it seems; how does that happen when I never intend to send you a bitter word? But let us see; may it not be because you translate my thoughts incorrectly? For instance, amongst other things, what struck you so much regarding the difference of nature and education—I meant to convey by that that my education was rather a wild one, such as is got in the woods, and that my retired tastes would have little charm for a woman of the world, which made me fear for myself. . . . Was there anything in that sentence to make a dragon of? Come, come, you are subject to alarms; another difference between us, for I have no fear of your friendship, and would have it know, timid as it is, that, after I have once bestowed affection, 'tis done once for all; there it is till Heaven, where we go on loving. When God wills that we should love, 'tis eternally: holy friendship is nothing but an overflow of that charity that never faileth.

Now, then, will you be satisfied? Will you repeat without hesitation the *Credo* of friendship? Oh! throw aside doubts, those cares of the heart; be very sure that *Mary* can never forget *Martha*, whom God has confided to her. She loves her, will do all she can to console her, to bring her back to the Saviour when believing hersel repulsed by him. But is it not rather she who retreats, leaves him for others, goes off into various agitations, and then complains that Jesus does not speak to her heart? Does she not know that God speaks only to the soul that keeps itself lovingly tranquil to hear Him, that at least makes an effort to detach itself from the world?

Listen: "Oh, when shall I be sufficiently disengaged from earth to see thee, oh Lord my God, and to taste thy sweetness? Now I can do nothing but groan and painfully endure my misery." Thus exclaims the 'Imitation,' in that beautiful chapter that converted La Harpe. Would you like to see it? 'tis the 21st of the third book.

What an admirable work it is! what knowledge of the heart! There are in it passages suited to all situations of the soul, remedies for every passion, a divine gentleness. I meet with a great many things adapted to your case, and I say to myself, "Were she but there thou shouldst read her that passage." Any one whatever might read that book with profit; I should recommend it alike to the sick, to the world's happy ones, to persons given up to the darkest despair. Had Judas read it he would never have been able to hang himself.

You read a great deal I imagine,—could you not find room for some pious books? It would do you good, would calm you; nothing is so sweet as those saintly voices that speak to us of God; nothing is so beautiful as what God inspires. Romances make on me the impression of gunpowder; they burn, blacken, rend the heart; religious works enlighten, sustain, nourish it. Good books are the manna of the people of God, the celestial food of souls on their journey to heaven; let us gather it up. The world does not know the taste of it, but you will tell me if it be not made for you, if that tender heart, that ardent intellect of yours, do not appreciate things divine. My dear friend, I am enchanted to be with you, but yet must leave you now to go with my sister to see a sick man.

*The* 5*th.*—I resume, to the song of a nightingale singing under my window; 'tis delightful to hear him, to write as it were to his dictation. Sweet musician! I wish he were in your room in Paris, you would be charmed with him; but these bards of solitude will not leave us; they make up the concerts we hermits have; God will not let us be without pleasures of our own. The fields are full of such; flowers, verdure, beautiful plants at every step; birds everywhere; and then an air, an air all perfumed! What a delight to walk about, to wander as partridges do.

Yesterday we went to see the invalid, a poor friend of ours, suddenly attacked with a brain fever. It was piteous to hear him rave, and his poor wife and little children cry. Oh, my God! it was heartrending indeed; but there is one way of consoling these poor souls; 'tis to speak to them of God, who afflicts in this world to make us happy in another. They seize hold of that at once; one has only to point out where consolation is to be found, faith enables them to find; sweet religion calms and reconciles them to everything. What would become of these poor creatures, without bread, without linen, without necessaries even, if God did not remain to them? Accordingly, as if to forearm himself, this poor sufferer asked for M. the Curé, and received the holy viaticum in the night. The next day delirium came on. He seemed to have a presentiment of it, and made haste to prepare his soul.

A little time ago I was with another invalid, a cousin, a friend who is now in heaven.* She was a saint, a most beautiful soul indeed. Oh, yes! my dear Lili is happy; she had suffered so much, and suffered so well. On Calvary for ten whole years she said with Jesus, "My God, thy will be done." Accordingly God abundantly comforted and sustained her in her last agony. I saw that agony, I know how saints die; and how beautiful and angelic she was with her hands crossed and her crucifix on her lips! That was her last kiss! She went away, as says St. Theresa, with the one she had loved best. The impression that death made will long abide with me; I shall long remember that failing form, that bed against which I leant repeating prayers for the dying, and above all, that moment when the priest came to say in the night, "Depart, Christian soul, depart out of this world."

Oh! if that soul had not been ready! My God, how many there are who without being ready depart into eternity! 'Tis harrowing to think of poor, unhappy souls! I own to you I look upon those as mad who live without faith, without practice, who go away hence without thinking that God is waiting for them. To neglect the only thing needful, is not this inconceivable in beings endowed with reason, in Christians instructed in the truths of that Gospel which tells us, "What shall it profit a man to gain the whole world, and to lose his own soul?" To *lose!* When one meditates on that word *lose*, and on what it is that is lost, the soul grows terrified

* See 'Journal,' p. 192.

like one who finds himself on the point of being cast into the sea, and attaches itself to God who saves; learns to love, to serve Him, to obey His law. Fear is the beginning of wisdom.

Forgive me so many serious reflections, my dear, but they occur to me, and between friends 'tis out of the abundance of the heart one speaks. Now a pleasant word or two; let us talk of Mdlle. de Rivières. Have you still that kind friend with you? What you tell me of her and her good influence makes me wish she should long remain. Speak of me, I am very glad you should, 'tis telling me you love me; but don't go too far, I beg of you; you do not know me; you view me in too favourable a light.

"Too often Love embellishes the loved."

I fear the effect of reality when you actually see me as I am. But who knows when that may be? My journey to Paris depends upon events still to come. And then to leave my family, my father, the dear father, the dear desert where I have always lived—all this keeps me back.

I put up many prayers for your health. If you only knew how flourishing I would have it, and how free I would have you from this enthusiasm for ugliness! What can make you suppose that thus pulled down and suffering, you would please me better, than fresh, healthy, and handsome, since God has made you so? To like ugliness is contrary to a woman's nature; you cannot like it, nor I either; it always seems to me as though 'twere sin that had made it. I should like to see you as beautiful as a saint. Therefore tell me: "I am better." Recover as fast as possible if you want to please me, dear one. Suffering and thinness will not take you to heaven, 'tis through the heart we get there.

Go back then to taking proper care of your health; do as you told me the other day: *I will only occupy myself with my recovery.* Think of your mother, so afflicted by your condition; think of your friends and your children. That little Valentine! I would not have her make you uneasy about her health, or anything else; yet all mothers have these uneasinesses, but then they have so many joys as well!—a child is such a pretty, innocent, tender thing. What happiness to kiss, educate, teach them, to make them loving little souls for God! I long to see a baby in this house, that I may play the mother, may rock and caress at will. It would be a great delight to me to have the care of a little creature, to bring it up; I should be entirely occupied by its future, its happiness, the development of its nature. My heart would be absorbed in this. What blessedness God confers on mothers in giving them a child; how precious a treasure!

Adieu! I do not know Italian, and therefore could not understand the end of your letter, nor did what went before help me much. Will you have two Cayla flowers in remembrance of our spring? One is for Mdlle. de Rivières, as a friend's friend. We call them *Ladies of eleven o'clock*, because they open then. We have others that open out at other hours, pretty field timepieces.

One thing alone calms and sustains me; 'tis Holy Communion. God has enabled me to feel that He is the

sovereign comforter, the only support of a sick soul.
Oh! but for that what would become of one? what could
be done with a broken heart, too ready to run away
every moment after the creature? If God do not keep it
all is lost. 'I can comprehend despair in the absence
of faith; but with it, with this divine aid, everything
changes within us; one does not suffer less, but one
suffers as a Christian, one suffers in God and for God,
one suffers while loving, which softens everything. My
dear and much loved one, I open out to you my whole
soul, which is indeed an object of pity. If you prayed,
I should say, pray for me; but yes, you do pray, it
is impossible that you should not more than ever have
recourse to prayer. Oh, we want heaven, want the other
life to console us for being upon earth! Unhappiness
alone is sufficient to make us believe in immortality!

To THE SAME.

*8th June*, 1838.

Poor child! poor mother! how I pitied both you
and Valentine during those three days of suffering,
anguish, agony! It was a trial that God was submitting
you to; He willed that like the mother of Jesus a sword of
sorrow should pierce through your soul. But your child
is saved, she is given back to you, the dear little one, the
*precious treasure*, you so much love; oh happiness, twofold happiness, for you too are given back to me! I
seemed to see you dead beside that mournful little bed.

How I bless God, my friend, for this recovery when I think of that fearful faculty of suffering that is in you! Alas! this it is that consumes you, that destroys your health, your always having something to suffer;—without speaking of what you add, by your way of thinking, to your moral sufferings. No doubt it is well to look upon our pains as trials, chastisements that God sends, for they can be nothing else; I am comforted to see you thoroughly understand this; but now I fear your going too far, and, instead of submitting with resignation, sinking into despair. I meet with that word in your letter, and do not like it—God does not allow that fearful despair in the mouth of a Christian. 'Tis the language of hell; never use it again, I pray you, you who ought to have so much hope, whose heart is turning more and more heavenwards, who are so evidently loved and sustained by God.

Such as I see you, you appear to me a very miracle of Divine help. Without it, could you have resisted so many assaults of all kinds, falling one after the other, now on the heart, now the health? Stronger than you have succumbed; something superhuman is keeping you up, enabling you to live. I speak morally and physically. One may, indeed, venture to say this when the faculty give you up, and medical science is wholly at fault. Must we not believe that there is a higher faculty that takes care of you, and prolongs your life? But you think that science has been of use to you; very well then, let her go in peace, and leave you now alone; it would be much better, I think, not to afflict yourself with so many different kinds of treatment. Only you suffer, and remedies must needs be sought for. My dear invalid, you will find them in calm, in heart-peace, in the cessation of all that has disturbed, deranged, destroyed your health. In you, as in so many others, it is the soul that kills the body.

However, you are better, much better than a short while ago; even the enthusiasm for ugliness is passing away! 'Twas a reaction from another extreme, that is the light in which I view it, however good the mood in which it appears to have visited you. The love of beauty is too natural to us to change thus suddenly into a love of ugliness, unless in the case of a miracle of conversion such as has been seen in saints. Sublime transformation, unveiling of the Divine beauty which ravishes the soul, makes it forget the beauty of the body, nay, even hate it as an occasion of sin; but what purity, what detachment this! Which of us women has got so far? I, who am not pretty, cannot wish to be ugly. You see where I stand with my *sublime contemplations;* they have not been able to raise me above vanity.

Oh, dear friend, do not let us talk of contemplation, that is the state of the blessed in heaven; for us poor sinners it is much to know how to humble ourselves before God in order to groan over our wants and sins. It may be beautiful to soar, but looking into one's heart is very useful. One discovers what is going on within, a knowledge indispensable to our spiritual progress—indispensable to salvation. Is this not much better worth than ecstacies and transports, than a piety of the imagination, which rises as in a balloon, to touch the stars, and then collapsing, falls back to earth? There is an ideal side in devotion which has its dangers, which fills the fancy with heaven, angels, seraphic thoughts, without infusing any solid principle into the heart, or turning it to the love of God, and the practice of his law. Without this, even if we spoke with the tongue of angels, we should still be nothing better than *sounding brass and tinkling cymbals.*

This passage of an epistle has always impressed me, and made me fear to speak about piety without having my soul sufficiently imbued with it; but you keep assuring me that my letters do you good, which encourages me and leads me to think that God wills me to write to you. I will not, therefore, be any longer ungrateful, but happy to believe that I render you happy, all inconceivable as that may be. I should never have suspected it, nor that I had scattered flowers over the arid hours of your life. How can this have happened? Charming mystery, that the heart can at once solve: you love me, I love you; that gives a charm to everything, even to my little *Lady of eleven o'clock*, poor floweret of the field, quite bewildered and overjoyed with all the pretty speeches made to it by you and your friend. But you may praise it without flattery, 'tis a lovely flower. I am very fond of it. If I ever come to your Coques garden, I should be much inclined to plant some for you; it would be a something of that Cayla that you so like, where you sometimes dwell, where you take refuge from the world. You saw me quite correctly in my little room, writing, reading, looking out from my window upon a whole valley of verdure, where sings the nightingale. That was quite right for a little while, but afterwards see me out of doors, surrounded by hens and chickens, or spinning, sewing, embroidering with Marie in the great hall. We are much occupied with household matters; from one thing to another the day gets filled up; life passes; afterwards will come heaven, I hope.

Meanwhile I find myself happy where I am, elsewhere I should perhaps be less so. I acknowledge that, as you say, I am born to inhabit the country. God has placed me well; He orders all things lovingly and wisely; He does not bid the violet spring up in the streets. 'Tis in my nature to be happy here, far from the world and its pleasures, with no need of courage to change what you call my misfortunes into happiness. What misfortunes? I cannot see that I have any. I have only known family sorrows. Do not go and imagine that I must have suffered much to have arrived at my present state, at the calm condition that you look upon as a victory. It is that of the soldier who is not called out under fire, nothing more. There is no moral in it, or very little, for always there is some little warfare to carry on in one's own heart.

My dear Marie (am I to call you Henriette or Marie?), you would have been the same if you had lived far from the world. The double woman would no longer be seen. The one who discerns the emptiness of all pleasures, despises them, sighs after an invisible good unknown here below, who understands that there are no true enjoyments save in the love of God—Oh! that one, that woman after God's heart, would prevail over the woman of the world, full of vanities, proud of her triumphs, searching after every sort of enjoyment, and, in short, preferring *pleasure* to *ennui*. What an expression! how well it tells what the soul craves,—failing God, *pleasure*. Well then, this double nature, whose conflicts you feel so keenly, which we all bring with us into the world, would be changed into a good one, had you nothing wherewith to sustain the bad. It is the world that feeds it; that is why the Gospel says, "Woe to the world, because it destroys souls." Happy they who are far from it! Only see how true this is, and consider whether that friend of yours who used to be called the angel of angels would have received that appellation had she lived in the whirlpool of Paris. *She knew nothing of the world;* happy ignorance, which will have taken her to heaven, where nothing enters but what is pure as a little child.

But is there no safety except in a desert? Let us beware of affirming this, or limiting heaven. We may save our souls everywhere, serve and love God everywhere; even the throne has had its saints. We need only recall St. Louis to believe in the most difficult of salvations. I read with especial delight the history of his sister, that blessed Isabelle, so humble in the midst of grandeur, so averse to pleasures, so innocent and penitent, confessing so frequently, giving to the poor what she might have spent in decking herself, the delight of her brother and of his court, through the gentleness and gracious qualities which made her wept by all when she retired into her house of Sainte Claire, at Longchamp, to die. Lofty and touching instances these of what grace can effect in willing hearts, of the triumphs of faith over the world. We who see them should despair of nothing, however perilous our position may be. We are never tried above our strength. In the matter of salvation will is power, according to the motto of Jacotot. Who was that Jacotot? Some one, no doubt, who thoroughly understood the potency of the will, that mighty lever that can raise men to heaven.

---

TO MDLLE. LOUISE DE BAYNE.

*22nd July,* 1838.

Dear and very dear friend, it is with tears of affection, sorrow, and emotion of all sorts that I reply to your letter of the 19th of June. Such is the date it bears, though it has only just now been brought to me. That is why I yesterday wrote you a letter that may perhaps have pained you, because it will show you that I feared I was forgotten by you, by you, my intimate friend—by you, Louise, whom I love more than any friend I have. The idea of your forgetfulness, your indifference, is insupportable to me, and the heart's sad experience makes one sometimes tremble without any reason. I was wrong then, very wrong, to place yours amidst the number of friendships that pass away *with time.* Yes, *I* was wrong; so much the better, I feared so much that you were so.

How touching your letter is! how full of sorrow, of regrets, so true that I felt them as I read it. You have made me weep for your father, that kind friend of mine; you have taught me to feel what a similar loss would be to me. Poor friend, how I pity you when you look at that arm-chair set apart, that empty place at table, in church, everywhere where you used to have your dear, excellent father with you, and where now you let fall your tears! 'Tis all nature can do, to weep, to lament! But faith! faith imparts strong and consoling thoughts, shows you your father in heaven with God. Heaven is the home of our spirits; let us remember that whenever we see any depart hence. As you say, we shall soon follow them.

Oh how satisfied I am with your letter in a religious aspect! Never has your mind appeared to me so much turned heavenwards. One sees, indeed, that religion towards which you say you were not going has itself come to you. This is shown by your resignation to the will of God, which does not, however, prevent tears. Submission is a heart affair, and it is the heart that prays " Thy will be done," as Jesus did in the Garden of Olives. Console yourself thus, dear friend, draw strength and comfort from their source in God, in God alone. Become pious; see how you feel the need of it, how God has taught you that you *must not depend upon the joys of earth.* Indeed, what disappointments there are for you now! I have very often thought of this reverse.

Dear friend, how I would I could see you! but I cannot. In my next letter I hope to tell you why, and to acquaint you with many heart-interests.

Adieu! *through necessity.* I have only had a minute given me. Let this convey to you more than I say. My love to your sisters. Dear orphans of the mountains, you are greatly loved at Cayla.

Say something endearing to your sister Marie; I almost confound her with you. I wish much I knew her, you represent her as so good and amiable. God has sent her to you to be your angel of consolation.

Always all your own, dearly loved one.

*St. Magdalen's Day.*

---

To Madame la Baronne de Maistre.

*3rd August,* 1838.

*You have been sweeter than yourself to me.* Nothing so true as this expression when I apply it to you, when I feel the delight you confer on me now, and ever since I had your last letter two days ago : a charming, loving, consoling letter; such as one now never sees. My friend, what a friend God gives me in you! Oh! how I ought to love you, to love you well! I do so with all my soul as a duty; I mean a celestial, sweet, and sacred duty. I devote myself to your happiness, to all that I can do for you; I know not very well what that may be, but say it were only to dispel some one little cloud from your stormy sky!

A word, a nothing, will sometimes suffice to restore serenity; and calm, my friend, is a great gain; I wish I could see you attain to it, but 'tis difficult with your moral and physical constitution. Both alike throw you into an almost permanent state of fever by their constant reaction. Now it is the soul that kills the body, now the body that tortures the soul; a state common, alas! to us all, more or less, but which in you, with your extreme nature, turns into violent conflict, positive combustion, and leads to what you call your stormy sky. This is what often makes you so ill, so suffering every way; how much I pity you! but how I hope for a better state; everything promises it, I discern it on several sides, more especially in your anxiety to recover. Facts prove it. Courage and confidence, my friend! Obedience to the doctor brings its reward; God will help you, will maintain you in the favourable condition in which the happy crisis has placed you.

See how many blessings received from God! The morning after that night I saw an invalid that I love as I do you, at the holy table. And I saw her there as by a miracle, so entirely had her sufferings shut her up, distracted her, and kept her away from all external relations with God. How true that God is the life of the soul! I used to see her languish and fade away, while at present she is full of life and energy. I cannot express the joy this gives me, it is so sweet, so comforting, to see those one loves on the way to heaven. My God, what a boon! And, oh! if all those I am thinking of at this moment were in this blessed way! They will come to it, perhaps; God is so gracious; He is so reluctant to see creatures made for heaven throw themselves away, that He does everything to reclaim them, employs all manner of means to lay hold of them, even by their passions when there is no virtue left. One sees this in the conversion of the saints, and nothing makes one love God so much as these instances of mercy. Accordingly I seem to love Him better since the change in our friend, who, however, was not a lost soul; far from it, only led astray, seduced, swept away by the whirlwind of the world. Of all those past pleasures she tells me now that *friendship suffices;* words made up of letters of pure gold for me; so precious are they to her own happiness. Then she adds that "the consolations of prayer, tears before God, are denied her." Poor friend, who is not aware that weeping is not loving; God looks far more at what comes from the heart than from the eye.

I left you for a moment, but what a charming interruption! A letter from the charming Indian,* with a magnificent altar-cloth and a picture of the Virgin for our church at Andillac. I tell you this most joyfully, because I love Caroline and everything that comes from her, and because you will see by this that she is going to be my sister. Yes, she will be in spite of reverses of fortune, because she is an angel of virtue and goodness, and will make Maurice happy. They will not be rich, but we have known how to dispense with fortune, and are, I can certify you, happy with the happiness ot family union and family love. Maurice will do like his ancient race; will put his trust in God, and place his happiness elsewhere than in wealth. Nevertheless I will own to you that this reverse distressed us much at first, fearing there might not be enough to raise them above

* Mdlle. de Gervain, betrothed to Maurice de Guérin. See 'Journal.'

want; but all things explained, it appears that the family is still in honourable circumstances, so the marriage is a settled thing, and soon to take place.

These numerous details are in response to your tender interest, my friend! This dear brother gives me much anxiety, but much affection as well, which repays a hundred fold. He wishes to have me at his marriage; I too want to be there, and cannot set out, cannot go away from here, and leave my sister and my father for a long time. That saddens, saddens and makes me say No. All agree that I needs must go, yet I know not who will be able to tear me hence. If Maurice came to fetch me I should be less reluctant; then, too, I should see you, could make a halt at the Coques, embrace you, become acquainted with you, which would be a happiness for me too. As for you, do not paint me too fair; expect to see nothing but a pale, fragile girl, little accustomed to society, thoughtful rather than conversible, all concentrated in her heart-life. 'Tis by that I love you, think of you, cling to you; 'tis thence, in short, that springs what makes me loved by you.

The little present you speak of gives me extreme pleasure. How slow printers are! They don't know what the expectation of women and musicians means. Those musicians are no doubt much taken up with your pious chants. Oh! sing, sing for the Church; sing for God like a celestial bird; you will get a return in grace, in divine emotion, that will overcome your depression. The soul identifies itself with the subject that occupies it so as to lose itself therein; to lose oneself in God, what bliss! 'Tis to this that religious music leads, or should lead. Self-love may indeed come and blow some of its soap-bubbles over your work; but nevertheless it is not through vanity that the work is undertaken, and the attempt made to regenerate religious music. No doubt some celebrity results from it, seeing one's name in the newspapers, hearing churches resound with one's melodies, but human triumph is very small, and heavenly very great. Let us choose the best, like Henry IV.

Adieu; everything proves to you that I am yours with all my heart. A kiss, and two for Valentine. My remembrances to Mdlle. de Rivières. Yes, talk to me about Valentine and her twin sister, those two children that must make your happiness, your maternal happiness.

Reply soon; it is possible that I may have set out in a fortnight or three weeks, if I leave with a party of country travellers. I know nothing positively as yet. Maurice writes and does not tell us that he is coming to fetch me.

*Adiousias*—Adieu in my dialect. M. de Châteaubriand has passed by on his way to see our beautiful Alby Cathedral. How I should have liked to see the great genius in the great church!

TO THE SAME.

Moulets, 30*th August*, 1838.

It is from an old castle in the mountains, in the midst of elms and chestnut-trees, that I date the beginning of my letter, for I shall finish it to-morrow in another manor-house at Rayssac, the house of my friend Louise de Bayne. I am only here for a few days' rest with my good cousins.* And thoroughly now rested, I am about to jump into my friend's arms. Do you know, other and true friend, the reason of this journey, this departure from my desert? 'Tis that I mean to come and see you, and that I wanted before I set out to make a heart pilgrimage, a visit to our Lady of the Mountains, to my dear and very amiable Louise. The poor child! it was but fair to come and see her; for two years past she has been calling me, saying so tenderly, "Come, I love you, I am sad, orphaned; come and see me weep." She lost her father a short time ago—a father she much loved. All this it was that induced me to leave Cayla, and so your letter, my dear one, reached me on my way as though it dropped from heaven. Oh yes, indeed, from heaven, as to the happiness I get from it, that I hold in my heart and carry away with me. You will follow me during my whole journey; and were it possible to write in the saddle, I should, while riding on, write you many tender things, but, being unable to do any better, I scribble here on an old desk something, I know not what, which means affection, tenderness, thanks to be heard at Coques, so loudly and fervently does my heart utter them.

Oh! if only my pen would write! But there is always something wanting on one's travels. I left my inkstand in my little room; here I find my heart my only resource; that does very well to love with, but one wants

* The De Thezac ladies. See 'Journal.'

in addition to be seen and heard by a friend. What a divine thing writing is, speaking to each other from a distance! a delight which is about to escape me, for I am scrawling in a manner to make you lose eyes and patience both, that friendly *pazienza* that I have so much interest in preserving.

After this, judge whether I go to Paris or not! I owe this journey too much to you not to take it; I should do so even had I no other heart-reasons. But I have,—the dear Maurice who wants me, the dear sister who calls me, and then the conventional motives that you have expounded to me: all this impels, draws, carries me to Paris. Paris, which is so far from Cayla! Do not let us think of distances, departures, of those one leaves, else one would never set out. You cannot imagine how much I need to be confirmed in this plan of going away. We are so little accustomed to leaving each other that we don't know how. But when the tree will not give way 'tis torn up by force; and so with my poor heart, which would not give way either if I listened to it.

But God wills it; at this thought I take up my staff and depart. Pilgrim of friendship, I shall come in the first instance to knock at your door. Oh, the delight; the sweet welcome! I see you smile at me, I feel myself embraced; and your family, too, will receive me with cordial kindness. I am very fortunate, and say to myself, " Whence comes such good fortune? I cannot understand it, 'tis a dispensation of Providence." God be blest, and bless you, kind, good, excellent friend!

Do not imagine that Louise prevents my loving you,

do not indeed; the heart has more than one chamber. I compare mine to a honeycomb, all made up of little cells filled with honey, the honey being you, being Louise, sweet friends that God has granted me to find in my life-path. You say that I am a poet; I am not very sure what that means, nor what it is I have within me, but I feel a nameless something for you which could shape itself into pages of writing, words, tendernesses, kisses on your cheek, prayers to God.

Adieu for the present; to-morrow morning *the rose-footed dawn* will find me with you again.

This evening I love you dearly, my fair early riser.

*At Rayssac.*—Here I am on the mountains, with their camel-humps, their brows bristling with forests and rocks, a wild, rude nature that I love. Wherever the eye marvels and the soul admires one must enjoy oneself. I shall not however be here long, eight or ten days at most, in spite of the "Stay longer" of Louise. The dear friend! How fond you would be of her did you know her, could you hear her racy intellectual conversation, and see how tender, loving, and devoted her heart! She is you in many points, in ardour and elevation of character, in *faculty of suffering*, in I know not how many respects, that cause me to love you in her and her in you. When at the Coques I will tell you about this Rayssac affection.

But I entreat of you to recover yourself, heart and head both; don't let the sun tan you any more, let me find you beautiful with health, rosy as the dawn, not in order to please me more, but to make me happier. To find you ill would be a sorrow to your friend. You amuse me very much with your *fairy Carabosse*, and encourage my self-complacency in my appearance, which is sure to please you then, be it what it will. A delightful assurance for my pallor, though for the rest it has never afflicted me. Whatever the form, the image of God lies beneath, and we all have a divine beauty, the only one that does not pass away, the only one we should love and keep pure and fresh for God who loves us. Adieu! I am sure of your affection; depend equally on mine, that *common-place* is, and ever will be mine. Here is Louise; I quit friend for friend.

One word to you after my excursions, confidences, and lamentations over a fall from horseback. 'Twas my friend and I who had that fall, and a poet sang our disaster, a very common kind of accident, but not always so happy in its result, if it be happiness to be sung. There is a pleasant witty party here, which gives a charm to all that goes on; each imparts his ideas and his brightness. For this evening a visit is proposed to certain ruins, and to a church hid in a valley.* 'Tis a pity that I cannot draw and collect all these picturesque mountain views to show you. I picture to myself your Coques as very different, all amenity instead of asperity. To each place its charm, to each hemisphere its stars; admirable variety, which leads us to admire its Author.

I am going to ask Maurice what he decides about the journey. The marriage is only postponed on account of

\* The little church of St. John de Jaunes.

my eldest brother, who cannot leave Cayla earlier: perhaps he will not be able to leave it at all. Our future sister has made pretty presents to the church and to us, and all this with a touching sweetness. I shall be truly happy on the day that makes her my sister indeed. You will consider me very garrulous to-day: 'tis the fault of women and friends; therefore I shall be forgiven, and in any case I embrace you. My caresses to your children.

---

To Mdlle. Irène Compayre.

*15th September*, 1838.

We are too good friends, my dear Irène, for me to omit telling you all that gives me pleasure, and therefore I inform you that my brother Maurice is about to make a charming match. He is to marry a good, amiable, and pretty girl that the good God has brought from very far to make him happy. 'Tis the Indian of whom you have, perhaps, heard speak last year, who came from the banks of the Ganges to live in Paris, and will belong to us shortly. The marriage is to take place in November, and, as there is no doing without a sister, I am wanted there, and set out the 2nd of next month. See where Providence leads me from my desert! into the world, the world of Paris!

I shall probably spend the winter at my sister-in-law's. If during that time and in that locality I can be of any use to you, consider me at your service. Friendship does not change with change of place; thus you may be very sure that I shall think of you in Paris, dear Irène. You will, perhaps, be rather surprised at this translation of your hermit friend: but I am passive; events dispose of me, guide me—or rather Providence, who often sends us the most unexpected things. Could I ever have supposed that a sister would come to us from India!

I am very sure that these tidings will give you pleasure, that you will take part in my happiness as you did in my anxieties last year about this same brother then ill. How little days resemble each other! now sadness, now joy. For all alike let us bless the will of God, who does nothing but for our good.

I hope, my dear, that the air of Couvers suits your health; and your brother and invalid sister, are they thoroughly recovered? I inquired for them, and wrote to you not long ago. Often letters get lost, and make us suspect our friends: this happens to me with Louise. By the way, I must tell you that I have just seen her for a minute, *i. e.* ten days, that passed like a lightning flash. I could not resist the delight of this glimpse of her before my great journey.

Adieu, my dear friend! Marie embraces you. My love to your family, and believe me at all times and in all places your friend.

TO M. DE GUÉRIN, Cayla.

*Paris, 8th October,* 1838.

Oh, how well I have slept in the pretty little pink bed beside Caroline! Dear Papa, I wanted to write before going to bed, but they would not let me, and, besides, the post only went out this morning, and you would not have heard from me any sooner. But I longed so much that you should hear, that I would have written at every stage had it been possible. I kept saying to myself, "Papa is anxious; Mimi, Euphrasie, Eran are thinking of the traveller." And how occupied I was with you all! You followed me throughout the whole of the way. At last here I am, out of dust, diligences, drawbacks of travel, and welcomed, loved, treated in a manner to compensate a thousandfold for all the fatigue I underwent during these four long days. I want to tell you everything, but there are so many things—so many things, dear Papa—when one goes away, when one leaves you, when one rolls on towards Paris, when one finds oneself there, when one falls into a dozen arms at once! Oh! why were not you there, in that Place Notre Dame des Victoires, at the moment when, setting off in a hackney-coach with Charles, I saw Maurice, Caro, and aunt calling and running to me, all of them embracing, one through this window, the other through that? Oh, delight!

Never was there a sweeter entry into Paris! We soon got to the Rue du Cherche-Midi, chatting, laughing, talking of I hardly know what with Maurice and Caro and aunt, a hundred thousand things and questions about Cayla: "How is Papa? how is his leg? Is he as fresh as last year?" That poor dear Maurice! he wept while speaking to me, seeing me, and asking me all this. And Mimi and Eran, all—all of you—you are loved and inquired for. As soon as I got down I delivered your letter; then came breakfast, which I wanted; and then, breakfast half-over, there was Auguste, rather surprised to see me arrived so soon and full of affectionate kindness for me and all of you. His wife is very well; the children have hardly recovered from colds on the chest that followed whooping cough. That good Auguste came to beg these ladies, as a great favour, to leave me all this week with Félicité. I could not refuse; the more that the confinement is so soon expected, and that then I shall no longer be able to see Félicité freely. I shall be very glad to find myself with her for a few days. . . . .

I thought I should have arrived battered and bruised, and here I am as if just out of cotton-wool. We had, however, dirt enough to suffocate us in that terrible Soulogne, that goes on for ninety miles; and a noise like thunder on the road from Orleans to Paris, which is paved throughout. Impossible to sleep that night. On the other nights I had dozed and even slept for some hours. Last night I slept all through. And what a difference between the slumbers of the pink bed and that of the diligence! One is shaken, knocked about, swept along, and still it is the better when one does go fast. What a torture it is in the Soulogne sands, where one can only travel tortoise pace! However, fortunately it did not rain; when it does, the travellers have sometimes to push the wheels along.

After breakfast I was able to go to mass at St. Sulpice, and then to the Tuileries, which we visited in the King's absence. Oh, how grand, how royal, it all is! The throne is splendid. In my mind's eye I saw Louis XIV. and Napoleon seated there. We were a large party of visitors, English, brothers of the Christian schools, &c. A friend of Maurice's had got him tickets of admittance for yesterday, and, as I have not often the opportunity of seeing palaces, I accompanied these ladies with pleasure.

Adieu! dear Papa; to-day I only tell you these few words about my arrival. . . . . Maurice embraces you all as he embraced me yesterday; aunt and Caro the same. This is for Mimi and Eran. I add a hundred thousand loves for Euphrasie, both from myself and Maurice, who is charmed to know that she is at Cayla. All sorts of things to the Parsonage, and particularly to the makers of *gimblettes*,\* which have been highly approved. The attention gave great pleasure to these ladies, who asked me if Augustine was mischievous and grown? I answered Yes and No; Yes, as to the question of growth; for the rest, No, since the first Communion. She is all goodness. M. Augier is there, wishing me Good morning. We have already made acquaintance. He is a good young man, in looks and in reality. M. d'Aurevilly comes this evening. I positively must leave you, dear

\* Dry cakes, in the shape of crowns, for which Albi is noted.

Papa. Keep well, take care of yourself, have no anxiety about the absent one, who suffers from nothing except not seeing you and remembering that we are separated by six hundred miles. Oh, six hundred miles! but my thoughts make nothing of them, and return every minute to Cayla. We are in such quiet quarters that I fancy myself in the country, and slept without waking till six o'clock this morning. Tell Jeanne-Marie and Miou that inquiries have been made after them. My compliments to the whole house, and to each and all who may inquire for me.

---

TO MADAME LA BARONNE DE MAISTRE, Château des Coques.

Paris, *9th October*, 1838.

How I have longed, my friend, to write this date, to tell you that at last I am with the charming Indian: loved, made much of, treated like a sister by her and every one. Oh, the delight of being once more with Maurice! This is not to be told; but you will understand it, you who understand all heart affairs; but you must also understand that neither his delight, nor many others besides, nor the whole of Paris, can make me forget *les Coques.* I am there in thought every moment.

> "Would I a swallow were;
> Swift would I cleave the air,
> Perch on thy castle's towers!"

Yes, indeed, I would be where you are, for I love you

truly and long to see you much—much—much. I could go on endlessly affirming this, but you believe me without it. What is the use of repeating it to you? My friend, what grieves, distresses, torments me, and spoils this delight of my visit to you, is that it appears a long way off—very long to me who would have it happen tomorrow. Always postponed festivals! 'tis not my fault, nor that of any one else; 'tis the course of events, weddings, baptisms, &c. Let me explain all this. You know, perhaps—or, at all events, I am going to inform you—that Maurice is to be married the 5th of November. We are now nearly in the middle of the present month: see how little time I should have to come and stay with you! Alas! we should be obliged to part again in a week; that is much too soon, is it not? At least I should consider it so. But even this is not my only hindrance. I have been here but two days, and already I am chosen as godmother by one of my cousins, who is much attached to us, and I could not refuse her the pleasure she requested of seeing me hold her baby at the font. She expects her confinement in about a fortnight; the day is not fixed, but nevertheless here I must remain, waiting the arrival of the little angel.

Most certainly I never looked forward to this festival, but how many unexpected things I come in for now! I no longer recognise my life, up to the present time so uniform, hidden, peaceful, far from the world, from cities, —and here I am in Paris! Accordingly, what surprises me above all is to see myself here, as the Doge said. They show me wondrous things. I have been over the

Tuileries, have gazed on that throne, those halls, that palace where so many kings have passed. One comes away from it with sad and lofty thoughts. Poor Marie Antoinette! Poor Royal Family! I have crossed the Place de la Révolution, and how can I tell you my emotion in thinking of the 21st of January! What different impressions one receives in these Paris streets! There a church, here a theatre, there again a hearse. These funereal cars freeze my blood. Oh! death in the midst of such animation crushes one: I am not accustomed to contrasts of the kind. But, nevertheless, nothing surprises me over-much; when one has made up one's mind to expect the unknown it astonishes less.

In the midst of all this I think of Cayla, of the dear father, the dear sister, who parted with me so regretfully; I think, too, of you. Maurice showed me a house you once occupied, which caused me to say, "Would to God she were still there!" I should not then be no one knows how long without seeing you. We have talked all over, and arranged how it is to be. As soon as the baptism and the wedding are over I shall set out for Les Coques, and there remain with you as long as you like to have me. Nothing then will prevent the two friends from being together. Just now it would be impossible for more than a week. I prefer later and longer; be of my mind in this, my dear. Do not be vexed; let your friendship repress its impatience. I suffer enough from these postponed festivals of mine, for the happiness of knowing you is everything to me. That is why I say *my festivals*. The others, too, will be very sweet; the happiness of Maurice is quite my own, and I believe it secured with the angel that God is giving him. The more I see, the more I love her, and the more I appreciate the qualities of her heart, of her very, very sweet character. She loads me with kindness, makes me charming presents, decks me out, dresses my hair, transforms me. I shall come to you a Parisian, but with the Cayla heart,—that changeless thing bound to you by so many spells. My friend, if you only knew how I have been trying to write to you! Not a single moment for two days past; visits to pay and receive, dressmakers, jewellers; in short, I don't know what else; which is not to be compared to the delight of sitting down and taking up a pen, to give you a sign of life and entreat you to write to me. Think for how many days I have been without a sight of your handwriting, and that I love it as my daily bread! One word —a thousand—never too many for your friend. Caroline is to sing me one of your melodies; I am going to listen to her as to a nightingale. When will you sing them to me at Les Coques? My thoughts always revert to that.

Adieu, my friend! I write and leave you hurriedly. This is a mere how do you do? a word on arriving. But I am glad to have written to you; my heart's conscience reproached me too much for not doing so. The first moment I could I wrote to my family, the second to you. All homage from Maurice to both "châteaux."* The sister unites with the brother, and embraces you her-

---

* That of Les Coques, where Mme. de Maistre lived; and of Saint Martin, the home of her parents, M. and Mme. de Sainte Marie.

self. Find me out a name for my godchild. This occupies us a good deal; we consult all the litanies without making up our minds. Your health—do tell me what is still threatening? My God! how many prayers there are for your recovery! Do not tell me the case is incurable. Everything may be cured with God's help. Ever yours.

---

TO MDLLE. LOUISE DE BAYNE.

Paris, 15*th October*, 1838.

Alas! my dear friend, here I am in Paris, full of sadness in the midst of joy, surrounded by friends, loaded with presents and all sorts of pleasant things. But Maurice, my dear Maurice, is ill! This is enough to rob me of all happiness, all pleasure. What a pang I felt when I saw him looking so pale as he ran to me across the Place Notre Dame des Victoires when I got down! It was such a delight to see each other, and now this delight is very sad, but only to me, for he believes himself quite well, and begins to laugh when I tell him to take care of himself. If we were in summer, I should make him set out, immediately after the wedding, for Cayla, where the air is milder than here; but the nights are too cold for that delicate chest. My God! what mourning I foresee in this marriage! I open out my heart on this subject to you only, but fears and very dark forebodings oppress me. Caroline, too, is very pale and weak, no appetite, no strength, and less pretty than last year, when she was so rosy. Her brother coughs, their aunt complains of her leg; a sympathetic suffering affects them all. It is only I who am well, who have no other pain except to see them, the dear ones, in so sad a state on the eve of their happiness. But as for that, this does not sadden them the least in the world. No one knows so well how to take life as these ladies, who have known so many of its phases. Hence I lean upon their cheerfulness and laugh with them; but alone or in church I return to my own way of thinking. I will not say all that comes into my mind: I speak of it only to God and my good cousin Raynaud, my other brother.

I am writing to you from his house, where I have been for a week. The morning after my arrival this kind relative came to see me and to request leave to carry me off with him and keep me some days. As it is vacation time, he has busied himself in showing me Paris, and with him one learns as well as sees: he gives you the history of the building and other things. We have traversed Paris in every direction, have taken daily walks of three and four hours, and that without my feeling any fatigue, without even remembering that I was walking. One has no body, one has only a soul to see and admire. What marvels to be sure! In the first place, our ascent to the lofty towers of Notre Dame, whence one sees the great city as a whole, whence the panorama of Paris admirably unrolls itself before your eyes. Standing there, one observes the public buildings, churches, steeples, the two arms of the Seine, Montmartre, Mont Valérien on the horizon, and in the distance royal dwellings and the dwelling of the dead, the Père la Chaise, where rises a white obelisk,—some monument, no doubt. I have not yet visited that side of the town, which is very far off; we have confined ourselves to the centre, to the churches, which in general are very fine, and the palaces which abound.

But the grandly beautiful features of Paris are the edifices, the churches, the ancient and wonderful Notre Dame, St. Eustache, the Sainte Chapelle, which ravishes eyes and mind; yet nothing excites admiration so much as the dome of the Invalides. They tell me 'tis the finest architectural work that there is; all full, too, of sculpture and paintings, and these explained by an old "Invalide," himself another old glory. It made a great impression upon me. From the dome we went to see the kitchen, where dinner was being prepared for three thousand men. The saucepans were like tubs—Marionette's is a miniature in comparison. The salad was steeping in an urn as large as the *max* in which Marionette still kneads barley-bread. On leaving we went through a garden bordered with cannons; I observed some splendid ones from Algiers, into which I thrust my arm.

From thence we skirted the great and famous Champ de Mars and got up to the Bois de Boulogne. 'Tis a very pretty scene: gentlemen riding, and even a few ladies. But the fashionable world has not yet taken up its winter-quarters in Paris, and yet there are crowds everywhere: streets, promenades, churches, theatres, all are thronged. This ocean overflows on all sides. I have been much edified in the churches, which are much frequented, and where there is every appearance of devotion. There is a larger attendance at the parochial mass than in our churches. I just arrived in time on Sunday to hear mass at St. Sulpice. Yesterday—another Sunday —I was at St. Louis,\* the parish of my Raynaud cousins. Here I heard a perfect discourse in the morning, and at St. Roch, in the evening, the famous Abbé Deguerry. We were not well placed, though, for hearing, and the reverberation of his loud voice made us lose three parts of his sermon, which was on *progress*,—a subject of the day, but above his audience, which was partly composed of ladies. There were many of the clergy there, the Archbishop of Bésançon quite close to us. Everything is mixed up together in Paris; at St. Cécile† an archbishop would not have been among the crowd. Here whoever will may lose himself. The music was enchanting. There was an angelic procession of young girls in white and with veils down to the waist; it was beautiful, very beautiful. M. Deguerry's style was quite new to me: I prefer the lecture of St. Louis to the sermon of St. Roch. This morning again I have just been to a mass of the Holy Spirit, and an address to the pupils of the College Bourbon by M. Abadie, who spoke very well to those youths. You see that I have no want of spiritual things.

Indeed, I want for nothing, my friend. I am loved and treated in the kindest manner at my future sister's, and here, at my good cousin's, he and his wife vie as to

\* St. Louis d'Antin.      † Ste. Cécile d'Albi.

who shall make most of me. My sister-in-law arranges my dress, gives me a pink bed, and, by the side of my room, a gem of an oratory, where it is a pleasure to pray! Oh! there is enough to make one happy; and yet, my dear, I find myself getting weary, and saying privately that happiness is nowhere. Write to me. Tell me what you do in the mountains. I am impatiently expecting news from home; I long to know what they are all doing there, and to see them again in thought. Write sometimes to Marie: you will please her as well as Papa, who loves you, as you know. Do not tell them anything about Maurice's health: I do not mention it; it would only alarm them, and perhaps it will improve. I hope it from his youth and the mercy of God. This Paris city is not healthy, I see none but pale faces. 'Tis not the life that one leads with these ladies that can do the mischief; no parties, no sitting up late: at ten o'clock we say Good night. Positively, I am quite perplexed by this poor health of theirs.

---

To Madame la Baronne de Maistre.

Paris, 23rd and 24th October, 1838.

Yes, no doubt, dear friend, I have always in the midst of my *festivals* leisure to think of you, but not to write whenever I wish. This must explain my delay, nay, my silence, and all besides, which will not have raised me in your estimation. But no, you are too good, sweet friend, to form hasty judgments. This is how it is. To begin with: I got your two letters, the first at my cousin's *of the baptism* during days of incessant walks and excursions. I hardly ever sat down except at table; impossible to write, unless I could do so running about. Then, hardly at rest with our dear Indian, a Curé in the environs of Paris engages these ladies to spend a long-promised Sunday with him, and I had received your last letter, and had a morning of mingled pleasure and regret, for I was obliged to give up hearing your *Salve*.* It was not that we had any lack of music at the Bagnolet Vespers; organ, and bass-viols, and choristers did their utmost; but your *Salve*, your music that I might have heard, was perpetually recurring to me; in mind and wishes I found myself at St. Eustache. Indeed, this country excursion would have given me much more pleasure on any day when I had not another pleasure in my head. The one spoilt the other.

A sweet spot it was, however; a beautiful church, good Curé, excellent dinner, charming garden, still full of flowers and greenery; and such weather!—a soft, bright, smiling sky, like that of the South. When I looked round I fancied myself at Cayla. This fine air did us all good, Maurice especially, who needs so much care on account of his chest. You speak of his cough, that cough identified with himself, which distressed me so much when I first saw him again in Paris. But at present I am more at ease. I hear hardly any cough; I see that it was only a passing irritation, brought on by imprudence and

* Performed at St. Eustache; the first composition of Mme. de Maistre ever executed in public.

parties. If he wishes to have good health he must be a hermit, must say farewell to the world, that wicked world which would soon kill him. Am I not right, my friend?

I delight in being approved by you; but, after all, I nave not to complain of *proofs of assent*. We shall always understand each other I hope, whether far or near; above all, we are going to understand each other near. Ah, what happiness! I often long for it, and all the kind things you say would make me take wings if I could to arrive sooner. But we shall arrive at last. My eldest brother, whom we are expecting for the marriage, might, perhaps, accompany me to your house on his way home. He would not, I am sure, say No. But the marriage is, on more than one account, put off to the middle or November, which will bring our meeting a little later. Things go on so slowly in this Paris. Nothing is ever ready. The papers have occasioned all sorts of diffi culties. But yours, yours! were we going to forget them? Have I not got to tell you that your engraver has done nothing because M. Dietsch has not taken anything to him? This seems strange after what you tell me. You have made all your arrangements, and these printing gentlemen don't seem to know what one is talking to them about! Only they declare that they will set to work as soon as they get the manuscript. If we had the address of this M. Dietsch we would have an explanation with him. I am very sorry for this mistake, both for you and Nevers; but, fortunately, there is some time yet to St. Cécile's Day, and if you write to me at once we shall be able to recover your music: 'tis an instance of artistic absence of mind; but really it is rather too bad.

I have already seen several churches old and new. I am for the old. Notre Dame, Saint Eustache, Saint Roch, and others of which I have forgotten the names, please me better than the Madeleine, with its pagan forms, a church without a steeple, without confessionals, the expression of an age without faith; and Notre Dame de Lorette, pretty as a boudoir. I like the churches which make one think of God, whose *lofty arches dispose to meditation*, where one neither sees nor hears the world. I find my taste suited at l'Abbaye-aux-Bois, a small, simple church, that almost reminds me of that of Andillac. It is our parish, that is why I have chosen it; and besides I have found in it just such a priest as I like; gentle, pious, enlightened, a disciple of M. Dupanloup. I should like to have addressed myself to him, but they told me he was far off, and I want something close at hand, for I am still like a bird just out of its cage, not daring to put my foot out of doors; I should lose myself a hundred times in our own "quarters" if I had not always some one with me. And yet I have run about finely and explored Paris in every direction. In the first place we went to the top of Notre Dame, upon the towers, where the eye stretches over the immense city, and takes in its plan. From thence they took me to the Invalides, the Louvre, the Bois de Boulogne. The dome of the Invalides, Notre Dame, and the picture-galleries, are the things that have struck me most. You ask about the impression Paris makes upon me. One admires, but nothing amazes. At every step eye and mind are arrested; but in my own country I used to pause over flowers, blades of grass, and wonderful little creatures. To each place its own marvels; here those of men, there those of God. Oh! those last are very beautiful, and will never pass away. Kings may see their palaces fall, but the ants will always have their dwellings. Upon which reflection I leave you, to go and sew a gown. I must not forget that Maurice lays his homage at your feet; as for me, I throw my arms around your neck, charging you to give my respects to the rest of your family. I have been asked for news of your brother; will you tell me where he is, and if you hope to see him soon again? I shall go on Sunday to St. Eustache. How are you? One may say this as one says a how do you do; but in this case it is not a mere polite formula.

---

To MDLLE. LOUISE DE BAYNE.

Paris, *All Saints' Day*, 1838.

Louise, my dear friend, do not you hear me, out of the midst of Paris, calling to you, saying, "Write to me"? I am expecting news of you, I think of you every day. I ask myself why it is that I hear nothing, that more than a month passes away in silence. This grieves me; do not you know that I have the same anxious heart in Paris as at Cayla? I can endure it no longer, and, though it be All Saints, I begin to write, and shall write on from now to vespers.

But before all, amidst all, above all, I want to know, my friend, why my friend does not write to me. Let's see; are you ill, attacked with sick headache, or toothache, or with some torpor of the fingers? I say nothing of the heart, the good little heart of Louise, which is incapable of being cold and dead all of a sudden. I do not accuse that, am not angry with that; I only ask it why it will not say a word to me? to me, who made such a festival of your letters, who promised them to others; for I talk of you here, I tell my sister from India that my mountain friend is very loving and much loved. The answer made me is, "When shall we have a letter from her?" My friend, do write to me; your letters are necessaries of mine; I feel the want of them in Paris, where I have so many things. But nothing replaces the old habits of the heart; for the last eight years our friendship has been an accustomed thing; we must have our messages, our chats, our letters every day; they are our cups of coffee, *spiritual* coffee. Do you remember laughing at that expression in one of the long corridors, where I happened to use it in talking of something or other that I have forgotten now? I am glad to find it recur to memory àpropos of you, very dear one, and of your very dear letters that I enjoy in hope. Do not wean me from them, I pray; recollect my address, Rue Cherche-Midi, 36.

Everything leads me to hope that Maurice will be happy with the charming little wife God has brought to him from such a distance. "This is a providential affair," said one of our friends to us, nor is it possible to see it in any other light. I am not very fond of looking at these matters with a human eye, which always fixes itself below. I am going to leave you at the first stroke of the bell of my church, l'Abbaye-aux-Bois. 'Tis there that I have *my chapel*, whither I go daily to mass, and just now to vespers. We shall have a sermon and music, that church music I so delight in. This is one of my Paris enjoyments, in which one may often indulge. All the services are solemnly performed. To-morrow the Abbé Deguerry is going to preach to us upon the dead. I shall go and hear him, and we shall see in what new manner he will treat this old subject. My memory would fain retain something of it for you; I should like, dear friend, to make you hear what I hear, see what I see, and to share all my Paris with you.

What I send you of it, however, is not much; I ought to write simultaneously what goes on without and within me to give you any insight into my life; this would be charming to write to you; but time fails me, time which flies like a bird, and sweeps us along with its wing. In the morning—church, breakfast, a little work; in the afternoon—a walk, dinner at five, a little conversation, a little music, and the day is over; nine, ten o'clock, surprise one, without one's having been aware how the hours were passing. We go to bed at ten. Just as in the dear province, in this and many other things I continue the usual habits of my life, which is why I am in Paris as though I were not. Adieu! the bell rings.

Seven o'clock.—Here I am, pen in hand, the fire on one side of me, people reading around, the piano playing,

Pitt (our Criquet) settling himself to lie down, and your memory, amidst so much besides, in this Paris drawing-room; but what is there of pleasant that I can tell you now? I hardly know; 'tis always and everywhere the rarest thing of all.

Let us discuss the sermon if you like, which was no rarity either; I found it long, the longer that I was afraid of keeping back these ladies' dinners by remaining to the end. These services are of eternal length, from three to half-past five or six o'clock. This would be all very well were I alone, but I fear deranging these ladies' ways, and that takes away my pleasure in going to church. At this moment, were I free as at Rayssac, I should go to the service for the dead, which is celebrated with full pomp, and must be beautiful at night.

It is very evident that I date from a holy day, for I only talk of church. I shall add a little news, and tell you that, since my last letter, my god-daughter has arrived, and is to be called Berthe-Marie. You know already that Madame Raynaud would make me god-mother. The baptism will not take place till Sunday. Why are you not nearer? I should send you "bonbons." I like to share all my sweet things with you. Do you remember the butterfly? Oh! I shall never forget the epoch when I sent you that! It was on an autumn day, when I was much occupied with you; but what am I about to recall? You did not, perhaps, receive it, or you have forgotten; a butterfly passes so quickly, a sugar butterfly especially.

This is not "àpropos," but I take my memories as

they come, and I must not omit to tell you the pleasure, the sweet pleasure, you gave me yesterday, at the Spanish Museum of Painting, where I found you restored to me. It was your very self, Louise; an animated head, oval face, arch expression, your eyes looking at me, your cheeks, that I should have kissed but for a bar across. I was struck with the resemblance, and so charmed that I went there again on purpose to have another look at my dear Spaniard. Decidedly you have something Spanish about you since I discovered you in St. Theresa, and in this other woman, whose name I do not know. She is richly and statelily dressed.

That museum amused me a good deal, or rather interested me, for one is not exactly amused in presence of beautiful pictures—amongst them admirable monks, most ascetic figures—that compose this museum. And what shall be said of the mummies, of those myriad Egyptian gods of strange and grotesque aspect, cats and crocodiles; a whole paradise of idolatry, which gives one not the least inclination to enter in? I looked long at linen four or five thousand years old, muslin, and a very small ball of thread, all framed under glass. What centuries above them! I should never come to an end if I were more learned and could describe a thousand curiosities and antiquities,—Etruscan vases charming in form and colour. One would say they were finished yesterday. The ancients had the secret of making their works eternal.

Such is my life: to see, to admire, then to retire into myself; there to seek those I love, in order to tell them what I have seen and what I feel. If I could, I should be always writing to you, which means very often. Who knows what I should scribble to you? Who knows what I am scribbling? Remember that I am writing surrounded by musicians and under the eye of Maurice, who laughs at my Journal, and, to embellish it, adds his homage to all the Rayssac ladies. It was he who pointed out that picture to me, which he had been the first to observe. He is sure to know what will please me, and takes me to it.

We always go out together whenever it is fine; now to the Tuileries, now to the Luxembourg; but I go by preference to the Tuileries, where there are so many pretty things to see,—sculptures, flowers, children at play, and swans in the artificial water; and all this dominated by the royal dwelling, and lighted up by the setting sun, produces a very beautiful effect towards the evening. I begin to be a little acquainted with the streets and gardens; I look upon it as a great triumph to be able to find my way all alone to l'Abbaye-aux-Bois, which is very convenient for the week-day mass, where I go now without taking any one with me, which used to hamper me; indeed, one can go out without any risk, as at Albi or Gaillac. I had been frightened about the dangers of Paris; there are none except for the imprudent or the insane. No one says a word to those who go quietly on their way. At night it is different. Not for the world would I venture out then, especially on the Boulevards, where they say the devil has his own. We sometimes pass through them at night in returning from Madame Raynaud. Nothing struck me but the blaze of gas in the cafés; and the perspective of the streets, with their brilliant lines of lights, is very fine; but I affronted a Parisian by saying that our glowworms in the hedges had just as beautiful an effect. "You are insulting Paris, Mademoiselle, by such a remark." This made us laugh, for one laughs at trifles every now and then. I have still to go to a concert. I may go there, and I shall; I want to know what music is, and I will tell you.

We went in a body, the whole Indian household at once, to see the Yversen sister, who is charmed with our bride elect. "Why, I already love you much, Mademoiselle;" and there was our Caroline all delight at this religious declaration. We hope that the good sister will attend the wedding mass, which is fixed for the 15th. We expect Erembert; his coming is not very certain, but probable. Then the dear Papa and Marie are all alone. You ought to write to them; do so, 'tis a work of charity and kindness. I am going to bed, wishing you good night, assuring you that I love you, and forget neither the Countess nor Léontine, nor your sister Marie, nor any inhabitant of the mountain. Tell this to M. Charles, and even to M. le Curé. Marionette and Marie the little nun are also present to me.

This letter is of old date; I will not finish it till after the marriage, that I may give you some details. I have received yours, so long expected, and took great delight in reading it on a bench in the Tuileries Gardens. It was Rayssac in Paris, Louise with me.

To M. DE GUÉRIN, Cayla.

Paris, *5th November*, 1838.

Never was there a more beautiful day; begun with seeing Erembert, and ended in writing to you, dear Papa. I know not which gives me most pleasure, or whether I am in Paris or at Cayla, so thoroughly do I feel with you all, so much do I read your letters, and see you, and hear you, and embrace you, and find myself in your midst. This would be unmixed happiness but for the anxiety that I gave you, or rather that the delay of the postman did. And yet I wrote to you it seemed to me sufficiently soon after your letters came, and even hurried myself to do so because of your *paternal impatience*, that I so well know, and also, it must be owned, somewhat on account of the turkeys, which, spite of all, have arrived.

The wedding-day is fixed for the 15th of this month. Last Sunday concluded the publishing of the banns at l'Abbaye-aux-Bois: one of these days we will go and deliver up the papers Erembert has brought. As for that, there is no difficulty; 'tis enough that some one known should know you, and certify that you have been baptized. This is what was told me by M. l'Abbé Legrand, to whom I spoke on the subject, and who was quite willing to believe upon my word that my brother was neither Turk nor Moor. This worthy Abbé is the one who has to do with marriages. I told you that he was one of the vicars of our parish, and my father *Set-to rights.* You inquire with so much interest about my conscience, my dear Papa, that I will tell you everything—everything that can be told, that is, for your holy curiosity does not extend to the private affairs of the soul I imagine, very little interesting as these generally are. You wish, then, to know whether I have all I want, if in every particular I am satisfied with my Paris life. Yes, dear Papa, quite satisfied, and, above all, as to this point. I admire the way in which Providence takes care of us, and surrounds us with aids. Nowhere are aids to piety found as they are here in Paris: they abound; each day sermons one side or another, associations, benedictions. If the devil reign in Paris, God is, perhaps, better served there than anywhere else; good and evil alike find their supreme expression; 'tis Babylon and Jerusalem both. In the midst of all this I lead my customary life, and find all I want in my Abbaye. M. Legrand is a friend of the Abbé de Rivières, like him holy and zealous, and unequalled in kindness. He furnishes me with books and good gentle instruction; it will not be his fault if I do not get better. One may work out one's salvation anywhere.

But here I am only talking church: I belong, however, to the world, and have much to tell you about it which interests you. First of all, there is born to us at Auguste's a fine little god-daughter, whose birth I am commissioned to announce to you. Félicité is going on perfectly well; we have just been to see her. I embraced her for Mimi, and the dear cousin returns it to her. I don't know when the baptism will take place; meanwhile the little girl is called Berthe. I should have liked Valentine better, but the other name was preferred, to which I shall add that of Marie. We have been to see her at her nurse's at the Fontainebleau barriers, through pouring rain; such weather! Oh! the Andillac roads are "parquets" compared to these. The environs of Paris in that direction are frightful every way.

Our quarter of *Cherche-Midi* is charming. M. d'Aurevilly calls it *Trouve-bonheur.* 'Tis not ill appropriate as regards Maurice. He will be happy, as happy as he can ever be : at all events everything leads us to hope so. 'Tis impossible to ally oneself with better souls. Caroline is an angel. Religion and piety fill that pure and tender nature. You will be pleased with this, and with Maurice too, who, to be sure, does things a little slowly, in his own way. But still we have to bless God for this conduct, which is rare among the young men of Paris. M. Buquet gives us a very good report of him; he means to bless the marriage, which is a satisfaction to us all. That day occupies us in a thousand ways, that great day which is to begin a new life for our Maurice. He, however, is the one who takes it most quietly, who looks on all these things and on his future with wonderful composure. The *agrégation* does nothing for him. M. Buquet himself has told us so; he will endeavour to find him something else. So look at him in the good nest in which Providence has placed him, without making yourself uneasy.

Have I told you everything, made you see everything—thoughts, words, and actions—in the way you like? Maurice is there on one side watching me write.

Eran is reading the 'Gazette' and warming himself; everybody embraces you, and Caro sends you her filial love. You will do well not to go to Rayssac while it is cold and wet. Now, having given both bulletin and advice, I give you a hug, and pass on to Mimi.

My dear Mimi, I thank you a hundred times more than I can say for your night letter stolen from your sleep. Poor Mimi, how busy and harassed you are, while I am playing the Princess in Paris! This thought, which occurs to me many times a day, a little interferes with my repose, my sweet *quietude*. I keep saying to myself that our hours are differently employed, but I help thee in heart. We are as comfortable as possible, both at Auguste's and here. Do not let Euphrasie leave you, I implore her; your solitude would be too great without her laughter and affection. I embrace her with both arms to retain her. M. le Curé pleases me much by coming to see and amuse Papa. 'Tis an act of charity and friendship which I shall remember in his favour. Give my regards to him as well as to Mariette. The same to Augustine, Jeanne-Marie, the shepherd, Paul, Gille, to all, in return for their messages. Eran wants a little room. Adieu! I embrace thee for Maurice, Caro, and myself.

---

To the Same.

*7th November*, 1838.

I mean to write to you every day till I get your letters, and to show you that I do not forget you, dear inhabitants of Cayla. The *whirl of Paris* will not sweep me away just yet. That expression of Papa's made me laugh, and showed me he does not know me. I am very sure that you, Mimi, never had such a notion. I told you that I was leading here the same life as at Cayla, and better still, having no worries, the church close by, and perfect liberty. We are all engaged in spiritual affairs just now, these ladies on their side, I on mine. Maurice is relegated to the Sunday, M. Buquet's only free day. Everything goes well in that direction; Caroline is edifying, she is very near following in Mimi's steps. In this, too, I admire how Providence has made this marriage a means of salvation.

It is fine to-day, one of those fine days so rare in Paris, where the sky is almost always dull and low. That struck me at first; now I am accustomed to it as to all else I see. I have even got accustomed to the carriages, and am no longer any more afraid of being crushed by them than by Gille's cart. We shall take advantage of this sunshine to go and see Auguste, and I know not who besides; when once one has set off there is no lack of people to visit. On their way to the cousins at M. Laville's, Erembert and Maurice met M. de Lastic, who is in Paris with his family. It is surprising how many acquaintances one meets in this great world where one believed oneself unknown.

Here there are always Indians dropping in. A friend of Maurice's, M. Le Fevre, has been spending the evening, a nice-looking little young man with a gentle and acute expression. He asked me when I was going to see my good friend Madame de Maistre. The fact is, he himself is a friend of M. Adrien, who, as for that, is disporting himself in the snows of Norway. He will not be able to attend the marriage. We shall be a pretty large party, though it is made up only of indispensables.

*The* 8*th.*—We have just been, Maurice, aunt, and I, to M. Legrand's, to take him the Andillac banns, and arrange the marriage ceremonials. We shall have the organ and great pomp, all at least that can be had in the simple Abbaye-aux-Bois. A word that I let fall made M. Legrand cry out, "What, you know the Abbé de Rivières!" "Certainly, and very well too; we have him in our neighbourhood." And there we were discussing the Abbé, and his zeal, and Cordes, and how anxious all had been to keep him in Paris. I thought that this title of friend's friend might not be without use to us, and it gave a little impetus to conversation between strangers.

Accordingly, after that, we launched forth on churches and music. We spoke of Saint Roch, where opera choruses are sung at mass; very beautiful but very worldly. This gentleman had travelled in Switzerland, Germany, Belgium; he had intended to pay a visit to his friend at Cordes, only there was no time for it. I believe him to be very learned and lofty-souled, and to have a capacity for great things under his almost infantine aspect. He is my ideal of Saint Louis de Gonzague. Raynaud tells me that he has done incredible things in the parish he has just left. Generally speaking, the clergy of Paris are very zealous and active in doing good.

Here more than elsewhere, even, it is by the priests that faith and piety are upheld.

At last a letter from Louise! I throw aside everything.

It was on a bench in the Tuileries gardens that I read the mountain 'Gazette.' Others were reading political ones, much less charming, doubtless, than mine, which was all made up of heart and talent. I shall tell you no more about it than that. We have no lack of letters, they pour in just now on account of this wedding, and there is one for me every now and then amongst the number.

10*th*.—A holy Sunday, spent almost entirely in church. In the morning at St. Thomas d'Aquin, where Caroline goes to confession and performed her devotions; and the evening to vespers and the sermon of Mgr. d'Algiers. We came home much pleased with the services and the preacher, who preached with a quite contagious enthusiasm. He is the most missionary-spirited missionary I have ever heard, the true Oriental priest, full of fire and poetry. It is possible we may hear him again, as he intends to hold a retreat at Stanislas, where he was brought up. M. Buquet sent us word of this by Maurice. So you see good care is taken of our souls. Preachers abound. I wait till evening to add something more; perhaps we may go out if the weather, which is very bad, holds up. Eran scours Paris more than we do.

13*th*.—We have just come from the Pantheon, that church which has passed over from God to the devil, from Ste. Geneviève to the heroes of July, to Voltaire and

Rousseau. It is still, however, a magnificent structure; the interior—the dome, the crypt, that sombre, remote crypt deep down underneath arches, and lighted here and there by lamps—produces a certain effect upon the mind. The imagination might easily be terrified in this gloom of death, or glory if you will, for there are only illustrious dead there, as in the Elysée, of which Voltaire and Rousseau are the gods. At the end of the crypt one sees the statue of Voltaire, which seems to smile at his tomb, all covered as it is with magnificent emblems. Rousseau's is severer in style: one sees a hand coming out of the sarcophagus holding a torch, which *lights and ever will light the world*, according to our guide, a cicerone about as luminous as the lantern he carried. The summit of the dome is of prodigious height, twice that of the steeple of Sainte Cécile. Paris is very fine seen thence, but the picture wants sunshine, and we had none. Adieu! to-morrow, at this hour, Maurice will be married at the Mayor's—the day after to-morrow, in church.

*16th.*—Yesterday was the great day, the solemn day, the beautiful day, for Maurice and Caro, for all of us. We only wanted you, dear Papa, and Mimi, to complete our happiness. We all said and thought so with infinite regret. You would have been enchanted with this family festival, the prettiest I have ever seen. Everything went off perfectly; the weather was mild and pleasant; the good God seems to approve this marriage, so Christianly and decorously was everything conducted.

How charming Caro was in her bridal robes, her orange-flower wreath and Indian veil! And Maurice, too, looked very handsome. M. Augier wanted to paint them as they were in church, kneeling on their crimson *Prie-Dieu,* so delighted was he. The church displayed all its pomp—the organ played very well during the mass. It was M. Buquet who gave the blessing and said mass, assisted by the Abbé Legrand. We had a great deal of company, and good company too,—a dozen carriages stood round the church; the Yversen sister was to be there. M. Laurichais, the confessor of these ladies, in short, all friends and relations whatever, came to unite their good wishes and prayers at this ceremony. I send you M. Buquet's discourse, which every one agrees is perfect. Would that I could send you as well the cordial sound of his voice, and his look of joy and tenderness in speaking to Maurice, whom he truly loves!

You will like, dear Papa, to know all that happened during this memorable day, which I take such pleasure in talking to you about; it seems to me as though you would be able to take part in it, and to see your children in church, at table, and during the evening party. The dinner was a success like all the rest, very well and fashionably got up, with meat, fish, cakes, wine, &c.; the turkey, ornamented with truffles, being the king of the table. We drank Madeira and Constantia copiously and joyously, and everything went off as well as at the Marriage of Cana. I sat between Auguste and M. d'Aurevilly, two chosen neighbours; and so we chatted and laughed away. Auguste scolded me for the absence of poetry, which he professed himself ready to read aloud, but we had none, nor had even thought of writing any. There is something better than that in store for Caro: what springs from the heart is and will always be hers. How modest she was in the church, and pretty in the evening! She was quite the queen of all. We had a dozen ladies, all of them very elegant, and I know not how many gentlemen, many of them friends of Maurice. They were very gracious to me, and all insisted on dancing with me—yes, dancing! Let M. the Curé take his holy-water sprinkler and exorcise me. It was imperative, and I could not have refused without making myself conspicuous and having to sit out drearily all alone. Auguste fulfilled his paternal functions to perfection. He charged me to say a word or two from him, I might well say a hundred about his friendship and devotion to us. He and I talk *sense* a great deal when we are alone. Our dear bridal pair retired to their own room at two o'clock, rather tired with the fatigues of the day. This morning Caro read a chapter of the '*Imitation*' in her bed, and then got up and came to embrace us. That is better than the *soup*. Your new daughter wishes to write to you in this envelope, so I stop short not to make it too voluminous.

One other word. I know not how to stop. I should like to tell you, to make you see, to send you our yesterday's happiness, the friendly faces round, the flowers we wore. This must be for when we meet again, for Cayla, all this minuteness of detail, the thousand small things that will get said when talking to one another again, after the

marriage of a son and a brother and a six months' absence!
Here is one and a half of the six already gone! In a
fortnight I shall be setting out to the Nivernais, another
absence in absence, for in leaving Paris just now I shall
seem to be leaving Cayla, so much at home here do
I find myself with a sister and two brothers. Eran
carried off the prize as a waltzer, but there were only
two ladies who showed off his talent. I had no idea
of what a ball was like, 'tis a pretty piece of childishness.

I wish M. Bories had come, you would have had so
much pleasure in seeing this good friend and talking with
him about Maurice. The dear Maurice! you will be
pleased with him and his angel of a wife. Last night
I was contemplating them both kneeling in their oratory.
Did I tell you that the morning after her marriage Caro
read, before rising, a chapter of the '*Imitation*' to her
husband? I repeat perhaps, but these are things one
likes to tell over again. Adieu! Let us bless God,
whose goodness is evidently displayed in this event.
My pen can no more. Our remembrances to M. the
Curé and to Cahuzac.

---

To Madame la Baronne de Maistre.

*Paris, 19th November, 1838.*

I am really unfortunate in happiness, dear friend; the
baptism—there is still the baptism that awaits me and
postpones the pleasure of seeing you. But for that
I should have been able to set out a week after the

wedding; my brothers, my sister, and your friend had so arranged matters—but there is that little girl still there to disturb my plans. But, however, heaven before all, and to make her a Christian what is there one would not sacrifice? It is this godfather who keeps us all waiting that I am annoyed with; and accordingly, unless he brings very pretty " bonbons," I shall owe him a grudge.

It is really a misfortune for me to arrive after the departure of Madame de Sainte-Marie, who is good enough to wish to know me. A very natural wish, which will not, I hope, be baulked, unless Saint Martin be at the end of the world, and even then! Impossible is not French, is not *heart*. You have been the first to prove this to me by bringing about for me a sight of Paris and yourself—two of the most impossible things, as far as I was concerned, a year ago. Oh! there is a Providence, and a great deal of Providence. I like to look upon what happens on earth as coming from heaven.

But the journey—there is still the journey; we must turn to that and tell you all about it. There are obstacles in the way—what is to be done? Trample them down; that is what I am going to do by setting out alone. My brother, on whom I had depended, cannot accompany me, Maurice ought not to leave his wife, so there I am without any fellow-traveller. But the journey is not long, and the one to Paris has initiated me; I know what rolling in a diligence is; so away with doubt and anxiety, we shall meet in spite of all.

I shall write to you as soon as I am able to set out. I can no longer dispose of myself: events drag me from place to place, from festivity to festivity, from one thing to the other, and always my heart keeps turning towards you, and I ask myself, "When wilt thou be with that friend?" For I give you no other name, *creature of reason* though you be. I don't know how to deal metaphysically with those I love; I instantly see them heart and face both, so to make them more wholly mine.

I have very often pictured you, and a sweet picture I have made. You really lay me under the obligation to be wise, you praise my wisdom so much, which however makes me laugh. You will be able to judge of it, but very certainly it will not judge you, whatever you may say, or however you may place your *follies* in opposition. Has not every one got his? Could we be morally dissected, do you think many organs would be found perfectly healthy? You, at all events, possess that physical advantage, upon which I compliment both you and your doctor. But alas! where is the use of science and perfection? With all that, you are ill. The state of your health is a painful mystery, which, joined to those of Calvary, will bring about your redemption, for it is suffering that has redeemed the world. Blessed are they that mourn, for theirs is the kingdom of Heaven. Not however that I wish you to suffer, oh my poor dear invalid, but only to reap the fruit of your sufferings.

After that we may converse about festivities. Let us do so. The one follows the other in this world; now tears, now joy. Thus life wears away under different aspects. Thursday was a very sweet, full, important day to me. I saw in it the accomplishment of so many prayers! A new epoch, a life for my dear Maurice beginning under the benediction of Heaven. Oh! how deeply moved I was by his side before God, before the priest who united them! The ceremony was really beautiful; a great many people, many friends, the bride charming through her modesty and grace. In the evening she was quite the queen of the party. The other women, most of them coquettish, were far from pleasing as she did, were not half so pretty as her simplicity. There was dancing, and I danced for the first time in my life. Now I know what a ball is; a pretty piece of child's play, and as I am not a child . . . . But let us leave it uncommented upon as an episode in my life. Thanks for the prayers you have put up for our young couple; do not call them the widow's mite, I know their value in God's sight. Before I come to my last word let me send many to your mother, with the expression of my regret at letting the time pass by when I might have met her at your house. You will feel this absence a good deal, after being accustomed for three months to her maternal care, to that tenderness you tell me of. How happy I think you in having a mother to love! Adieu! I embrace Henriette, Valentine, and the mother.

---

To Madame de Sainte-Marie.

Madame, Paris, 26th November, 1838.

Had I only my own heart to consult I should long ago have been with your dear and amiable daughter, but I depend, or have at least depended, on several things which have detained me hitherto far from her and from you, Madame, whom I include in the happiness that awaits me at Les Coques. I hope much to see you there, if it be possible for you to postpone your journey a few days, I ask it as a favour; let me become acquainted with you, let me find you at Les Coques, let there be nothing wanting between your daughter and me. It would be so sweet to me to receive her from your hands, to thank you for her, to replace her *mother!* I rejoice in the high charge, the maternal mission that God and you intrust to me, and which I promise to fulfil in the best way I can in spite of my age; there is indeed no such thing for the heart, for friendship; it is mother, sister, —it is all that exists of most tender and loving.

I hope to prove this to my dear Henriette both soon and ever. Weddings, baptisms, and all other festivities over, I now think only of that of joining you, Madame, and responding to your equally flattering and touching expressions to a poor unknown like myself. I was going to write off this to my friend when your letter came, Madame, still more to press my early departure. I should really consider it a heart-*sin* to defer it any longer. After executing a few commissions for some of my countrywomen to-morrow, I shall go and take my place in the diligence, and will announce the exact time of my arrival to Madame de Maistre. I hope it will be towards the end of this week, either Thursday or Friday, that I shall set off.

As to the time of my return, it in no way occupies me nor need disturb you. Whatever the happiness that awaits me with our dear Parisians, it will be replaced by an equal one; friends by friends, sister by sister; this is the name I give to my dear and amiable Henriette: a name she has won from me by her cordial and precious affection. I can understand, Madame, how you must love her as well as the only son who remains to you. Maurice is fortunate in being his friend, as I in being the friend of his sister, and in this character the object of your benevolent regard, an advantage that I highly prize and long to enjoy beside you.

Meanwhile, pray receive the assurance of my respect, and a great deal of love to my friend.

P.S. My new family desire me to express their sentiments, and my own often speak to me of you.

---

To Madame la Baronne de Maistre.

Paris, *Friday, 30th November*, 1838.

At last, then, I shall see you on Tuesday next, my dear friend, or I shall be dead, for nothing more can interpose itself betwixt us. Maurice has just taken my place in the diligence, that place occupied in heart so many days back. One would say that something envied me my delight in coming to you—always some difficulty or other in my way. Yesterday I thought I should tell you that I was to set out to-morrow, when a gown came to get itself made up for me and to put off my departure. I was ready to inveigh fiercely against dress, but the dear sister was bent upon having me nice to go to you, and I could not say no. This fancy, then, is the reason why I can only set out on Monday, but on Monday most certainly, *at three o'clock in the afternoon.*

Maurice tells me that I shall arrive about the same hour on the following day at La Charité, and shall be able to reach Les Coques that evening. What a sweet "good evening!" and how I long to arrive, to wish it you, to embrace you for the first time! It will be the anniversary of our acquaintance that I shall come to celebrate with you. It is just a year since that first letter of yours that took such hold of my heart. What a pleasure together to see the season return! to find myself in the scenes from whence you have dated so much that is kind and charming! I should like a language made expressly for the heart, capable of uttering all one thinks and feels, that I might speak it with you.

Madame de Sainte-Marie will, I imagine, have received the letter I sent her yesterday, and will you be so kind as to repeat my respectful and tender sentiments to-day? Shall I have the happiness of finding her with you, and of receiving you from her hands, as I entreated? If I were likely to be heard I should ask this again while asking pardon for letting myself be so long waited for. Indeed I am not worth it; at least, I should say so if you did not love me; but affection gives value, which makes me quite proud when I think: She is expecting me. To be expected, what a joy! to be *expecting* is no small one either; and here I am between the two till Tuesday. Adieu! a beautiful day, a beautiful night; never mind how late it may be, it will be one of the sweetest of my life!

Everybody presents respects and homage to all. I shall wait at the "Grand Monarque," at La Charité, for the carriage you kindly send for me.

All your own, my friend, and please do not be too ill.

---

TO MDLLE. LOUISE DE BAYNE.

Paris, 1st *December*, 1838.

M. de Frégeville is the most gracious, amiable, obliging of men. At length I have found him out; I recovered his address, and left my parcel there with a little note for him, to which he immediately replied, and came to see me on the morrow. The worthy man gave himself infinite trouble to find out my address, even applying to the police! This idea made us laugh. In short, here we are brought into contact, but without my being able to avail myself of it, nor of his offers of service *for all within his power*,—such were his expressions to these ladies, for I was out when he came. Fate has a spite against me. Mdlle. Laforêt* found him very pleasant, and exquisitely polite. I shall leave him this little *souvenir* for you, dear friend, and avail myself to the last moment of the opportunity of writing to you.

I am going to set out and to see green fields once more: another Rayssac, for Les Coques is on the mountains. Will there be another Louise there? She has, I do believe, much in common with you; but, my friend, you will be my friend always. I will write to you

* Aunt of Maurice's wife.

thence if you like. Who knows what I am going to see, who are expecting me? Everything promises most pleasantly, and yet I approach these unknown acquaintances with timidity. Pity my wandering life—dragged from place to place. No, do not pity me, 'tis Providence wills it so. We have only to be passive, and without disputing to follow the hand that leads; this alone sustains, consoles, and turns everything to profit as regards Heaven. I feel myself more disenchanted, more disgusted with the world than ever. Oh, how far more calm and happiness there is behind Sister Clementine's door than in all worldly scenes! I went to call upon her yesterday; she is in retreat till Monday, a loss to me who love to see and hear these good nuns, these souls apart from the world.

Is it true that M. and Madame de Bayne have left for Goritz? I pity you in your solitude, you at least do not like it as your sister does; I wonder neither at her taste nor yours. Dear friends, who comes to amuse you now? Have you Léontine, at least, the three sisters together at all events? If she is with you, tell her I love her; if she is away, tell it her all the same.

I should like to send you some pleasant news worthy of Paris, but the pleasant is rare everywhere, so much so that I have none of it to-day. I have, however, seen Versailles, but only the exterior, for, the King being expected, the doors were shut against us. Have I told you of this and our *royal* fury? Perhaps so in my last letter.

I should have had to tell you about this morning's concert if Maurice, who was to have taken me there, had not had an attack just as we were setting out. Pain instead of pleasure, a sudden transition very frequent in life! His little wife, flushed with emotion, took to nursing, sugaring, composing him, and everything grew calm beneath that sweet influence. Maurice will, I hope, be happy with her. I know no woman with such a character, heart, and face. She is a *stranger:* I study her, I examine her, in order to grow more intimate, to enter into her, if she cannot enter into me. We all owe each other concessions of taste and opinion for the sake of family peace and affection; this is everywhere the case, and we shall find them easy where there is so much goodness and generosity. Not a day that I do not receive marks of affection from this charming new sister. People always talk of her as the Indian. Madame de Lamarlière pronounced her much to her taste, pretty, and well dressed. That very day a bulletin of the visit and the toilette was despatched to Gaillac, and I am sure it has gone the round of the town, and that every one knows that the Indian wore a dress of brocaded silk, a black satin shawl trimmed with blonde and lined with blue, a lace collar, and a black velvet bonnet with an ostrich feather, *astounding heaven and earth*, according to Madame de Lamarlière's expression.

Adieu, my friend! I embrace you and say, Love me, think of me, believe in me, write to me, speak of me. Always all your own.

One other word: 'tis with you I especially like to converse, because we understand each other I think. I am going very soon to wish you good bye; it is striking two, and I have an appointment at my Abbaye-aux-Bois chapel. I should like to set my conscience in order before going away. Alas! I know not to whom I shall have recourse in the country, so far away from a church. Happily we are to go and spend Christmas at Nevers, and I shall try to get myself calm, for I am not so to-day. I tell you this believing you to be alone with Pulchérie, whom nothing surprises. Pray in your Rayssac chapel for your poor friend the Parisian, who will repay you in kind as well as she can. Adieu, adieu! till when?

I cannot help postscripts with you, dear friends. I have to tell you, each and all, that the General is your devoted friend. He came again to see me, not having found me on Tuesday. He took me out of the chapel just as I was going to pass the grating, which made us laugh a good deal afterwards, about my leaving the church for a Protestant. It is a great pity to see so good a soul in error; but it does not prevent his partiality for mountain Curés, those at least of his time, who he tells us were delightful. And his castle neighbours, oh! there were no bounds to his praises of them! A hundred questions were put to me respecting each of you ladies, the little Henriette, whom we call Louise, and the Countess, who rides so well, &c. I cannot tell you all we said during the hour and a half that he remained chatting. He admired our Indian, and spoke of my journey to the Nivernais to visit Madame de Maistre, who is *dévote*.*

---

\* It was Mme. Armand de Maistre of whom the General spoke, not Mme. Almaury de Maistre, to whom the letters in this volume are addressed.

The General knows that family: who is there, indeed, he does not know? He offered to accompany me to the interior of the Palace. We shall see when I return. I am sorry not to have been able to avail myself earlier of so much *obligingness*. Thanks to Pulchérie for her recommendation. I see she must have spoken very *ill* of me to him.

Of necessity I leave you.

---

To THE SAME.

*Christmas Eve, at Nevers,* 1838.

I have hardly time to do more than date this letter, dear friend, being summoned by the bells to midnight mass. I listen to their loud voices, and think of the little bell at Andillac with its pretty tinkle, tinkle. Who would have told me last year that I should be so far away? Thus God leads us whither we know not. I am going then to the Cathedral to pray for those I love, I need not say for you.

Two days have passed since those lines were written; two days of festivals, prayers, offices; letters written and received; all these! things that took up my time without preventing my being with you, dear, very dear friend. There is a way of seeing each other in everything and everywhere; 'tis in the heart and before God. We shall never have a better way of meeting, nor indeed any other for a long time to come. I shall only return to Cayla in fine weather, when we have flowers and a blue sky to show our Indian. And we are still far enough from that, as I need only look up to the pale sky, and white earth all frost and snow, to convince myself of.

As everything, or most things at least, remind me of those I love, this weather turns my thoughts to your mountains, dear friend; I see your white rocks, and you, poor prisoner, in your chimney-corner, eyes and heart wandering away. Come sometimes where I am, where you have seen me so loved and happy, beside my charming Baroness, who loves you too, and often says to me, " Let us talk of your friend Louise," and we talk of you. This happens more than once in the course of the day; for you know the heart has a way of returning again and again to what it prizes. After Cayla, Rayssac; nothing in a worldly life pleases me so much as these thoughts of family and friends. I delight to rest in them, and constantly revert thither both in thought and words. 'Tis with Henriette especially that one talks of one's country. What is agreeable to me is sure to occur to her; she has that fine instinct of the heart that guesses whatever pleases. Accordingly I have no want unfulfilled, I have almost too much happiness, for it is about to end; and what regret we shall feel at parting, at no longer seeing each other at every moment, we who have been accustomed to live together for a month!

We are, you see, at Nevers; we were at Les Coques when I got your first letter, the seeing, reading, and talking of which was no small pleasure. The passage about Goritz and Madame de Montbel touched everybody, the more that the Montbels are well known to

Madame de Maistre, who used to attend the soirées of the Toulouse Minister, while her father, M. de Sainte-Marie, was intimately connected with him politically. You are in a familiar neighbourhood; I have been talked to a great deal about the marriage of those poor orphans, asked whether they were rich, and various questions prompted by sincere interest. Henriette was charmed to hear that one of these young ladies had become your sister. How you would love my friend, dear Louise! how amiable, kind, attaching, and highly intellectual she is! I congratulate myself more and more on loving and being loved by her. It is a happiness in my life for which I bless God, for there is something providential in our meeting, and in the good I do this dear invalid. It is what I cannot understand, but there is no mistaking it; what I say to her, read to her, whatever, in short, I do when we are together, pleases, makes her cheerful and less suffering, so that she is already much better than when I came, and that, beyond a doubt, her family love me. Her father takes such care of me as to come into my room to see whether I have a good fire when I say my prayers. He is afraid of the northern air doing me harm, and said laughingly, during some severe cold that we had, "The Flower of the South will be frozen." Excellent and holy man that he is! I am very fond of him; he reminds me of your father. He has the same way of thinking, the same information; he has read everything, and written as well. He was good enough to read me some parts of his works, which one would have attributed to a Benedictine. He is intimately connected with Carmelites, Trappists, charitable institutions, with all that is pious and learned. Charles X. was partial to him, and saw much of him. If only he had listened to him!

We have visitors here from Goritz, amongst others a M. de Ch——, who comes and goes for the exiles from St. Petersburg to Vienna, sometimes into Spain, from court to court, indeed, and who charms you by his narratives. I have never seen a more agreeable, handsome, witty, and learned man. A great geologist, he examines excavations, descends into volcanoes, establishes himself amongst ruins. He slept and lived for a week in the chamber of Sallust at Pompeii, drove through its streets, went into its theatre; had excavations made in presence of the Duchess de Berry, and saw a thief surprised by the lava in the act of carrying away a purse. This caused a good deal of laughter, and made us all own that iniquity was sure to be found out sooner or later. I have seen his cabinet of natural history and mineralogy, as well as his cabinet of antiquities. I have seen the borders of the walls in Cicero's dining-room, charming paintings of inimitable or unimitated delicacy. With so many other qualities, M. de Ch—— combines those of the thorough Christian. He turns all his studies and discoveries to the support of religion, proves that science and faith harmonise, that geology and the Book of Genesis agree. You will think me very learned, 'tis that I have seen Paris, and that at Paris intelligence is in the air; nevertheless it is in the neighbourhood of Les Coques that I have learnt all this.

Madame de Maistre has charming surroundings, which, unfortunately, her health and the badness of the roads prevent her enjoying as she would like. As to the roads, they are left mere rock and swamp. We have hardly been able to walk to mass in the village. No week-day mass. Here I have all I want, two churches right and left, quite close to us, and a white-haired father, a saint, one of those who escaped the Nantes *noyades*, who speaks of God like a martyr. I went to him with Henriette; she was in the vestry, I behind the most closely-curtained grating. I pitied my poor friend for having this broad-day *tête-à-tête*; but she cannot confess in any other way, being unable to kneel. It is double penance and double merit.

Nevers is an ancient city, famous for its dukes and their palace; and the Cathedral, too, is very fine. I have seen the Sisters of Charity, and among them one sister who was much amazed at seeing me, Elisa Viguier of Gaillac. I really thought she would have fainted. " Oh, Mdlle. Eugénie, where do you come from?"—" I am coming to join you." But one glance at my bonnet with flowers, my gay attire, led her to another conclusion. I told her of the marriage, and of what brought me to Nevers. But all the same, is it not wonderful to see me there, and this life I am leading just now?

Louise, dear friend, whatever I do, whatever becomes of me, you will be always in my heart. Your two letters gave me much pleasure; the one brought by M. de C—— reached me one of these last days. He was gracious enough to leave a card at the same time, which well deserves a call from my brothers. They will go and see him and thank him for his kindness. I very often have letters from Caroline; this good little sister is full of attentions and affection for me. Maurice tells me that he observes her qualities develop more and more, her piety strengthen, and that he shall be happy with her. Everything goes well, except this dear brother's health. As for me, I am as at Cayla, changed only in externals—smart dress, hair curled, a thousand pretty little things, sweet little books, magnificent collars : so much for the outward woman; and for the mind, distinguished acquaintance—M. Xavier de Maistre, author of the 'Leper,' whom we are to see in Paris, and other celebrities of the day with whom Madame de Maistre is connected. She is bent on making her friends known to her friend, nor do I say no.

We return to Paris early in January, and then it is that I shall see the world's grandeurs; as yet I only know the pleasant, pretty, simple side of it. Now, however, baronesses, duchesses, princesses, and as many geniuses as you like. They amuse me to look at, as would a gallery of pictures; but, my friend, let us not fix our hearts, still less, our souls there. God and the world do not harmonize. Alas! how little one thinks of heaven in its whirl and glare! This is what I am told by my friend, who knows and is detaching herself from it.

Adieu, dear Louise! I do not know where you will be found by this letter, which takes you my new-year wishes—heart and soul wishes that I daily form and pour out before God, now that another year is at hand, with increased fervour. How sad the closing one has been to you, dear friend! This day last year you could embrace the father for whom you can now only pray! This recollection occurred to me in thinking of you, and I prayed God to console you under these sorrows, and all the others which life brings. Embrace your sisters if you are together, and tell them that I comprehend them, and all belonging to you, in these good new-year wishes. Thanks to the Pastor for his blessing on Babylon, 'twas not ill placed. What do you know of the travellers? That good sister and dear brother, what news of them?

---

To MDLLE. DE GUÉRIN.

Nevers, 12*th January*, 1839.

Still at Nevers, but not for long. We shall set out one of these fine days, and I want to leave thee, dear Mimi, a last "souvenir"—a long account of all I have done, said, and thought; as Papa says, of all those little details, that sand of everyday life that the pen tries to grasp. 'Tis, however, when I return, when we meet again, that I shall relate all particulars, small and great, of my journey, that I shall be able to tell what there is no writing, what can only be painted by the voice: such as the countless kindnesses of Henriette, the goodness to me of M. de Maistre, my conversation with Madame de Sainte-Marie, my whole intercourse with this excellent and amiable family.

I have thought much of thee and of Papa during the recent festivals. On Twelfth-Night I could see you turning box-leaves for the absent, for their return, and so many other pretty things staked on those turning leaves. The account of this Twelfth-Night evening, of the box-leaves, and the cake with the bean in it, much amused these ladies, who do not know our customs. Henriette takes pleasure in hearing me talk of the South, which she has always wished to visit. We shall see her, if her health permits, and from Cayla she will go into Italy, to Venice, to Nice, where her cousin de Maistre is governor; and she will take me with her. What say you of our plan, Papa? and thou, Mimin, dost not thou think one separation is already quite enough? O, no doubt it is! But while far away from you I like to travel on paper and follow Henriette.

Fortunately, we shall not be far, for Paris, and I have promised her the Thursday out of every week. Then it is that she will introduce me to her distinguished friends. Madame de Vaux, a most marvellous woman as to energy, stature, and intellect, who carries on a controversy with Lamartine in writings full of truth and power—for she is very pious—used to correspond with M. de Lamennais before his fall. Maurice, who knows her, has introduced Caroline, who writes me word that she is enchanted with the Baroness de Vaux. I long to see her in her own house: I have often done so in church. Then I have still got to know the Duchess de Damas, a correspondent of Henriette's; M. de Neuville, who wanted to write to me; and the excellent and unfortunate M. Xavier de Maistre, who has lost his four children, and is accordingly much out of spirits.

Here I have paid some visits, seen some company,

and even dined with Monseigneur, who is very agreeable. As he comes from the South, and was told I did so too, he talked to me of our neighbourhood, even of Cayla, which had been pointed out to him on his way to Gaillac, and asked me whether there was not a bishop in our family. "There was, Monseigneur; but I never saw him."\*
It was a charming evening. There is a very select circle at Nevers, all made up of great names. I was introduced to drawing-rooms, churches, and convents. M. de Sainte-Marie took me to see the Mother Superior of the Sisters of Charity; and on the same occasion, I asked for Elisa, whom it is not very easy to get down into the parlour, but that day we spent a whole hour together, talking of our own country, to which she desires kind messages, her brother, M. the Curé, and Cayla included. She is very happy, and will win her wager if God grant her life. From thence we went to the Carmelites, and I had a long chat with a young lively nun, who ended by inquiring my age—reckoning upon a candidate, perhaps. This sacred conversation, carried on, through the curtained grating, without our seeing each other, had a charm of its own. M. de Sainte-Marie has passports for all convents: for the last twenty years he has been the temporal father of the Carmelites, so you may imagine the greetings and compliments that went on.

This sheet is like a journal, all full of my own news; and yours—yours, dear Mimin: how much pain and pleasure both it gave me! That poor Euphrasie left you so suddenly and unexpectedly! I much regretted

---

\* Mgr. Naudo, Bishop of Nevers.

her departure: she shortened the time, cheered you by her mirth; you were not alone. Poor recluses, how often I think of you! How constantly I place myself between you, as Wolf does! We must look forward to my return. Not that I am dull, or very seldom, my life is so varied; but yours, all alone, without any variety this wintry weather, distresses me, and I think of it very often. I long that you should have Erembert again, and fancy you will soon be recalling him: but still I should be very glad to find him in Paris, and he too, I expect, is waiting my return.

Caro, the charming, presses me very tenderly to come home. I shall no longer find good M. Augier there; he is gone to Boulogne, and Maurice will miss him at dinner and in the evening. There is a charming little nephew of his, who is a great favourite with us all. This little *Bill* is very pretty, and a great friend of mine: he is ten years old. Caro, too, is very fond of him. Maurice writes me word that he daily discovers new qualities in her; that her piety becomes more enlightened; that she is charming in her gentleness and attention; and that he foresees happiness with the little woman. God be praised! We have been so anxious for this.

The news of the day is made up of glory and mourning both: the capture of Vera Cruz by our troops, and the death of the Princess of Wurtemberg—the young Princess Marie of Orleans—whom everybody regrets. She was good, beautiful, attractive, and pious. We have some Goritz visitors here, who tell us wonders of Henri V. On the whole, however, our politics are calm.

And my poor aunt came in the bullock-cart! Tell her how this idea pleases me, and that I think of her when with an aunt of Madame de Maistre, who is aged and amiable, and who likes me. I make conquests of old men and old women—'tis very easy. My remembrances to Marie: we shall resume our correspondence in Paris. Louise speaks of having had two letters from you. I embrace you both four times. Elisa* has been very good in giving you three weeks; accordingly, she shall have a beautiful watch. Mine will soon point to eleven o'clock. Good night! I am going to bed. Kind messages to all the neighbourhood.

---

To M. DE GUÉRIN, Cayla.

Paris, 20*th January*, 1839.

I have written you a word or two almost daily, my dear Papa; to-day I want to write at greater length. The good General came to see me as soon as he knew I had returned from Nevers. 'Tis not—truth to tell—entirely on my account these visits are made. Caroline suits him so well, he thinks her so pretty, and likes so much to say so, that I cannot doubt that our Indian has a large share in the friendship of the dear old man. One of these last days he was here when Caro was making up an Indian doll for the little De Maistre girls. He was sufficiently enchanted to take to working at the doll himself, and to wish to remain till the completion of the toilette,

---

* Mdlle. Elisa Fontenelles, a cousin of Eugénie's.

which unfortunately was interrupted by visitors; so the Marquis left us, and the next day Caro wrote him word that the Indian lady was ready and would be charmed to be presented to him, and at once the worthy man returned to us, spent the afternoon here, and offered to accompany us to-day to M. Aguado's museum of paintings, which is said to be very fine, and to which we mean to go. From thence we shall visit the interior of the Palais Royal. Nothing is too much to expect from the good Marquis. Pulchérie did us a great service in introducing him: I have thanked her for it. A letter to Rayssac will accompany this.

My dear Papa, we have no lack of friends in Paris. What shall I tell you of that good, perfect family that I have just left? Always some fresh kindness on their part. To-morrow, Saturday, a large brilliant evening party at M. de Neuville's, to which I was invited; but I shall give up my place to Eran, who will accompany Madame de Maistre. There is to be a sort of gathering of beauties of all lands—English, German, Spanish, and the lovely ambassadress of the United States. 'Tis a pretty sight for one who is fond of society. I refuse, as much as possible, to go out, but I shall not be able to excuse myself from going to M. de Neuville's, who has been so kind to Erembert. I have seen the Baroness de Vaux, the Joan of Arc of Henri V., who in 1830 only asked an officer of the royal guard for fifty men, in order to get rid of Philippe, she herself to head them sword in hand. This woman is a man in energy and stature; now she is entirely devoted to God, visiting prisons and exhorting those sentenced to death, and this combined with a charming simplicity. I am to be introduced to others, too, of whom I shall tell you. But all this does not prevent my thinking a great, great deal of Cayla, and impatiently waiting the month of May; I shall even set out, if I can, with Erembert the beginning of Lent.

Mesdames de Maistre and de Sainte-Marie send you all manner of kind messages. They think Caro charming —the most enchanting creature that can possibly be seen, Henriette says. The evening she saw them first she really was radiant: she is prettier than before her marriage. She is an excellent little wife, full of little attentions to Maurice, as is Maurice to her. They are happy. Maurice behaves perfectly. He is worth a hundred times more than last year, as he himself tells me. There is always the same confidence in me, and we often have private chats. This dear Maurice longs to see you, and often reverts to the *Mimin*. We shall all be happy to meet again at Cayla. On Saturday I shall be thinking of thee, Mimin, at St. Thomas d'Aquin, where I go to hear M. Dupanloup, who, by the way, is to preach there during Lent. There is no lack of godly teaching in Paris, but the taught are very rare. The more one sees of the world, the more one is struck with its ignorance of things needful. The Yversen sister comes to see us every now and then. She told me of Madame L——, who would like to know us, but we have already so many people to go and see that I lose the wish of making new acquaintances. All the time goes in dressing, in visits to be paid or received; there is hardly any left for reading or writing. The Lastics are here, Madame de la Renaudière, the Barrys, an English family who are very fond of Maurice, and an infinity besides, whose very names I do not know. Then there are the De Maistres and those they introduce me to—more than enough for me.

Oh, how I shall rest at Cayla! The contrast will be all the more appreciated because so striking from the whirl of Paris to the calm of the country; from the roll of carriages to the low rumbling of carts; from the Paris sounds to the *coucouroucou* of our hens. I see great charm in that, my dear Papa, to say nothing of you and Mimin. How much I long to embrace you! They go on treating me very well here: everywhere, indeed, I am quite a spoilt child. My health is good: have no anxiety of any kind about me. How are you getting through the winter in the new drawing-room? Better, no doubt, than in the hall. Is Wolf banished from it? Maurice wishes to know. Passing thence to the kitchen, tell me if our servants are well. I regret the partridge.

Thank M. the Curé for having drunk my health—'tis a proof of remembrance. How I long to return it him in Cayla wine! Here we drink Bordeaux. However the wine may turn out, you will do well to send a barrel. Here I have got far away from M. the Curé, and I wished before I left him to recommend myself to his prayers, and ask him why the chapel is still open? Adieu! luncheon is ready, and then we must set out. Much love to my aunt, to Gaillac, to wherever our friends are. I am going to write to Antoinette. Louise tells me you are soon to be at Rayssac; I advise you to wait for her return from Castres, and, besides, it must be very cold just now in the mountains. What do you hear of Euphrasie and poor Pulchérie? I take it for granted that Madame Facieu and every one at Andillac are well. Impossible to write more. Caro and all of us embrace you.

---

To Mdlle. Louise de Bayne.

*Paris, 9th March,* 1839.

Why are not my arms long enough, my beloved Louise, to embrace you wherever you may be? Always good and affectionate, you write to me from Lastours; you find time to think of coming to divert me in the midst of all your own diversions. You discovered that I was sad: it is true, my friend, I was so, and still am. Maurice, my *so* dear Maurice, has long made me uneasy. Fever, emaciation, pallor, sleeplessness, loss of appetite: my God, what suffering all this causes! Shall we have to lose this dear brother? This dread is within my heart, and feeds itself on presentiments, absurdities that it goes on raking up—such as having dreamed of coffins as soon as ever I fell asleep, every night during my journey to Paris, and meeting on the day of the marriage a funeral procession that had to make its way through our bridal carriages. 'Tis in vain that I dismiss all this, sweep it away; it remains with me like a vision. Say what you like of my dark fancies, and pray God for your Paris friend.

I was uneasy about you, in suspense, and your dear

note does me infinite good just now. It is so sweet, so comforting to hear you. Your narratives have a charm that you liberally bestow on me. O thanks, friend, thanks! it is so precious to be thus loved. After God, there is nothing better on earth, I assure you. I have made trial of the world, which has no value for me. One finds in it nothing but emptiness and show. My ideas have greatly enlarged on that head, and more than ever my tastes tend to the country, a retired life, the small home circle. If only there be no blank made there! If God wills it, we shall be all together this summer at Cayla.

We had intended to set out in the spring, but business and his poor health keep us back. He will be incapable of bearing the journey for some time to come. He is getting over the attack, his doctor reports him better every day. There is hope still. Hope! What would life be without it? The little wife nurses her husband with admirable care. Love and devotedness make up this Indian angel, to which add fervent piety, and you will have an idea of the charming creature. The world which she would enchant in no way enchants her. She is almost an ideal being. A quick wit, a penetrating intellect, large eyes that see everything: happily, they are blue, the colour of the sky, which renders them celestial, and is why . . . I will tell you this *why*, which concerns myself, and will not write it. I was going to do so, but there it is safe back into the quill. This quill contains many a thing, else what should we have for our tête-à-tête?

But you—your fall, your double fall—and have I

said nothing about it then? Forgive me, dear friend, my bad charity began at home. Tell me, do tell me, what traces you and the Countess still bear of all those upsets, scratches, and bruises. Do you know that it is frightful to think of your being run away with by the horses, and overturned, flung I know not where in the dark? My God, what a misfortune might have resulted from it! I am going to say a Te Deum, for if you are alive it is through special mercy. Your good aunt must have been much alarmed at those cut faces; but what care, attention, kindness!—remedies that cure everything. You enjoy your life at Castres in that worthy and intellectual family of Lastours. I am glad to know that you are there. Stay there long; comfort the afflicted—that poor mother who cannot console herself. This will be both a Christian work and a diversion from your own sorrows, from that *mourning which has prevented your taking pleasure in the pleasures of the world*. These words of yours picture to me your heart, all full of regret and *world-weaned*. "Prayer," you add, "comforts me; when I have prayed I feel better." May God bless you for thus speaking, for having been made to feel experimentally that He is the soul's only support. We are advancing in piety, my friend; foster it by regular reading night and morning. There must be order in all things. The religious in their monasteries only sustain themselves by rule; so it is with every soul, and still more with those who are much in the world and rather excitable and changeable by nature.

This reminds me that there is now at Castres a pious girl, whom I know well and am fond of, Françoise Limer, the sister of our former Curé. She would be pleased to see you, and you would please me much by taking her a message from me. You will find her in Mdlle. de Villeneuve's house. Tell her that in Paris I forget no one. Never doubt this, Louise. Oh, my friend! could I but see you, speak with you, find some lime-tree avenue to walk in, I should tell you and ask you many things; you know how we blend ourselves, give and take in our conversations. So we do with my Louise here, Madame de Maistre, with the difference not of affection but of broken health—an organization which compels me to take the most delicate, most timid precautions. My least griefs do her harm. This good family is about to leave Paris, and my dear Henriette-Marie presses me to follow her to the country, promising that Maurice shall join me there on his way to Cayla. I had another plan, of going back with Erembert, who is about to leave us. Out of Paris my thoughts take pleasure only in Cayla, and my Paris is not the great city, it consists of three persons. Affection urges me to follow one of these, my charming invalid. I do not know what I shall do, but one thing is certain—I shall soon leave. Do not reply to me till I tell you where I am. My dear Cayla hermits will not be sorry to see me again. What happiness if we could all arrive there at once! These Benjamins one leaves behind a good deal spoil the delight of returning to one's father. Such is life—thorn and flower!

I attend churches and sermons as much as possible; they do one good, one always comes away with some holy thought and better courage. On Sunday we heard M.

de Ravignan at Notre Dame. 'Tis a curious thing to see such an assembly of men, a sea of heads flooding the immense cathedral, to listen to a voice; but what a voice! From time to time some smitten soul, some young man in doubt or under conviction, seeks out the orator that he may confess. As to that, however, people flock with equal ardour to the play, and Mdlle. Rachel attracts at least as great a crowd at the theatre as M. de Ravignan at Notre Dame. I am not surprised at the infatuation of the Castres people for this young marvel: those who have seen her are enraptured. Yet she is ugly: I hear this from those who have seen her near. Alas! how profane what I am writing in Lent! . . . .

I do not forget the dear sisters in the mountains. Adieu! Love me, and write at once if you wish to find me in Paris.

To M. DE GUÉRIN, Cayla.

Paris, *March and April*, 1839.

This fragment of a letter will tell you, my dear Papa, that I am by the side of my poor invalid friend, awaiting the arrival of M. Dupanloup. It is while thus waiting that seeing an inkstand I continue to write to you at the expense of the vestry. But I shall put a penny into the box for my ink and paper, &c., for I stole a sheet to follow this, if we are left long alone. From time to time some peaceable abbé or sacristan passes through, looks at us, and seems rather perplexed by this improvised office in a vestry. But the protection of M. Dupanloup is over us: we have but to name him here as a universal safe-conduct. He has already been, and has left us for the retreat at the seminary of which he is the superior. I shall ask him to let me see the little Combes. This will make you laugh, 'tis an episode in my Paris life that I shall remember.

Never was there such a holy week—always excitements, excursions! Andillac is more favourable to meditation than Paris, but God is everywhere and in all, if one is bent on finding and seeing Him there. My poor dear Papa, I have prayed much for you in these beautiful fanes of Notre Dame, St. Roch, and others that we have visited. I have thought of the simple little Andillac chapel where you were. The new chapel will, I imagine, have served for tomb, or Paradise, as they call it here.

If ever there was anything unconnected and scribbled, 'tis assuredly this letter, begun, left off, taken up again in so many different places. Just now at Maurice's, after sitting five hours for my portrait; that good M. Augier was quite determined to take it for you. It was for you, too, that I let myself be taken, that I might at least return to you in some fashion! My dear Papa, you will see a painted me arrive with Eran, who also has been painted, and, more fortunate than I, is about to see you again, to embrace you, talk to you of Paris, of so many, many things, of his journey and long absence.

Mine is going to be prolonged further than I had intended, but you see yourself, could I refuse these kind friends what they requested with so good a right to expect? They will thank you for it, I assure you.

I shall bring you back the little copybook* which you so much value. It is now in the hands of Count Xavier, which will constitute its highest distinction. I have, you see, been presented to this celebrated man, and he appeared to me as charming as he is good. He is fond of his cousin, and under her patronage I was sure to be well received. We found him alone in his room, reading the Offices of the Holy Week. The worthy brother of his brother Joseph, he ought to be religious. It is thus he consoles himself for his paternal sorrows, for the three children he lost between the ages of eighteen and twenty.

The very evening of this visit I was taken to Valentino, to the great concert of eighty musicians, which I had heard once before. I have still a good deal to see, but one might spend a thousand years in Paris without having seen everything. I lay great stress upon acquaintance made with persons, even more than with things.

Your health makes me anxious, however well cared for it be by Mimin. Do nurse yourself, therefore, I pray you, that I may not be unhappy about you. Adieu, very dear Papa! adieu, very dear Mimin! I have not time to write to thee. Maurice sends Papa 'Reflections on the Gospel,' by M. de La Luzerne. Goodbye to all. I send a waistcoat to Pierril, and an apron to Jeanne; to thee, to all, all that the heart can devise. That kind M. Augier! do thank him well in your next letter to Maurice. My portrait will be finished at Cayla. I found

---

* A book in which Mdlle. de Guérin had written down some of her poems.

it impossible to sit to-day. I do not like leaving you; but, for all that, adieu! I will write from Nevers. Erembert is delighted at the thought of seeing you again. I already picture to myself the happy day of his arrival.

*Evening of the 2nd of April.*

---

To MDLLE. LOUISE DE BAYNE.

Nevers, 13*th April*, 1839.

Again at Nevers, my dear Louise, again remembering you in my encampments and travels. Never did Arab lead a more wandering life. Monday in Paris; to-day here; in a few days somewhere else. But that will be at Les Coques, in the country, in repose, in a place most completely to my taste. There will be nothing lacking but a church, which is too distant for daily visits. Something is always wanting to travellers, but God can make up for all, as was told me by my holy Curé of St. Cyr, the old man of the Nantes boats, of whom I think I spoke to you at the time of the Christmas festivals. Who would then have told me that I should see and hear him again? I fully believed I had said Good-bye to him till we met in heaven, and should never more find myself at Nevers. I little thought then that my dear Maurice would again be ill at the time fixed for my departure; that he would be unable to set out with us. Erembert is gone off alone to Cayla, and I am waiting here till Maurice and his wife come to take me up on their way. Madame de Maistre and her family have arranged it all, and I left it to them, finding pleasure in pleasing them, and also in being still near Maurice, able to have frequent tidings of him, and to go and see him, if necessary, in case of his becoming worse. Who knows, my God! The doctors have pronounced him in a very critical state: two cauteries and the air of the South are the only chances of safety held out to us. I say nothing of the care lavished on him in every way, of the perfect devotion of his wife. Alas! if that could cure, if the heart could confer life, we should have no anxiety. Is it not too sad to see him in this state since his marriage?

My dear friend, pity me. Do better still—pray for him and me. Our best hope is in God. I believe this: I have experienced it, and that everything in life is illusory, and yet I do not feel the consolations of piety; my heart, which is weaned from the world, cannot attach itself to heaven. I appear to have no feeling left, like one completely stunned. My dear friend, write to me; words of yours will do me good. Do you suppose that I am losing friendship too? That is a thing which never passes away. I am determined to make you believe it. See how I love you, and tell you all that grieves, all that goes on in me. My last letter was very unreserved, very miserable, rather too much so; I reproached myself for having written it. What is the use of communicating sufferings that can hurt others? Tell me the effects of it—that I pained you? I believe I did; I know what your heart is towards me, and then, from my further knowledge of it, I fear I may have done you harm in another way, may have thrown you into the state of excitement and sadness in which I myself was. We ought to guard against this. Whatever happens, our soul ought to rest so firmly upon God as neither to be troubled nor overwhelmed.

I left my dear invalid surrounded by friends: among them I number the d'Yversen sister, who has given us many proofs of real interest, and the Baroness de Vaux, of whom I told you — that energetic woman, full of devotedness and religious feeling. She goes to the prisons, to exhort the condemned; on her way she will visit our invalid, and speak of the good God to him. I have had tolerably good accounts since I came here, but there have so long been these alternations of better and worse that one can trust to nothing. Erembert must be arrived at Cayla; I can fancy the embraces that are going on and the joy of the two recluses. They had depended on seeing me too. I wrote them word that I should arrive with Maurice, who had a fancy to keep me, and that I was spending a few days at Madame de Maistre's country-house, waiting till we should all set out together. One must not tell them everything. What is the use of knowing all when one can do nothing?

I am writing very egotistically: not a word of you or about you, just as though I were forgetting you. Very far from it, however, for I think of and speak of you with Henriette, one friend leads to another; sometimes too she has a way of looking like you which charms me, for then I see two in one. I make this remark to her, and she congratulates herself, knowing how loveable Louise is in my eyes. One might go further, but conscience checks the heart: it is not right to expose any one to the danger of vanity. You tell me I once told you so, and I hold to my principles. My dear Louise, one word, two words, a thousand words from you, I beg, of your life at Lastours or at Castres. How has your time—your Lent—been spent? Mine has been the most disturbed, the most mortifying possible: mortifying, that is, in a spiritual sense, for we eat meat half the week; but God has given me my dry bread—my penitential diet—in the form of anxiety. My poor friend, how I have experienced what the *Imitation* tells us, " The cross will follow you everywhere." Paris was to be my Calvary—Paris, where I expected so much happiness. You have not, doubtless, written to Rue de l'Arcade? Do so to Les Coques, near La Charité (Nièvre). I have a longing for tidings of you, of your sisters, of M. Charles, and Marie. How about their journey to Goritz? Will you present my regards to Madame de Gélis and the family that loves you? . . . .

Does M. Louis de M—— happen to be in Paris? The shadow of an acquaintance becomes noticeable in that world of strangers. Poor Paris, my promised land! how hast thou deceived me! Let us only reckon with *certainty* on Paradise. We must remember this, my dear friend :—

>Happiness will flit,
>Fool who trusts to it!

Variation on a saying of Francis I. But let nothing prevent you trusting friendship and the friend who will never change.

To Count Xavier de Maistre.

Monsieur,                      Les Coques, *April*, 1839.

"A rose-leaf is never in the way," was the saying of, I think, a Persian poet. A graceful idea, which might seem yours, with which this sheet of paper invests itself in order to form part of the bouquet addressed to you by my friend. Will you deign to accept it, and also my grateful homage touching those manuscript poems that you have been so indulgent as to read? Nothing more felicitous could befal them, and your flattering opinion will ever be my fairest poetic crown. I did not hope for so much, and could never aspire to more. I have no wish for fame, and the advice you are good enough to give me on that head is in perfect accordance with my own ideas. Celebrity is not happiness, as more than one great man can testify: and to woman, more especially, wide spheres are unsuited. God has made them small for us, as for the flowers. Oh! I would not exceed mine, but I had been told that God made nothing in vain, and that every mental gift should subserve His praise, or else was thrown away.

Oh! sing, sing then, you whom He made to sing.

It was thus the thought of my *Enfantines* arose: little poems within the scope of children, a useful aim for my inspirations, and then a hope, too — the hope of poor Homer — "Give something for my songs." A useful resource this to my father, a secret idea that I nurse in my heart, as Prascovie did that of going to Moscow.

Such, Monsieur, is my little dream, which you have flattered by your favourable opinion till it almost turns to a reality. You impart life to the talent you have found; it learns from your lips that it is able to do what it wills, and is quite proud and very strong in your expressed approbation.

Accept, I pray you, the homage of all my hoped-for laurels, and—what is more certain—the feelings of profound respect with which I have the honour to remain your very humble servant.

---

TO MADAME DE STE. MARIE.

Les Coques, *May*, 1839.

This time the *rose-leaf* shall be for our dear mamma, since she likes them, asks for them, accepts them so graciously, and says such pretty things. 'Tis enough to lead me to make up a large paper nosegay, which will be easily done if I gather all my heart holds for you, all that I feel, think, and say of your very great kindness. O thanks, then, thanks for the note of tender reproach and for the little cap with *hope-coloured ribbons* (the colour I have adopted since I have been with you) that you have bestowed on me, together with so much besides! This cap delighted me: I received it as from the hand of my mother, who interested herself in my head as well as my heart, which you do not deck out unsuccessfully either with all your affection.

I find myself quite happy, just now, thanks to you, my

heart's mother, to your loving Henriette, and to the good news I have had from all quarters. I must tell it you. Maurice is much better: he says so himself, and writes me a letter of convalescence, spring-time, life, after a walk in the Bois de Boulogne. There is hope! There is something to bless God and Ste. Philomène for! Hallelujah! hallelujah! . . . . 'Tis a resurrection! And then again his Indian brother-in-law, M. Dulac, is on his way to Europe, and comes to settle affairs. Everything is turning out better than we expected for our dear Maurice. I was longing to tell you this. Happiness and unhappiness both get told to friends, and no one deserves that name better than you.

One word of our life, our sweet life at Les Coques, in the open air, *amidst the flowers and verdure*, like La Fontaine's rabbit. A great delight to all and to me to find myself here, to enjoy it beside the queen of the place and of my heart, as says some tender author, not a whit more truthfully than I. In truth, I love your loving and loveable daughter ever better and better, and can no more conceive our two lives separating than I can my two eyes. Do not let us think of what I see still far, far off, and would postpone to the end of the world. It is so happy to be together, to be with one so full of heart, intellect, and charms of every kind!

Would you believe, in spite of this, that she has still to complain, to pronounce me too *reasonable?* Who would have supposed it? And thereupon we dispute frantically, and also upon *rose-buds*, and Andryane the republican Adonis, whose face I find the only thing to admire in him. I am reading those Memoirs of his which have been so praised, reading them without any enthusiasm, always expecting it to rise, and with a prejudice against republicans which perhaps prevents it. Prejudices are so powerful! Our Henriette is indignant at such "sang froid," especially when I tell her I would gladly spin the rope to hang republicans and republic both. Oh! then it is you should hear her, should see her throwing her indulgence over

> The gibbet
> And the gibbeted.

Thus arguing, disputing, time flies its fastest in this castle, in the little drawing-room, seated on the sofa, before a table covered over with books, stockings, tapestry-work, music, a confusion continually worse confounded. We pass from one thing to the other. Man likes to spend his life in change, and so do women, as far as their fingers go. This reminds me of St. Martin, which I am very anxious to see—not for the sake of change, but to rejoin you and with you enjoy those beautiful gardens and flowers I hear of. M. de Sainte-Marie will tell you whether this be not true, and how much we yearn to embrace you. We consider that he is leaving us too soon, which is what I should always say on seeing him go away.

Adieu! a word I do not like to say to you, kind and dear mamma. Do not be angry with me, I pray you, for not having written to you; 'tis too kind to complain of it, and then I know what is for *Riri* and what for you. The dear child, how I embrace her! Her papa has told you how pretty and happy she was at Saint-Martin.

*Titine* is not a little so, either: always trotting about, and also very good and very well. 'Tis only the poor mammas who suffer. I did not fail to sympathise in all your anniversary sadness. Can you love me? Love me for my happiness, and accept my respect and affection.

---

To MDLLE. LOUISE DE BAYNE.

Les Coques, *2nd May*, 1839.

A letter from you at last, dear Louise! 'Tis a real happiness to me, who love you at all times and in all places, to find that I too am loved by you. I hardly knew what to think of this long long silence in return for two such great letters and all that I confided to you about Paris and myself. My friend here used to ask me whether you were dead, and I assured her there was no danger of that, for you would never have left this world without announcing it to your friend. I had partly guessed what prevented your writing during your Castres life: visitors, talking, expeditions. I know how time passes in society. There were days in Paris when I had hardly time to look into my own room.

That agitation is over; now, a life of complete calm externally, for within 'tis still much the same: anxieties, increasing alarm about our poor invalid. But for that I should be happy here, where affection, care, most loving attentions abound, to which add intellectual delights— books to any amount, an enchanting country, the view of the Loire and an immense horizon, a room with a white muslin bed, a desk to write at, and you may believe that I am fortunately placed here. This hill is for me a Mount Tabor, a place of vision, where a voice tells me "You are beloved." There is nothing comparable to this tender friend and all her excellent family. M. de Maistre is a model of goodness, a type of devotedness; neither his wife nor children are ever ill without his spending the night by their bedside, warming linen and giving them draughts. I admire him, and ask whether he was the sick-nurse of his regiment. 'Tis one of the cases where the heart teaches.

This brings me back to my habitual thought, to that other invalid that I would fain nurse, that I long to see. Another does so, does so perfectly, with all the devotedness of conjugal affection. Poor dear sister! I fear she will injure herself by over-fatigue and not save him. She wrote to me lately, "All my hope is in God. He will have pity on me, I trust; meanwhile I submit to all."

It is really admirable, the piety of this young woman, brought up almost among heathen — not, indeed, her own family, who are thorough Catholics, but the people of her country. If you could but hear her speak of the month of Mary, how much charm she finds in the services, the instructions, which are so well done in Paris! That is one of the things I regret; but I have had a room given me here, which the little ones fill with flowers, where master and servants come every evening to pray to the Blessed Virgin. In the country one does what one can. The church is very far off. Madame de Maistre can never go: the roads are so bad there is no taking a carriage there. Accordingly, she is a prisoner in her pretty house and her beautiful desert. All that she has done has been to go out once in a sort of litter; but it makes so much fuss, she must have so many men about her, that she has little pleasure in it. But we two alone—she leaning on my arm—do sometimes walk a few steps into the wood, where we seat ourselves in the shade. This reminds me of being with you under the limes.

My dear Louise, we often talk of Rayssac, of you, and your sisters. In absence, the thought of those one loves keeps recurring, and one likes to utter it aloud. There is no sweeter enjoyment, especially when shared. Have I told you how much Henriette loves you? As much as one can love a charming unknown. And for me, who know you well, I love you neither more nor less than of old. There are some things which cannot increase: how add to what is already full?

There you are, my dear sheep, back in the fold, to the mountain pastures, under the care of the Pastor Amalric, who will be charmed to see you return so white. You have done wonders in your La Platée chapel,* and your soul seems to me in a condition that I much approve— —more calm, more free from illusions than ever. O marvel! Courage, friend! Perseverance! perseverance! as Father Guyon used to say, as your Castres father has said to you. Calm within, affection without; a family gathering, always so sweet a thing; methinks I see you happy now with your good sisters and that dear Marie

* One of the principal churches at Castres.

that you were longing to embrace. Yes, there you are happy, but uneasy about her state. So it is always; but let us hope that this little angel will arrive safe without causing you too many tears. I promise to pray for your dear sister. This child will be your delight. I had hoped for the same, and wished it much, for Caroline and for all; but I hear nothing of it, and in my brother's distressing state dare no longer give it a thought. What would become of that poor little woman, who is so delicate, and, though made strong by courage, so afflicted? The weight of anxiety is almost beyond her strength.

Alas! you see, dear friend, I do not tell you that he is better, as you hoped to hear. Very far from it: the complaint goes on increasing, and I receive more and more alarming accounts. After a momentary improvement he has fallen back again; had frightful relapses, which make me miserable. I do not know their full consequences; they conceal his state from me, or, at least, think they do so, by vague expressions which do not mislead me; and, besides, other letters confirm my fears only too much. Yesterday, good General de Frégeville wrote me word that he had seen my brother the evening before, and had thought him very ill, or words to that effect. They talk of Eaux-Bonnes; but how is he to get there, how set out, when he does not leave his bed? If it be possible—if only he can be got into a carriage—I shall go and join him at Orleans. Sad return! In a few days I shall know what there is to hope. He is dying to set off, to find himself once more at Cayla, at home with his father and all of us. Paris can no longer be anything to him, as you truly say; 'tis the place for the healthy and gay. My poor Maurice! shall we have to take him back dying to our poor father? You may write to them now about his illness, it is impossible to conceal it any longer. O have him prayed for, dear Louise! lift some other young girl's veil to recommend to her intercession this young invalid, the brother of your best friend. I am inexpressibly grateful to you for all the interest you have shown and felt, and for having led me to think of the Prince Hohenlohe. I am going to write about it to Paris, to a friend who will perhaps be able to inform us how we may get at the Prince. We have already had a novena at Nevers to the relics of Ste. Philomène which have just been sent over from Rome. I believe in the power of the saints; I depend upon the succour of our friends in heaven and on earth, and on God, who is wholly good, and knows all our needs, whether of life or death. His will be done! I do not know whether I perform this act of submission rightly. Adieu! all kind remembrances to your three sisters, whose prayers I also request. One can never have too many pious ones. All your own.

P.S. In reading the newspaper I came upon the Algiers article, and saw the death of poor Zoe Maznéjouls, crushed by a beam! Death has all sorts of ways of striking us; but this death, at all events, was not unexpected. Thirty years of preparation have led that soul to heaven. I hope much from the Christian sentiments of my dear invalid. My respects to the pastor.

To Madame la Baronne de Maistre, Château des Coques.

Tours, 22nd *June*, 1839.

At length at Tours, dear friend, and the dear invalid not so ill as I thought. God be praised! 'Tis a mercy to have any diminution of anxiety! He is, however, very pale, very thin, much changed, with a loud hollow cough, no voice at all, and given up by M. Petros. He would not undertake the case. You used to tell us that he was an alarmist. But M. Buquet and Providence brought unexpected help: a doctor, who, having heard of the young invalid, asked to see him as a friend of M. Buquet's. At once a complete change of treatment: ether thrown to the dogs, almost cold baths—of which the good doctor was himself kind enough to regulate the temperature—drying the invalid with his own hands, and paying him six visits in the course of the day, so as to watch the disease in all its hourly phases. Was he not indeed, my friend, sent from heaven? The proof of it is that Maurice is sensibly better. He came to me in the drawing-room, and seven or eight days before, he tells me, his legs could not support him; and now comes the journey, which amuses without over-fatiguing him.

We shall travel by Bordeaux with post-horses, so I know not when we shall meet again at Les Coques. I shall write to you at greater length from Bordeaux; this is a mere line on arriving, hastily dashed off in an hotel room where I am alone—alone indeed, I give you my word, after having left you! My brother, his wife, and Charles are at Mesdames Mansell's, handsome, elegant, graceful Englishwomen, who received me too most kindly, but had no bed to give me. If I had known that they meant to spend three or four days here I should not have left Les Coques, my paradise.

Adieu, my angel! I never left any one so suddenly nor more tenderly. All sorts of love to all Saint-Martin.

P.S. The invalid remembers you all, and tenders you his homage. He has seen your brother often. Oh! what heat! I put up many entreaties to the clouds. Ever yours.

The rose-tree is quite well.

---

To MDLLE. LOUISE DE BAYNE.

Angoulême, *Saturday*, 29*th June*, 1839.

Your letter reached me just at the moment of my departure from Les Coques, dear friend, as though to comfort me for the loss of a friend. You always arrive opportunely, but never more so than when I am sad and need consolation. You speak so me so sweetly, tenderly, and piously, that there is charm and profit in listening to you, and some suspension of sorrow. All the time that I was reading your letter I fancied myself at Rayssac, by your side, during one of our confidential conversations, which you know I like; then I folded up your loving words in my heart and my pocket, and set off on my journey in the diligence towards Tours, where I rejoined my poor brother.

What a mournful journey! To begin with my departure from Les Coques, my farewell to the kindest friend, the resource of my heart, of everything, my con soler during six months of sorrow: in short, she to whom, after God, I owe everything! It is only when we are together that I shall be able to tell you how indebted I am to this friend and her family. Her mother insists positively on my returning to them next year. The heart says Yes; but how can I promise? My whole life depends on my poor Maurice, so closely are we bound one to the other by family ties. My God, if he were to be taken from us! I cannot dwell upon this thought, which yet occurs to me with every heart-beat. Without being actually despaired of, his state gives the greatest alarm. He suffers from hunger, and cannot eat. I dread the throat ending by being entirely closed. Such, my friend, is the state of the poor traveller whom we are taking by short stages to his native air, to that dear Cayla for which he sighs.

Since Tours, where we remained eight days, we have done nothing but sleep at an hotel. We have passed through Châtellerault, celebrated for its knives; Poitiers, whose battles you are familiar with; to-night here we are at Angoulême, where you have an abbé who will not, I think, make the place famous, but whom I would go to see had I time. I write to you in my room, ready to go to bed that I may be up to-morrow at five. We travel early in the morning to avoid the heat, and post, the the most convenient way of transporting an invalid, but ruinously dear. Nothing less than the Indian purse is required to meet these expenses.

The poor loving wife would give all the gold of Bengal for her husband's health. Her devotedness knows no bounds: always with him night and day, and often getting out of bed. She writes daily reports of the sufferer's state to the doctor who is treating him. This new doctor, only recently consulted, has changed the whole treatment, done away with blisters and all that could exhaust, and substituted baths and good broth, forbidding bleeding, which had been abundantly tried. Some slight improvement has resulted from all this—a little more strength; but the chest fills, the throat gets inflamed. My God! do Thou come to our aid. What an alarm we had when we saw him spit blood in a wretched wayside shed, where our only resource was water and a fresh egg! This little woman is an angel of piety and resignation. You would love her dearly. We expect to get to Bordeaux the day after to-morrow, and, when we can, to Cayla, the last station on our *Via Dolorosa.*

Pray for us, my dear friend, and do me the kindness of writing me word at Cayla, as soon as possible, what steps will enable us to apply to the Prince Hohenlohe. The priest to whom I wrote is at Rome; I have therefore been unable to send my request for prayer, not knowing how to set about it. Be good enough to tell me this, and soon, that I may do so on my arrival at Cayla. There is no time to lose in asking for a miracle and a recovery.

Adieu! my very dear Louise. I am exceedingly touched by your letter, by what it tells me of yourself, though I do not quite approve of all. Oh! how hard I am to please! for you are really on the way to perfection, and edify me like a preacher. But I love calm, even with God. This is not so easy as people suppose. My love to your dear sisters: I do not forget their affection for me. Never did I need marks of interest more than now, and I ask them for these in church especially. I include you in this request, dear friend, and leave you after a sad embrace.

In a week or so we shall be at Cayla. What a bridal return! Alas! poor life of ours, if God did not sustain. Write to me immediately, if you please. Let us try all means of saving this poor brother. I know it would be happiness to you to contribute to this. That poor Elisa Lafont is to be pitied. I have just heard, too, of the death of a young wife of nineteen, who was at Maurice's wedding, very pretty and very healthy. But what of that? Death stops at nothing. Let us be ready; the misery is only for those who are not prepared. Every day Maurice asks me for some religious reading. Nothing but these sentiments consoles me.

At ten o'clock at night, and always yours.

---

To Madame la Baronne de Maistre.

Hôtel de Nantes, Bordeaux, *Tuesday, 2nd July.*

At length at Bordeaux, dear friend: very far from you, and still far from Cayla, merely a station of rest and full of charm for the eyes. A delightful country, a large, handsome, populous, animated town, the Paris of the South, with a more beautiful sky. We are going out to have a look at all this and walk about a little; but friendship before everything. I think of you more than of buildings and curiosities. You have never left me during the whole of our journey, my dear friend. I seemed to see you making the fifth in our carriage, or else we were at Les Coques, on the sofa, or in the wood or the dairy, but, at all events, always together, you in me and I in you. Distance only separates bodies, and that, alas! is quite enough.

Why is there not a telegraph for purposes of friendship? You should have known at each moment what was befalling us on our way, our alarms or our calm, according to the state of the invalid. He has borne the journey very well—I even think the motion of the carriage good for him, as he seems to suffer more as soon as he leaves it. We have only had very intense anxiety once, when he spat blood in a state of extreme prostration, with the throat so irritable as hardly to be able to bear a drop of water. This was in a village tavern, where we could get nothing but a fresh egg and some water. He swallowed the egg, and got better. The simplest remedies are often the best: this, I believe, is the secret of homœopathy. My poor Maurice would not be so ill if he had begun by it. They have exhausted him with bleeding and cauteries. The present treatment is much better: to do nothing but rest, take nothing but broths and nourishing things, beef, mutton, and poultry. Is this not sensible, and completely in accordance with your system? You do only good. Certain it is that this new treatment agrees with the invalid. May God be pleased to spare him to us! I do not know whether he will go to the waters: we wait the orders of the doctor, who could not decide upon anything before we left. M. Petros would not undertake for so short a time a case that he might perhaps have successfully dealt with six months ago. Why was it not thought of sooner? Incurable misfortune! Oh! let us take hope from what still remains—a little life, country air, and peace of mind.

. . . . Oh! my friend, how often I return to Les Coques and to you! How I live there since I have left! The Jordan could not remount more rapidly to its source than the heart to the place it loves, which for me means beside you, where we have been together, where you are. I picture you at Saint-Martin, where you have arrived, I suppose, from Nevers, after having embraced your aunt and the interesting Madame de R——. Did you give any message from me to those ladies, whom I well remember? I have met many in these parts of the world where we are travelling, but none equal, none of your family.

At Tours, however, I much admired Mrs. Mansell and Miss Melina, her sister, two pretty and agreeable Englishwomen, with distinguished manners, who received us with most cordial hospitality. They, too, are Indians, but they remind one of the noble and interesting women in Scott's romances. They are friends of Lady Bentinck, the wife of the Governor-General of India. You see we were fortunate in our acquaintance. These ladies are very fond of Caroline and her aunt. Nothing can be more captivating than our Indian: she is beautiful as a May rose, with her fresh cheeks and fresh toilette! It is a happy thing to be young: one can glide over sorrows in which the old sink. Caroline, though always beside her husband, seeing him suffer continually, getting up often in the night, most active in her devotedness, is yet in perfect health. The fact is, she is not aware of the full extent of his illness. She goes on hoping, and does well. Hope is so good for us! All mine is in God. When I see him so pale, so thin, I have hardly any human confidence left. He is there beside me in his bed, sometimes sleeping, sometimes saying a word or two to me. I am alone: Caro has left me to be sick-nurse for a few hours, which I like as well as seeing the town of Bordeaux. That can be done later. We are to go and see the vessel in which M. Dulac, the brother-in-law, is to embark. This will be a pleasure to me: I shall talk of sails and rigging; I shall have seen a little of everything when I get back to Cayla. '*Tis thus in travelling we learn.* The rest of the couplet does not concern me.

Shall I soon hear from you? Oh! that is what does indeed concern me intimately. Give me full particulars of yourself, your health, your (I may say our) dear mamma, who must be happy to have her two children with her! You will soon see M. Adrien. If he is with you, give him much love from Maurice, after accepting his affectionate regards for Madame de Sainte-Marie and yourself. Adieu! This is a sad word compared to those we have been exchanging of late. My best respects to your father, and warmest remembrances to your perfect husband. Is he still solitary? How I caress the little ones, and embrace you and your mamma!

P.S. We are here until Friday: too long, and not long enough, since I shall not have time to receive a letter from you. A year ago I was writing to you on this very day, the 2nd of July. Who would have said then that the same date would be penned from here? Life is full of the unforeseen.

---

To THE SAME.

*9th July,* 1839.

What is it you think, what is it you fear, dear friend, from the infrequency of my letters? Misfortunes, perhaps; and, if so, you are right. We have had papa very ill; this sorrow, and others which press upon us on our Maurice's account, together with the occupations consequent upon them, have slackened my correspondence with you—with you whom I so much love, and to whom I want to tell everything.

My kind friend, how often I speak to my family of your tender mother, of all those dear distant friends that God has given me! I admire how you have been sent to us at a season of trial, in days of affliction, as if to console us; as it were a balm at the foot of the cross. Already I feel this cross very heavy; but courage! God helping, one reaches Calvary at last, and from thence heaven. Yes, heaven, my very dear friend: let us look nowhere else: 'tis the only prospect that comforts and sustains when the heart sinks and fails.

Yours suffers, suffers much from the same sorrows as mine. I am sure of it. I know you; know how truly you love me. Oh, my friend, what joy and regret this causes me! On no account would I increase your sufferings—alas! great enough already—and yet I do so every time I speak to you, every time I pour out what I feel. What would you have proceed from me but tears? That is why I hesitate to write to you, that I write so little to-day. Write to me you. Oh! you will do me no harm; you know that my health is good and strong. I can suffer without dying. Tell me, then, what you are doing at Saint-Martin, that beautiful place, so replete for you with memories of childhood, which please so much, which for a moment can console for the sad and bitter present.

For my part, Cayla charms me: not a tree, not a path, not a little chink in a wall, to which my heart does not cling. As yet I have been out little, I have merely gone round the house; always occupied as a sick-nurse, and how long one would like to be so! There are sorrows that make themselves very dear. Alas! one so enjoys tending those one loves! My poor father is out of danger but still weak, and so he will be for some time to come. The fever is not yet over; but for the last two days he takes a little chicken-broth. With cooling diet and much care we shall save him, I trust. Why cannot I say the same about another sufferer? but for him we can no longer have any other than a heavenly hope. M. Adrien must have told you what the doctors thought. I cannot speak any more of this. May God sustain us, my dear friend! God loves us, and afflicts us in this world to make us happy in another. This is what faith teaches us: 'tis my support, my strongest consolation. Let us share it, my friend, as we share our sorrows; let us unite our souls as we unite our lives. It is not for nothing that one is a Christian. Père Quadrupani was very sweet and comforting to us on our journey, that long *Via Dolorosa*. Adieu! I embrace you and those who love you. Let us hear soon.

---

To the Prince de Hohenlohe, Germany.

Monseigneur,

The miracles of healing worked by the saints lead me to hope everything from your intercession. Permit me, with so many others, to implore it, to commend to your influence with God a beloved and dying brother, for whom we have few human resources left: those of faith are the best, and will, I believe, be efficacious for the sufferer, aided by your charity. As to the Christian the soul is more precious than the body, I recommend to you that of our dear Maurice. Not but that he lives a Christian life, but can one ever have love and faith enough? Let your charity, Monseigneur, deign to accept my prayer, and also to indicate the day on which we may unite with you in order to obtain from God the mercy we desire. But, whatever happens, we beforehand accept the will of God; and in the same sense I pray you, Monseigneur, to receive the homage of my gratitude and the assurance of my deepest sentiments of respect and, admiration.

---

To Mdlle. Louise de Bayne.

*10th July*, 1839.

Dear Louise! dear friend! I arrived yesterday, and have this moment received your letter—two happinesses of which I want to speak to you at once. I have quantities of things to tell you, of the journey, its troubles, fatigues, fears, and of the rest of this present time—rest as of the promised land. Oh! how far away it all seemed, this Cayla, this good father, this dear Marie, Erembert, and you too, my very dear friend. It is something, at least, not to be at different ends of the world, though 'tis merely an idea when once one is separated. But in that *so far off* there is an additional sadness for the heart, which does not like distance. My God! what must the separation made by death be, when those one loves are no longer to be found in any part of the earth? Then one turns to heaven, but all the hopes of paradise will not console us for those dear vanished ones; one weeps for them, which God does not forbid.

Who knows whether I shall not have to pass through this trial? I sometimes hope, sometimes despair. We have been hovering for three months between life and death. This poor brother! I am always speaking to you about him; I can speak of nothing else, and with you there is no restraint; 'tis as with a sister who shares family griefs. You show me this by your affectionate letter. God comforts us, at least, by the interest evinced in us. What am I to say to that kind Pulchérie, who hastened to write to Madame de Cazes on the subject of the Prince Hohenlohe. This has touched us much, as well as the details that Madame de Cazes has had the goodness at once to transmit to me with expressions of cordial sympathy. This letter, which I found at Cayla, had arrived by an express from Cordes from my uncle Fontenilles, which I do not very well understand. The Providence of Heaven and of your friend has brought it about. How I bless them! How grateful I am to my dear Pulchérie for the proof of affection she has given me on this occasion!

If I were not so afflicted I should have reason to be happy in all that surrounds me now. You can comprehend the paternal jubilation on seeing me again and the delight of Marie, but our poor Maurice struck them very painfully. They had not thought him so ill, though I had tried to prepare them for that dying aspect. At last here he is arrived, and saved from the many dangers of the journey. I was always dreading to see him sink on the way, but, on the contrary, the motion and the open air did him good. It is only now that he again droops: no sleep, and a derangement of stomach which, combined with sore throat, prevents him from eating. Poor martyr!

But he is very calm, very resigned. Before he set out he received the Holy Communion in his bed; that is a consolation, not, at least, to have to tremble for the soul. I have just written to the Prince, and I address it under cover to Madame de Cazes, who offers to forward it. When you write to her, do tell her of my gratitude and of the happiness she gave by telling me of the two cures in her own family wrought by the prayers of the saint. I think it was in her brother's case. You tell me so, I believe.

I am so busy, so cumbered, what with unpacking, visitors, and numerous letters received, that I am writing in a hurry. Need I tell you that the good General recently charged me to lay him at your feet, that he is one of our true friends, and that, as a proof of it, he got me a hundred francs from the Queen for our church? The last courier brought me the order of the Queen's secretary, payable at the receiver's at Gaillac in ready money, which makes our new chapel thrill with joy. The idea occurred to me of writing to the Queen, who is said to be good and pious. I was not mistaken: thanks, however, to the obliging recommendation of the Marquis, who is a favourite at Court. God be praised! good comes from everywhere. After that, a letter from my loving and loveable Madame de Maistre, and then yours, dear Louise. Here is enough to occupy pen and heart.

We have spent a day at Gaillac, and in that short time our Indian made a conquest of the whole town. All who saw her are taken, dazzled by her beautiful eyes. In truth, she is charming. Our cousins are delighted with her; Madame de Paulo put on her most gracious face.

How I regret your being so far away! It is to you all, to my best friends, that I long to show off our dear marvel. She surprises me in everything; I cannot understand how she bears grief and fatigue so well. She is the only one who watches her husband at night, and he does not allow her much sleep. I heard her get up three or four times last night. God gives her strength; she is so pious.

We remained six days, I think, at Bordeaux, half a day at Toulouse: in all, 'twas a twenty days' journey—an endless time for an invalid and for us on his account. But for that these halts would have been pleasant: they rested one, and showed one sights, but I could only take a hurried glance at anything. All the time at Bordeaux was spent in Maurice's room. When the weather was mild enough to have the window open I used to look out at the port, the omnibuses, and passers-by. In the evening, as we were opposite the theatre, Caroline and I used to amuse ourselves with watching the actors and actresses dress, turning themselves into kings and queens, and kicking each other the while. Poor wretches! A little further on, by way of contrast, was a charming church, where we used to go, one after the other, to mass. This is all I saw.

And now again the dear Cayla, which shall have me long. I want rest, retirement, want to return to my primitive way of life. These eight months seem a dream: I ask myself whether it be really true that I have just come from Paris? Alas! yes. Maurice proves it to me. One only wish remains—to see you. My heart is dead to everything but friendship. I embrace your three sisters: Madame de Bayne will permit me to do so. Pray for me and for him. All your own.

---

To MADAME LA BARONNE DE MAISTRE.

*19th July,* 1839.

I adore, oh! my God, thy eternal and impenetrable decrees, and submit to them willingly for love of Thee! There are now three years, dear friend, that I have put up this prayer, that it has upheld and prepared me for the most cruel sacrifice. The moment is come; no hope left; the doctor has pronounced the terrible " Nothing to be done," and spoken to us of the last Sacraments. We very easily got the sufferer to consent. I alluded to them in connexion with the prayers of Prince Hohenlohe, and, as he had duly kept Easter, his conscience did not terrify him. There he is confessed. I write to you during the preparations for the Holy Viaticum and Extreme Unction. I do not know why I am not in mortal agony of grief. Doubtless, I still hope. Oh! my friend, my poor friend, let us pray God fervently for this dear soul. Amidst all this I think of you; I could not help writing to you, uniting you with my heart, my tears, with a whole afflicted family. Let us think of heaven. I will have nothing more to do except with the other world. My God, thy will be done! I say it in tears, but tears are prayers.

How at this moment I feel the need of faith, the help

of piety. Oh! what will become of me? Your letter reached me yesterday; I did not expect to answer it so sadly. Exhaustion, sinking, came on suddenly. Perhaps it is a crisis; perhaps we shall save him. But at all events let him be ready; let him prepare as a Christian for departure at whatever hour it takes place. Let us place ourselves together at the foot of the cross: it is there I leave you, my beloved friend, afflicted as I myself am.

I press you and your tender mother to my heart. Adieu! We must be prepared for everything. Whatever happens, I will write to you.

---

To MDLLE. LOUISE DE BAYNE, Château de Rayssac, Varre (Tarn).

*22nd July*, 1839.

You must already know, dear friend, the loss we have sustained, but I too want to speak to you about it. I have to tell you of my grief, my affliction as sister, as intimate friend of this poor Maurice. Dear brother! there he is dead, *dead!* How describe what that word is to me, all of incomprehensible pain that it contains! No; I cannot reconcile myself to this thought of eternal separation, never more to find him anywhere upon earth. Oh! how our affections disappear! God wills that we should raise them higher than earth, and therefore takes those we love to heaven. He, my brother, is there, in heaven, amongst the blessed. I hope so, for he died the death of the elect. God be praised, who, in His mercy, willed to save the soul and let the body die,—that human semblance we so much love, which appears to be the man and only conceals him. Thus it is the Christian eye sees these things, and looks towards the life to come when the present breaks our heart. For me there is an end of all that one calls happiness. This death kills me, takes from me every charm that bound me to the world. My future was in his: his children would have called me mother. I had invested everything in him; too much so, perhaps. God does not choose that we should lean so heavily on the creature, a reed that breaks under the hand. My poor soul often suspected this, but in vain; we only attach ourselves more strongly to what is about to escape us.

It is all over, then. There he is in heaven, and I on earth. Oh! sudden disappearance! Was it not yesterday that his wedding took place? Alas! all connected with that past seems to me an illusion, as our poor Caroline says: "I feel as though my marriage were a dream." A very sorrowful dream. One month after set in the fears, the falling away, and all those sufferings which have brought him to the grave. Poor Maurice! I can say nothing but that name. For me it contained so much happiness, something electrical in its effect on the heart. Nor was this the case with me alone. The whole family were under the same influence; he was the delight of us all. My father used to say this child was his pride. Every one spoke well of him; nothing but tears and praises over his coffin. It was the day before yesterday, that sorrowful, lugubrious, heartrending, and latest parting in the cemetery. We all accompanied him thither—our dear Maurice!—we were with him as long as possible in this world. Oh, what a descent that of the coffin into the grave. I followed it with my eyes while praying God for the dear soul of my brother. I can no longer see anything, love anything, except that mound of earth. There we every day go to kneel with his poor widow. How dear this young woman is to us—this half of our Maurice, this marvellously energetic, strong nature, always with him, devoted to the dead as to the living. Poor young woman! an angel in prayer and tears for two days beside that bed, now holding the hand, now kissing those cheeks, that mouth. . . . . . Alas! alas! what a sad enjoyment! My poor Maurice! How we could not leave him! O my God! lying there so cold; the eyes dim—those eyes that were so brilliant, so beautiful! What death makes of us! We shall all come to that. My poor friend, what should we do with eternity on earth? Just to prepare ourselves well, and to go when God wills: that is all. There are blows that prostrate, leave nothing standing but faith. Pray that God will give me much faith; never did I need it more.

If you could come to see me, Louise! As for me, do not look for me; I could not endure to be anywhere but here, in these rooms where he passed away, in this house where everything recalls, everything mourns for him; and besides, we are not too large a family—my poor father has only three children now. How afflicted he is, never more to see his dear son, his Benjamin! This sacrifice is very great: may God accept it! We place ourselves at the foot of the cross. When the Prince puts up his prayers he will not cure him. It is too late: why not have thought of it sooner? I shall always feel this regret, but who could have believed death so near? I hoped he would last until autumn without knowing why, for I thought him very ill; but never, never did I believe I should see him end so soon. He sank, very gently, in five minutes after having received the Holy Viaticum. Up to that moment he was fully conscious: what proves it is, that after his confession he called back the Curé to speak to him of his relation with M. de Lamennais, in the form of a retractation. Oh, what misery had he died at that time! In everything there is some cause to bless God: this cross, this death, bears the evident marks of salvation! that is what consoles us on the side of faith, and ought we not to view everything as Christians?

Adieu, dear friend! I ask the remembrance and the prayers of your three sisters while announcing this sorrow to them. You were to be written to the day before yesterday; but there is more of the heart in this, this is from me to you. Marie desires to go along with me in my letter word for word and heart for heart. Her thinness and the change in her looks afflict me. This is the season of sorrows. How is Madame de Bayne?

---

To Mdlle. Antoinette de Boisset, Lisle d'Albi.

*23rd July*, 1839.

Pray for him, my dear Antoinette; pray for the brother, the friend of your friend. Here we are parted:

he is in heaven and I on earth, where I no longer behold anything of his but his tomb. O sorrowful disappearance! I cannot make up my mind to it, cannot believe that Maurice is no longer of this world, that he will never more return as one of us to this place, that arm-chair, that room, that bed! Oh! God, my God! it is true, nevertheless, and Thou hast willed it so; Thou hast taken this dear child from us, doubtless with some merciful design. How should we doubt this, after so many tokens of salvation, after his holy and blessed death? Yes, my dear friend, his end was the most sweet, most consolatory imaginable: the priest who attended him,—everybody, tells us that he is in heaven. Oh! how this comforts. But do not let us neglect to pray for this dear soul. Who knows? one must be so pure to see God. It is, therefore, as much to recommend him to your pious interest as to announce my own sorrow that I send you these lines.

Alas! I wrote you so different a letter so short a time ago—a wedding letter! . . . . How swiftly the things of this world change! God will not have us attach ourselves to earth, and only sends us shadows of happiness here. You have felt this as well as I, dear friend. You mourn a sister, I mourn a brother, both so loveable and beloved, the joy of their family. Maurice! to all of us it was a delight merely to think of him, merely to speak his name! All that dead! Poor dear sister!—I mean his wife—the most interesting creature to us, and, indeed, that can possibly be seen. We admire and wonder at her: so much courage, energy, and self-control in so young a woman! Never was there a more beautiful example of the power of faith and piety. Oh! what an angel God had given to my brother! The blow that separates them is fearful. A widow and an orphan at twenty! "If I lose my aunt, who will be my stay here below?" And then she commits herself to God, her great resource. I should not be surprised if she entered a convent, such is her piety and detachment from life. This marriage, this Paris visit, this death, all seem to me a dream. I lose myself in these events, these memories, these realities. Providence has inexplicable designs for us. Crosses at the end of everything; tokens of salvation that I adore. Adieu, dear friend! Pray to God for the brother and the sister who will never be otherwise than one.

Be so good as to impart our affliction to your own family, to our friends de Gélis, and to Irène. I cannot write to them to-day.

Your heartbroken friend.

---

To MADAME LA BARONNE DE MAISTRE, Château de Saint-Martin (Nièvre).

*Friday, 26th July.*

For the last eight days since he has left us, since he is in heaven and I upon earth, I have not been able to speak to you of him—not able to be with you, my tender friend, you who are also so dear to me. Shall we never have done with our human affections? Neither grief, nor disruptions, nor death, nor anything can change us. One must love on, love even what is in the grave; love *remains*, clings to the body which once held the soul; but that soul! one knows it to be in heaven. Oh, yes! up on high, where I see thee, my dear Maurice! where thou art waiting for me, whence thou callest, " Eugénie, come up here, where with God one is happy !" My dear friend, it is all over with happiness on earth : I have told you so before; I have buried my heart's life, I have lost the charm of my existence.

I cannot say all I found in that brother, nor what happiness I derived from him. A future, hopes, my after-life spent beside his, and then a soul that understood me! He and I, we were the two eyes of the same brow. And now, here we are separated, God has placed Himself betwixt us. His will be done. God took up His station on Calvary out of love for us : out of love for Him let us remain at the foot of His cross. I find this cross very heavy—all circled, indeed, with thorns—but so was that of Jesus. May He help me to carry mine ! At last we shall reach the summit, and from Calvary to heaven the way is not long. Life is short, and what should we make of eternity on earth ? My God ! so only we be holy, so only we profit by the grace to be derived from trials, tears, tribulation, and anguish,—the Christian's treasures ! O my friend, we have but to look at these things, at this world, with the eye of faith, and everything changes. Happy Father Imbert, who so eminently possesses that eye ! O that I had something of that spirit of his, so full of faith, so radiant with love ! I need support, and I often wish for this holy man, who would instil into me an enthusiasm for martyrdom and the cross. Alas! he has been prophetic. He told me, "You are the child of sorrow! make up your mind to many trials." I, who at that time was not, as it seems to me now, speaking to him of anything sad, I was struck with those words, which God has just fulfilled.

My friend, I have thought much of you in all this. The share you take in whatever concerns me, that *oneness* which there is between our hearts, made me feel that you were suffering too, that you were stricken and torn as well as I. I have prayed God for you. I am calm: I write to you without weeping; I throw myself into your arms. We have quantities of visits, but none are like what yours would be; and yet they are from friends, relatives, and neighbours, who are all very sincerely afflicted. But to have to occupy oneself about dinners, about daily household details, to be surrounded by the ordinary course of words and things, when everything within is changed, when one realises so great a void,—this is killing. And then the agonising contrast, the bitter thought that will keep occurring: "All these persons would have come to see him with wedding faces and congratulations!" Six young girls, yesterday, cousins of ours, with whom he would have laughed! How things change! Let us too change, my friend; let us wean ourselves from the world, from the creature, from everything. As for me, I ask for complete indifference.

He passed away without any struggle, quite easily, as if falling asleep, just after he had received the Holy

Viaticum. M. the Curé assures us that he is in heaven. But let us pray for this dear soul: we can do nothing else for him now. It is consoling to pray, is it not? to be able thus to succour those we love, to follow them with our affection even into another life. I pity those who have only tears to bestow upon the dead. It is very well to weep, but not without praying also. Prayer is the dew of purgatory : let us pour it out in floods ; we shall do so much good thereby. How I love to do so now! How comforting faith is to me! Dear friend, I wish you its sweet divine influence!

Write to me. I am anxious ; I am not dead to you, God knows! May your health be good, not too much upset! Tell me of all, of your dear mamma, who is also very dear to me. I recommend my Maurice, my Alphonse,* to her pious mother-heart. Dear mamma! I am heavily afflicted, and my father and all of us. He was the most affectionate of the whole family. You understand me, and sympathise, I am sure, in our grief. Why are we so far away? else I should this moment be in your arms. Adieu! very dear mamma, speak to your son of my brother who loved him. I pray M. de Sainte-Marie to remember this dear child before God.

Adieu! my dear Henriette. I return to you to leave you again : we do little more in this life. Love to M. de Maistre.

In heart and soul and thought eternally yours! Tell me of Sophie's brother, and remember me to her.

* The name of a son Madame de Sainte-Marie had lost.

I cannot refrain from mentioning our admirable Caroline, angel of devotedness, courage, and piety that she is! Near him, with him, in him to the very tomb. Oh! how this binds us to her!

---

To Mdlle. Euphrasie Mathieu, Albi.

*Saturday night, 27th July,* 1839.

It is to the sound of the bell ringing for the Novena of our poor Maurice that I come to speak to you of him and of our grief, my dear Euphrasie. I can speak of nothing else; my heart, my soul, my thoughts, everything in me is absorbed in this dear brother. You can understand this, you who knew him, who were aware of my attachment to him, of all the love that bound us to each other. God has separated us, has placed us at a great distance: one in heaven, the other on earth. But we shall soon meet again: life is not long, and crosses are what detach us from it and from everything, dear Euphrasie. You have experienced this before now. To each his season of trials, of tears; a precious season; a treasure to the Christian, when we take it as we ought. Oh! how soothing faith proves then! how happy are we to be able to console ourselves in the presence of God. Let us pray much, dear friend, for our loved Maurice, for those dear souls who leave us. Prayer is all we have to give them.

I thank you warmly, dear Euphrasie, for your touching expressions of friendship and of sympathy in our sorrow. Like us, you regret that dear, amiable Maurice. His name, that I used to be so fond of hearing, now wrings my heart, and yet I keep continually repeating it mentally. My God, what a sacrifice! what a mournful return from a wedding! Thus it is that everything changes! Providence has other views than ours: let us bless them, however sad they may seem. What now makes us weep will perhaps be one day our joy. In heaven all will be changed; but what will never change in my heart is the affection I have given you, dear Euphrasie. Mimi embraces you.

---

To Mdlle. Louise de Bayne.

*12th August*, 1839.

What are you doing? where are you? what are you thinking of at this moment, my friend? My heart has suddenly transferred itself to Rayssac—where it often is, for the matter of that, but more so than ever now that I have just been reading one of your letters, which, poor thing, had been relegated unread to my pocket. I put it there on opening it and seeing the date and the few first words treating of the Prince's prayers, alas! on the 12th —seven days before his death. It was only to-day that I found myself able to read this letter, kind and loving about me as it is.

My father brought it me from Albi, whither he went to implore the Bishop to leave us our dear pastor. A useless and most unfortunate journey! My father, overwhelmed by sorrow and fatigue, fell ill, and was threatened with an attack. For several days we were very much alarmed, but God has taken pity on us: our good and tender father is restored to us; he is better, much better now. I am writing to you by the side of the sofa on which he is resting.

O my friend, what dark passages there are in life! seasons when sorrows heap themselves upon the soul and seem to crush it outright! God permits this out of mercy. We have need of trials and afflictions, as the earth of hail and tempests. My poor dear friend, I maintain myself in these believing views as much as possible, but do you help me: I need a pious friend. I am weary; everything seems a desert, a churchyard. I find myself isolated in the midst of my family. My dear Maurice has left this blank to us all; to me, perhaps, more than to any other, owing to our habit of being together, and to the sympathy between our lives. He and I were the two eyes of one brow. This was too sweet, too much enjoyed by me. God has deprived me of what most delighted me on earth: accordingly, all I now see is utterly indifferent; yet I like writing to you, 'tis a heart-indulgence that I have long felt necessary, especially when I am unhappy. I am so in a human sense only, for, as a Christian, I am anything else. These afflictions, partings, rendings—all transitory things—are gifts of God for heaven. I keep telling myself so, and that this dear brother has been taken away from a vale of tears. "Why weep for him?" you ask. Oh! how much good those words did me, my friend! One needs to be recalled to God, to be lifted towards heaven; every moment the soul falls back into its grief; always I find myself at that grave, regretting what it contains. Oh! my friend, he is there! When I take to insisting on this terrible idea of death, I distract, I lose myself, I call out, "My God, have pity on me!"

In your letter of the 12th you said, while speaking of the beauty of Caroline, "Contemplate her long." Alas! how short it was! There she is, gone away, that dear sister, that admirable woman! Her soul is as enchanting as her face. Every one admires her, even the holy Abbé de Rivières, who simply told us that she had made a conquest of him—a conquest of a saint by an angel. In everything Caroline is an exceptional creature. Her aunt came to fetch her, fearing for her health in that room that she never left, in this place, amidst these associations fraught with him. Accordingly, here we are parted from her who seemed to have come from the ends of the earth to be made ours, to unite herself to our Maurice. Of this most brilliant and marvellous marriage nothing is left but a tomb! O nothingness of human things! sudden swiftness of Death, flying on festal wings. It was yesterday—was it not—but yesterday we were celebrating a wedding? What sorrow, dear friend, for your friend, in that past, in this present! My God! all was being arranged according to an eternal purpose!

Louise, I would I could see you! I love you! I only care to write to you and two others; not but what I would write to many, and with much affection, too, but not with my whole heart—a heart that pours itself out, weeps, falls down on this paper. My dear Louise, you will forgive me for selecting you for my sadness, for conversing with you so mournfully; but you enter so thoroughly into my feelings that it seems to me as if in speaking to you I were speaking to myself, to a stronger, a more sustaining, more pious self. Yes, you are more pious than I, and I bless God for it. You will be the less unhappy, the more ready for the trials that may come or are come; for, when all is seen and tried, there is no strength but in this. All human support is but so much sand; tell me not of it, and yet I am not yet detached therefrom. My God! what lessons have I still to learn! I keep dwelling upon his memory, his remains, upon all that I have recovered of his.

My Coques friend and her mother have been mother and sister to me. Like you, they have had prayers and masses said. Oh! he has no lack of prayers: all the priests of the district have come over to say mass. The holy Abbé de Rivières was also bent on praying near the remains of his friend. There is no end to visitors and letters. They occupy, but console little,— with the exception, indeed, of some friends and some writing that do one infinite good. Our former curé was with us to-day: that kind friend and gentle pastor, the one who received our Maurice's last sigh—there he is, removed far from us! His successor is a young priest from Albi, a perfect stranger to us. Tell my troubles to M. Massol,* that he may pray for us. We are infinitely grateful to him for his mass and his kind remembrances, and equally so to you. A fortnight after his death I

* The Rayssac Curé.

received the Prince's reply. Oh, my God! I had delayed too long. I have written again to that most kind Madame de C———. Oh! that I should in no case have forgotten to do. Tell me of your sisters and of Madame de Bayne, who is, we are told, at Toulouse. Lose no time in sending me tidings of the birth, and the state of this dear sister.

I embrace you with a heart broken, indeed, but alive to you.

---

To MDLLE. ANTOINETTE DE BOISSET.

*17th August,* 1839.

I know not, my kind friend, why I have so long delayed sending an account of myself to you who asked me for it in so touching a manner, who wrote me a letter, every word of which is graven on my soul. Oh, you love me truly! I see you do, you speak to me so affectionately, so sorrowfully. You tell me that we are sisters in affliction. Oh, yes! sisters, my poor Antoinette, that we may weep—you, your brother and sister; I, my brother —that we may help each other to bear this cross as God wills it should be borne. What a sacrifice, what a means of salvation is to be found in these losses for which there is no consolation on earth! It is thus God means to detach us from everything here below. These are blows sent in mercy, both for us who remain and those dear souls who have left us. Let all things be seen from the point of view of eternity; perhaps later our dear Maurice might have been less well prepared. There were evident signs of grace in his death which make me bless God and console me on the side of faith, for the heart still remains very sad, very desolate. We were so united, we lived so in each other! Poor, dear love! Oh, that he may be happy! We shall meet again. Life is not long; in our trials we have at least glorious hopes. How happy to be Christians! it is in affliction that we feel this. Have you not experienced this as well as I, alas! and twice for my once? Let us unite at the foot of the cross. My dear Antoinette, let us pray together for those we have lost. We can do nothing more for them here below, but how consolatory to relieve them in the other life! I therefore recommend this dear brother to you; pray for him as I have prayed for yours. I know I am saying what is unnecessary, but I like to say it: I like to ask you for the very things you do. You had foreseen my misfortune, then, the day of your visit? Alas! I had long apprehended it, but not so soon; and then I know not what hope, what faith in miracles and in life, kept up my illusion. Even the very evening before his death I was saying to Erembert, "If he can go on till the month of October we shall save him; he will spend the winter here." . . . . My God, how badly one calculates in this world! . . . . Let us leave off calculating on anything but death—it is the only certainty.

As afflictions follow each other, we had my father very ill two days later; and then that good Curé who consoled him, who had just received his son's last sigh, was suddenly snatched from us. Write to me, who am very lonely in my solitude : speak to me of heaven, of God, of those pious subjects you treat so piously and of which I have need; this is the moment for them, 'tis a time of trial, God be praised!

Adieu, dear friend! Be so kind as to express all my attachment to your mother, who loves me, and in her profound sensibility pities me. Oh! I am much touched by it. My father and the rest bid me tell you how they appreciate the share you all take in our affliction. Our Caroline is gone; her aunt, who was alarmed about her health, came to take her aawy, but with the promise of returning next year. What a return of a wedding party! 'Tis heartrending.

My love, if you please, to your sisters, to all friends. Adieu! love and pray.

---

To MADAME LA BARONNE DE MAISTRE.

*23rd August*, 1839.

You complain that you do not get letters from me; you tell me bitter things, my sweet friend. Sadness and bitterness, to know you sad and to be the cause! Alas! must I too, then, make you suffer—I, who would undergo martyrdom to free you from your pain—I, who am always thinking of you, and who often write! And yet you think that I omit writing to you! What can have become, then, of three letters addressed to you and one to your mother since the mournful 19th? My poor friend, blame the post, the officials—I know not who, the whole world

—rather than believe that I forget you. Then recollect that it takes sixteen days before an answer by return of post can be received. It was only the day before yesterday that I got your note from Nevers, together with the letter from Sophie—two very kind, very touching, unexpected ones. Blessed be such surprises, which charm and comfort! Come often! come, my friend, to your friend's side; come, dear letters, my favourites of all! No one enters so thoroughly into my suffering as you: you are my sister by tears; this is as sweet as being a sister by blood, and dearer still to the heart, for sorrow is the strongest of ties, nothing attaches more closely.

We love each other, therefore, more than ever. More than ever I think of you, long to see you, to hear you, to be with you. And all this can only be in spirit, so far away are we. Why is there not some one spot, some home for friends on earth? Oh! I for my part should never go away from it; I should live there with very few persons, but those very dear, very amiable, very sweet, very intelligent: a little paradise, of which you should be queen. Alas! my friend, let us not look for this on earth—that scene of dispersion, of death, where one hardly catches a glimpse of those with whom one would fain spend one's life. We just touch hands and separate, and go and die apart. It is not worth while—no, it is not worth while to form affections and plans here below. We know, indeed, that we are strangers and pilgrims, and that those are mad who would seek to fix themselves during their journey. We know this, but we forget it; and so God sends us these great lessons of death. Let us profit by them; let it not be in vain that we are addressed by the voice of the tomb. For a month past I never cease thinking of death, meditating thereon in the morning and in the evening, repeating a *De Profundis* beside the bed on which he died. If it distresses you to hear such melancholy things, tell me so; I will not mention them again, dear friend! I do not sufficiently spare you; I forget that you are not, like me, in good health, and capable of enduring the strongest impressions. I live in gloom, on a grave, and yet I live! Oh! how much strength there is in us for sorrow; far more than is supposed, we are so made for suffering!

Let us talk of yourself, of Les Coques, whither I follow you, and now see you on the sofa, thoroughly tired by the journey, and shaken as much in body as in mind, for the one depends on the other. What are you occupied with? not even any music? I should much like to see you return to it; I should listen to you, I should hear you from here; *the ear of the heart* is exquisitely fine. If you would like some poetry to set to music I will send it you. We ought, as much as possible, to ward off dejection, which is good for nothing — that consuming dejection which destroys the heart, leaving it without life or strength. And yet strength and life are necessary while we go on breathing, for sorrows do not absolve us from duties.

How are your children? Is Valentine delivered from her short cough and her loose teeth? I hope she is very good and keeps her little mamma company like an angel. Are you beginning lessons in good earnest? But there is your unfortunate health, which cuts everything short! At all events, M. Adrien remains to you. Oh! how much I like him to be near you, that good, amiable brother! Let him not leave you! there are departures enough, alas! I entreat him earnestly to suspend his roving tendency for your sake.

Adieu, my friend! I am incapable of telling Sophie how penetrated I am by her affection; however, I am about to write to her, little in the vein though I be. Once more, a thousand kind things to all belonging to you, father, mother, children, and the perfectly good husband. My whole soul loves and kisses you. My father is asleep on the sofa, Erembert is at Gaillac, Marie at Cahuzac, I am alone in a cloister of memories. O my God! my God! how events change places! Cheerful Cayla, how sad thou art grown! I should have drunk too deeply of happiness. Let us learn to dispense with it for a while, in order to possess it for ever. Nothing but the other world can console us for this.

We expect M. Raynaud the first days of September. Of all our visitors he is the most longed for—good and dear cousin that he is, the friend of my father, a father to Maurice. All the curés of the district came of their own accord to say mass; one, in particular, came from a distance, the Abbé de Rivières, his friend from childhood. He came twice, and has written us the most affectionate letters. Oh! if all this could console, consolations have not failed; the whole country has gone into mourning, and it does good to see that one is loved and that others loved those one sorrows for.

P.S.—That little green copybook which went off to America,* I was going to ask for it from M. d'Aurevilly. Maurice's wife has everything else.

---

To MDLLE. LOUISE DE BAYNE.

*27th August*, 1839.

Yesterday I received your letter, your kind "*write to me immediately,*" and I write to you to-day. Thanks, dear Louise, for this tender interest in my father and for so much affection for myself. Thanks for the one and the other, for they are one and the same. You have, then, felt for us much, thought that we were much to be pitied? In truth, terrible afflictions have befallen us, but God knows what we need. After the great sorrow comes a great mercy. My father is restored to us: I may indeed say restored, for death had laid hold on him too. For some days the doctor did not know what to do, and said to others, who have since told us, that he dreaded to see two graves open. Oh, my God! one is enough; but Thy will be done. Do we even know what we mean by our own will, imperfect and short-sighted as it is? I endeavour to detach myself from mine, which would fain not have consented to what has happened, to what afflicts, to what causes so much regret and so much

* The manuscript of Maurice's Journal.

suffering. Human feelings all these! We find this out when we stand still in the presence of God, when we read what is said of hopes and afflictions. A book that I am fond of, the 'Holy Desires of Death,' is of great use to me, soothes me, shows me what death is to the view of faith, and how the Christian, instead of weeping, should rejoice over this passage from earth to heaven.

Alas! and yet how difficult to me it still is to rejoice in the loss of my friend! How difficult not to say to God, "My God, wherefore take him from us? wherefore separate us so soon in this world?" 'Tis the heart which does this, the weak and suffering heart which bemoans itself. The good God will forgive me, I hope. Did not Jesus weep for Lazarus, his friend? I seek to justify myself by divine examples, which perhaps condemn me. Conscience throws itself on the heart, the heart on the conscience. I know not what I do, nor in what state of mind I am. No one to enlighten me! M. Fieuzet has been gone for three weeks, and his substitute has as yet only said mass on Sunday and gone off again, so that we are a flock without a shepherd. O Pastor of heaven, guide us thou!

My dear friend, experience makes me feel how good it is to lean on God, on God only. This is the one thing needful: all else is transitory and often deceitful. Look at our illusions of the month of September—where are they now? In the grave or in oblivion. Oh! these eight months have taught me more than my whole life at Cayla. I am sixty years old. In the same way my sister, the sorrowful widow, said, on the morrow of her husband's death, that she was thirty. "I have aged ten years beside this corpse;" for she had so contemplated it, had left it so little. Strong-minded and admirable woman! Her own hands prepared and dressed him for the coffin; alone with the curé, there on her knees, there kissing him, and praying for four-and-twenty hours. Angel of a sister that she is! She is to return next year; she has left her easel for painting behind her. It is possible that business may take her aunt to India, and, if so, Caroline will spend the time of her absence quietly with us at Cayla. It is so arranged, for the young woman does not wish to travel, nor does her aunt dream of taking her. Delicate and fragile, and worn out besides as she is, what has she to do but take care of herself? There is much to be feared for that health of hers, which was so constantly risked for six months. Alas! alas! my poor Maurice! his wife will ever be to us a sister, a sacred sister.

How I shared your alarms about your dear Marie, rumbling and jolting along your mountain roads! There she is, at rest now! What do you know about the other parts of the journey? When will the dear little expected one arrive? I shall remember his mother before God, and you, too, my friend. Let us address ourselves to the Almighty for everything and everybody. How happy I am made by the Christian tenderness you express! Always speak to me of piety, of the love of God, that this love may absorb me. Let heaven cover earth. When shall we meet? I should like, oh! how I should like to see you! but, as I have already said, I am not going hence. My poor heart, my poor father, everything detains me. Send my affectionate remembrances to the Countess, and tell her I am sorry to know that she was so near us, and thinking of us too, without coming to us. What pleasure I should have had—yes, pleasure (if such a word can be used)—pleasure in seeing and embracing that dear Pulchérie! Be sure you tell her how we regret her short stay. Adieu! to you and to Léontine, whom I love and embrace for Marie as well as myself. My father is sufficiently recovered to think of your kind interest in him and to lay his homage at your feet, ladies. As soon as he can he will come and see you.

Adieu in God.

---

To the Same.

*4th September,* 1839.

Sad as the solitary Night-Heron, I come, my friend, to converse with you, to pour myself out, to tell you of those nameless moods that pass over a crushed spirit. What torrents of regrets, memories, sorrows sweep across me! A year, very soon a whole year, since I was with you in the mountains, talking to you about my journey to Paris, the marriage, the future of that poor brother, of all things hoped for—except those that have come to pass! O treacherous human events! Oh, grievous catastrophe! My God, Thou hast willed it so in mercy I do not doubt.

One of these last days I found in a religious work, the 'Sufferings of Jesus Christ,' a very comforting thought: "Do you suppose that God, who loves us, would send us either suffering or death, if they were not the germ and the earnest of eternal life?" How true this is when one comes to think of it! But—unhappy that we are!—we do not think of it, and we groan over what ought to constitute our joy. Oh! were I sure he was in heaven, how tranquil I should be! But, my poor Louise, I am sometimes seized with terror in reflecting upon that awful eternity. The holiest tremble before God. However, we must rest upon infinite mercy, and do all we can to help our poor departed ones.

My life, my thoughts, everything is changed within me and without. I pray God to confirm me in Himself, who is immutable. To see what one loves, what one leant on, sink out of sight, and to remain behind, is frightfully painful: one is like a shipwrecked sailor left alone on the ocean. I am not alone, indeed, with a father, brother, and sister who love me, and yet I am conscious, as it were, of an immense solitude. I am writing you this from my little room, that beloved little room, turned into a vault by the objects and recollections it encloses. How many subjects of meditation in presence of this cross before which I write! How everything turns to dust and ashes! My friend, it is here that I listen to that great lesson of death, which teaches us more than all books whatsoever. They are nothing without experience.

Through all this my heart turns to you, and wanders off in the direction where it is loved. Alas! nothing can divert it from this; this will be its tendency so long as I remain on earth. I have a hope of tidings from you to-morrow, brought by the mountaineers, and perhaps you are at this very moment in the gallery writing to me. There is nothing unusual in friends meeting thus in thought. What is going on in your solitude? Do you know that we are three friends in three separate deserts—Rayssac, Les Coques, and Cayla? One might make a rather pretty novel, entitled 'Three Solitudes,' were one to take to writing down whatever of pleasant or of sad passes in these places. Sometimes the idea of writing comes across me, just to amuse myself, for a stocking is not enough for me. We are without books, without occupation, now that our visitors are gone. And you, dear friend, what have you to tell me of yourself, your life, your soul, your Toulouse sister, and those nearer at hand? To each and all my tender love, and, if you will be so good as to add it, my regards to Saliès. What Madame de Cazes did for me attaches me for ever to her. My God! why did not we undertake it earlier?

Adieu! much loved one of a very dead heart.

---

To Madame la Baronne de Maistre.

*My little room, 9th September,* 1839.

To the sound of the wind, and of I know not what that moans in the air or in the soul, I come, my plaintive friend, to converse with you and about you, to talk to you of your last letter, which reached me on the 5th, the eve of Saint Eugène, as if to make a festival of the day. Alas! as to festivals, there are no longer any on earth, if it be not those of the saints. But then, are not these the true festivals to the eye of faith? Their joy, at least, is not merely for a day, as is the case with those of the world. My Saint Eugène, who from being Bishop of Carthage came all the way hither to die for the faith, gives me the holy hope that from an earthly neighbourship we shall pass to a heavenly one amongst the blessed. I am quite rejoiced to have the relics of my patron saint so near me, to see the ruins of the monastery he built on the banks of the Veré, whither St. Carissime of Alby came to take refuge from the world's pursuit. Oh, how sweet and poetic this sacred story! Why is there not still a Eugène, with a cell in the woods ready for the Carissimes who might wish to take refuge there? One of these last days I was saying to my father that I was in a manner bound by duty to go over into Africa, whither my two patron saints Eugène and Augustin called me, like two loud voices, to join the sisters of Saint-Joseph, who are converting the Arabs. What do you think of this, my friend? You think like my father: I observe that your opinions often tally.

This dear father is touched, melted, penetrated by your affection for him, and the filial kiss you promise him on coming to Cayla. "Oh! tell her to come." Come then, dear friend, come, come! I wish that a speaking-trumpet could convey our voice to Les Coques. Do not say that you begin to be doubtful about it: doubt is good for nothing. Believe, and believe firmly, as I do, that we shall meet again. Amidst so many ideas that we have to banish from our hearts, let us at least preserve the innocent and cheering. I turn out a great many, but none that are connected with you. God does not forbid friendship. Oh! were that the case, one might indeed say, "Lord, thou requirest the impossible." But, how far from that! Look at Jesus, with his beloved John, with Martha and Mary, whom he loved. What tenderness! how his life was bound up in them even up to Calvary, where he chose to have them still! His holy mother, Mary Magdalen, the other women whom he loved, and the beloved disciple remained standing at the foot of His cross. Divine model of affection, of union in sorrow!

I observe that the more we meditate on Calvary, the more we find there all we need, all that enters into the life of the Christian imitators of Christ. I go on feeding increasingly upon the sufferings of Jesus Christ—ineffable intercourse of love and grief between the soul and its Redeemer! How much God has taught me during the last month and a half! What a sudden experience I have had of life and death! I am sixty years old, and yet I still find myself young. There is one side of the heart which learns nothing: God knows which it is, and how I both would and would not have it changed.

My friend, you too in your mountains have your own experiences, and I do believe no one will ever be more skilled in sorrow than you. Poor victim! poor martyr! Oh, it is indeed you who are most to be pitied, who are the largest link in the *chain of suffering!* Not even any music? that is too sad! Do compose some music. I had promised you some poetry, but, alas! what can you draw from a lute all wet with tears? Nevertheless, if you will, I can send you tears. You are going to have with you your dear and loving mother, who will delightfully relieve tedium and solitude. Then there are the two little girls, with their mirth, pretty ways, and games. If you could but go out this fine autumn weather! I never see the sun without thinking of you, my beloved recluse. How is it, dear friend, that those who would fain be together should be separated? Oh! 'tis because there is a place of reunion not to be found upon earth.

My *superhuman* sister-in-law, poor child! is suffering very humanly, having taken hence attacks of fever, according to what her aunt tells us. She herself only says, "I am always cold." In her last letter there was no mention of her health: I trust that it will only be an alarm. You inquire for one who is also very dear to us—for that good, kind friend of our Maurice, M. d'Aurevilly. He writes to me, he calls me his sister, and Erembert his brother. His letters—on a large scale, like his heart—are remarkably beautiful in feeling and expression. My father is charmed with them and with that tender and deep friendship felt for our poor loved one which bound those two young men together.

Dear friend, have I asked you to throw my arms around your mother's neck and to caress the little girls for me? All manner of respectful speeches to M. de Sainte-Marie and M. de Maistre. My father presents you his affectionate nomage. The only thing that he has still to complain of is the swelling in his legs. Marie is recovering her fine colour. On my arrival I found her frightfully thinned; presentiments had been consuming the kind sister. One suffers less, I think, from the reality, alas!

---

To the Same.

*16th September*, 1839.

Thunder, hail, commotion, calamity without, gloom, sadness within. Were the sky to fall, it would add nothing to my dejection. It is not because we are experiencing another reverse that I find myself in this mood: it is the tendency of my nature, do what I will. It would require an angel to divert me from it: accordingly, I come to you, my friend—you, who have been sent me from God. I write for the sake of writing, just to be with you in heart, the only way possible. As soon as I suffer I think of you, who suffer far more; I drive away my egotistical compassion, that plaintive *me*, that harasses us. But it is difficult to get rid of it: this I feel; let me then bring it to you to-day.

Yes, my friend, it is very *egotistically* that I write to you, seek you, call you, want you. I need to be consoled. Alas! why are you so far away? else we should have spent this day together. You would have replaced a friend who has just gone away, who has bequeathed us many tears. I allude to M. Raynaud, that kind and perfect relative. Never did he show himself so affectionate, so attached, so one with us as on this occasion. Affliction experienced or shared brings out the qualities of the soul: it is only on this black ground that man shows himself as he really is.

The fact is that our cousin has proved himself the most admirable of relatives, as well in what concerns the feelings as in the matter of other interests where so many dignities stumble and fall. There he is gone for who knows how long! Who can depend upon meeting again? and yet he has promised to return, and thinks of bringing us his children. God grant it, and also that the hope he entertains for me may get accomplished: it is that ot having me with him again in Paris, which—being at Les Coques—I shall reach in one bound, he says. He built this little enjoyment on that which I built on you, when I told him that I hoped to revisit you some day or other.

News of you and all your family were asked and given with lively interest. Why have I not daily some one to come and talk of you to me? I know of nothing that gives me pleasure; my heart is dead; but still in your direction it has living chords—*vibrating*, I should say, were I Sophie, the gracious, the too flattering. What do you hear of that other poor friend? Does St. Quentin console her for Vienna? And her brother—that fallen brother?

As for us, my friend, we are vowed to misfortune. I do not know whether the hail will have left anything for you to drink on your arrival. But never mind, only come; we will have *eau sucrée*—a sweet compensation. Why is there not such a one for all misfortunes? This hail came to make some variety in our calm. I listened to the noise of it, and should have enjoyed it but for the thought of its ravages. My poor little Nivernais rose-tree excited my compassion when I saw it, shattered, stoned to death, as it were, blossomless and broken—no possibility of rescuing it, the storm came so suddenly. We were at dinner, when a few claps of thunder were heard, and instantly a shower of stones, fortunately without wind, which makes me hope the damage done will be less great; but all the country is white, as in winter, with half a foot of hail. The corn-crops were ruined by the heat, there is a failure of potatoes, everything foretells a calamitous winter for the poor, for, after all, it is they who suffer. We shall not lack bread. In every sorrow there is a worse close at hand. God, who knows what trials each of us requires, distributes His gifts as His providence sees best. These terrestrial vexations cannot elicit a tear from me. After sword-strokes pin-pricks go for nothing. My friend, what are you doing? How fares that heart of so many storms, so many throbs *too many?* I should like daily bulletins of your health, and how rare they are, though you often write to me. What goes on at Les Coques interests me more than anything in the world: 'tis my home, the home of the heart. I am seldom away from you, I assure you. "What is she doing? where is she?" I even constantly add, "What is she thinking of?" Tell as much as you will of all this to your inquisitive friend, who is unceasingly and endlessly occupied about you. And the little girls and your dear mamma, everything around you interests me, more than that, touches me: my heart is in it. Let me, then, have tidings of all that belongs to you, the flowers, the garden, and the gardener. That poor farmer (tiresome pen !), that poor man, how is his bad leg going on? You see that I make the round of your solitude, passing through both thorns and flowers. But 'tis the flowers I pause at. Adieu! I stretch out my arms towards you. Why have I not that long neck that Valentine endowed me with? I should reach, should kiss you and her too, the dear child, and all the cheeks that would permit me to do so. I throw this into the post, with no other reason than the pleasure, the necessity I feel of being with you. After God there is nothing, oh, my friend ! so sweet as a friend. Although this be between ourselves, your good father and good husband always have a place in our converse as in our memory. Your mamma knows that she is mine too.

P.S.—Have you any tidings of Madame de Vaux? Caroline sees a great deal of her. The poor mourner has made a good choice of a friend in this strong and tender woman. I should dearly like to have the books and other things that she has carried away, but she lays as much stress upon them as I, and therefore I ought not to say anything; besides, so much was done for him, and even for us.

To the Same.

*End of September*, 1839.

I thought your music very religiously sad. Go on pouring your soul into your chaunts, like God's minstrel, David. Your compositions are much talked of here; one of my cousins has copied out your *Ave Regina*, which is to be performed with due pomp at Gaillac.

You pass for a great author, not in music only but books. You are associated with Count Joseph by reason of the talent and industry you display, and are spoken of as his wife. I rectified that anachronism, which rendered you too venerable. As to the praise. . . . praise does not age; you may accept it all; the De Maistres are associates in genius. It is in vain you call me flattering; but, my friend, the fact is that I come in for a sweet waft of the incense offered you, that people say of me, "It is that lady who is her friend." Oh, yes! indeed a friend, beyond all they imagine: amidst all that flatters they know not what flatters most, and that it is much more as regards the heart than the mind that I feel proud of being loved by you. I have not been to Gaillac, nor anywhere else, though our friends claim us, and we have had a shower of visits. I have no wish to see anything or take any journey with the exception of one, and afterwards that to heaven, where friends will no more leave each other. Consoling future! my bright hope! fairer than that of going *to Persia*. What a vagabond mood has got possession of your pleasant brother! There are people who do nothing like others, and I am not surprised at this in M. Adrien, who is an exception amidst the exceptional. If he is with you, do not argue with him any more: his is a dangerous kind of reasoning I see, since it *unseated* yours, made you jump up behind him, galloping after a thousand chimeras, contagious follies, witty and attractive. Nothing is so catching.

Let us dwell for a moment upon our dear little girls. Riri and Titine, if you are there, I embrace you both, and Titine twice for her pretty little letter; but I am going to answer her separately. That charming child's miniature gave me a very sweet delight: dear little one, who loves me, who writes to tell me so! I at once recognised her hand, her way of saying things, and the little idleness that came over her half-way down the page. What you tell me about her studies, amiability, and piety affects me inexpressibly.

The Duchess of Orleans was passing by yesterday, four or five miles from here, nothing announcing the fact but a few pounds of powder wasted. A sad kind of journey: at Toulouse—city of ice—no stir, no cheers, no onlookers to be had for money even! What does a northern Princess come to seek in the south? At Alby she visited the cathedral with the doors closed.

To THE SAME.

The postman was very rich, very kind, the day before yesterday: five letters came. One from our old cousin, two others, and those from Les Coques, which I now come to talk about, and say "Thank you! thank you!" to your dear mamma, and to you, my friend. I write to her and you at the same time, in the same parcel, with the same pen, and in the same words. I love you! yes, I dearly love you both. Tidings from you are what gives me most pleasure or most pain, according to their import. I am tolerably satisfied this time. I hope everything from time both for you and for me—not for my health, which cannot be better, but for other things which are not so well; for my conscience, which is without a guide, which ever since the departure of our good pastor has always been a stray sheep, going to seek afar what I cannot find here. You know how important a place a director holds in my life, especially now that I need a support. Everything fails me at the same time, and sometimes I am sad, overwhelmed. I am wrong: for God, who sends me these trials, only permits them for my good. And then He, the good God, never fails us, He is near to the afflicted heart; but often this heart is unable to see or feel Him, and then it complains. It was in one of these dark moments that I wrote you that sad letter which must have pained you. I was sorry for it afterwards. My friend, do not let yourself be affected by things that do not last. You well know the variations of the soul: mine now rises, and now falls back. One would fain have some stability, but 'tis impossible till we get to heaven. Oh! there we shall ever abide in the true, the good, the beautiful. This alone can console. All our hopes are there, all our happiness, our lost happiness

even: *for where eternity resides one recovers even the past.*
I leave you to go and join two cousins who await me in the drawing-room. Of all the places in the house 'tis my own little room that I prefer, but I often have to leave it. What a pity to do so now that I am in it with you!

Since yesterday we have had a tempest,—a fearful nocturnal storm which shook the earth. Our young people were alarmed at it, and so even was an old soldier of Napoleon's, who had not, he told us, been nearly so much frightened at Jena and Austerlitz. He got up, lit his fire and a consecrated taper, and went on praying to God all the time the thunder lasted. I thought this touching: an old Christian warrior on his knees during a storm, beside a little taper, the simple object of a simple faith. We again heard hail, but without trepidation, having nothing more out of doors. Do not pity us too much: the other day we only lost a third of our grapes, which appears to us miraculous after so much hail. But the leaves saved them.

Those added lines of yours, those Sunday lines gave me great pleasure. "How shall we arrange our winter?" say you. Ah! my friend, it rests with you to do this, to make me happy by coming south, to our mild temperature, which cannot fail to do you good as well as Valentine. To Nice, to the Eaux-Bonnes,—these are long journeys for your poor back. I have been thinking much about it, and trembling lest it should be unequal to the effort of reaching Cayla. Take care of yourself, make your plans, set out, and come here—here to this solitude, both well known and unknown, whither so many hermits are summoning you.

The greatest happiness I expect, the only one, it seems, that remains to me, is that of seeing you, my friend. This can only be here, for I cannot think of leaving my father for some time to come at all events. Returning to Paris got casually talked of as one of the impossible possibilities of life. No doubt I should go back to it with interest—a very sad interest, alas!—but never mind that; I should go back there to find tears, which attach so much. Nothing is settled on that head for this winter, or the next, or any other. Do not let this influence you the least; let *me* have nothing to do with *you*. Only come, if it be possible. This is all I *desire*. We will arrange future plans afterwards. Now, then, that is settled, you will come to us after Eaux-Bonnes.

Adieu, my dear one! Remember me to all, and embrace the little girls. If my visitors allow me time, I shall write to your mamma by this same courier; if not, assure her of all my affection.

P.S.—In order not to keep back my letter, begun, interrupted, returned to, I send it off alone to-day; impossible to write any more except by fits and starts, and when I am with your mother I like to remain there long. Good-bye for the moment.

To the Same.

*25th November*, 1839.

All your little papers reached me yesterday, dear friend. I do not say "Thank you" for this packet of manuscript tenderness, amiability, and so many heart-treasures—no, not "Thank you," but "Give! give!" Go on giving me your letters, your tidings, your life, all that I so love and would fain receive incessantly as the air I breathe. Sweet relations of friendship! is there anything better in the world? Are you not of my opinion, my friend? Do you not thoroughly prove to me that you are, you who are so loving, so good in writing, so desirous to have news of me? Well, then, we resemble each other: there is a sympathy between us. I love to believe it! I feel it without inquiring whether 'tis wisdom or folly. That which binds souls is always mysterious.

As to the "*folly of the cross*" that you attribute to me, would to God it were true! You would no longer need to wish me happiness. Those insane saints ask nothing from earth, their heart is fixed higher. Alas! you see that your friend is still far from that, however *Arabic*\* she be; but have you really taken this seriously, my timorous friend? You fear lest I should quit you. You tell me this so tenderly, that, had I one foot already in Africa, the other would return to Les Coques—yes, Les Coques—'tis *home*, 'tis a second Cayla, as you so gracefully say. I read that out to my father, who also

\* See the letter of the 9th September.

loves me too well, and will not any more than you consent to my going off to Saint Eugène and Saint Augustine.

Nevertheless, let us allow that it would be a beautiful thing, too, to go to Africa, to nurse sick soldiers there —those new crusaders of a new Holy Land—and to teach the Catechism to little Moorish children. I have always been very fond of Moors, and to save one of them, some little child-soul, would be my delight. Concede me this dream, my friend—hermits have so many dreams! We have little work going on just now; 'tis holiday time for the imagination, and, by way of amusement, it takes to building cells,—sometimes, too, other things, for I would not deceive you. We often leave the desert, we return to Paris, to the world, to the parties where I went with you. As was the case with Saint Jérôme, Rome comes to us in our solitude, but Rome in mourning. Alas! my past is all in tears. My God, 'tis thou hast willed it so! I might be yet more unhappy; there is no unhappiness to the eye of faith. Broken ties, dead hopes, lifelong regrets! what is there here but what happens to numbers? but providential trials sent for our future good? Everything for eternity: this is the grand view the Christian takes. Let us not forget that this world is but a stage towards the next; earth is only a stepping-stone to heaven, according to somebody's expression. When the soul turns thus towards the celestial side of things it grows calm, it can console, support itself. I know nothing else for it.

Interrupted by vespers yesterday, by preserve-making

to-day, Monday, and by a visitor,—I hardly know how the thread of our conversation is to be resumed,—a very slight difficulty either when connected with you. But what is to be said fit for you, suffering and alone as you are? It is not easy for me to do you good, in spite of my ardent desire of doing so. What a useless friend you have chosen! Accordingly, I advise you to let me wander off wherever I think fit, whether to the Caffres or the Moors; but, notice this, I shall begin with Les Coques. Dear Coques! dear Coques! This journey, however, will only take place after yours to Cayla. My father, who wants to see you, decides the matter thus. My father, the loving, loves you; he does but return you what I have received from your family and yourself. Oh, come! Take care of yourself for this purpose, for I am always trembling lest your delicate health should prevent it. I can foresee nothing happier than to see you. God will, I hope, permit this very legitimate enjoyment. . . . .

---

TO THE SAME.

*14th December,* 1839.

My last letter will have made you uneasy, dear friend. I was myself very much agitated. All is perfectly calm now. Erembert appears to be rather better, though he recovers slowly. So many shocks one after the other had overwhelmed me, I was quite prostrated. You will more than once have cried, "Poor Eugénie!" You, dear friend, who feel all that I suffer, share all my afflictions!

How much I should have longed for you, only I try to console myself with God, who is the friend of the afflicted! There is, indeed, no other that can sustain. Have not you experienced this?

It is now my turn to be impatient to hear from you: impatient to know what becomes of you in the great solitude of your desert since the departure of your mother and brother. In you I am saddened by this absence, this blank left around you by those dear relatives. However M. de Maistre and Valentine may try, they cannot make themselves four, and restore you the activity of Madame de Sainte-Marie and the sound and stir of M. Adrien, for I picture him to myself as restless and frolicsome as a sprite. Don't go and tell him so: I do not like men to know the opinions I form of them, because it makes me appear so observing. In this case it is you who have revealed him to me by your letters and by the recent conflagrations at Les Coques. And so then, my friend, this fine architect and designer makes and unmakes flower-beds and gardens, transplants shrubberies and lawns, and you applaud the enchanter's wand. I dwell at length on this because of the interest I attach to your solitude, to its improvements, to all indeed that you have and see, woods, flowers, blades of grass, that beautiful grass-plot where your little feet no longer wander. 'Tis no longer weather for walking, but that will return by and bye, and then you will be able to go out. This unfortunate sprain will not, let us hope, chain you to rest, the eternal rest of the sofa. You can hardly believe how this addition to accidents and sufferings distresses me. How often I think of it! ....

My friend, my dear Henriette, how immediately you and I understood and entered into and loved each other, and became sisters! God bestowed on my heart the consolation, on my life the happiness, of meeting with you on earth. If I, on my side, have done you any good, if I am in any degree a pleasure to you, I may sing *Nunc dimittis*. There is really something of heaven in our friendship. Oh, how much I think, speak of it! Oh, what prayers I put up for you! Louise is equally united to me, but in a different manner: in youth, at the age of sixteen, by bows of rose-coloured ribbon; you later, in sorrow, by a mourning crape, which binds so closely!

Are you busy with your music just now? I should like often to see you at your piano, and sometimes in prayer over some good and pious book; like every suffering soul, you need this, need it even more than others. Always these counsels, sent you from my heart! It is, you see, because spiritually I love you so much. I cannot understand an affection content to terminate here. I have nothing to read just now. I am re-reading Pascal, which may well afford one subjects for meditation. This passage, for instance: "It is a fearful thing to feel our possessions constantly slipping away, and to attach ourselves to them without seeking to find out whether there be not a something permanent." It is you who gave me a taste for this book.

Speak of me to Sophie. Be yourself my letter; I should never write so pretty a one. I have already told you I have too much correspondence for my taste; besides, what interest can be thrown into it by a sad-hearted anchorite like me? It is only to you that I can be attractive. Oh, how much so you are to me! Love and respects from all at Cayla to Les Coques and Saint-Martin.

---

To MDLLE. IRÈNE COMPAYRE, l'Isle d'Albi, near Gaillac.

*15th December*, 1839.

May God console you, my dear Irène! This is all that can be said in these cruel afflictions and separations wrought by death. I have learnt and can certify you of this, as well as of the share I take in your sorrow, so similar to the sorrow I experienced that I can measure the one by the other. I lose a brother, you a sister,—sad mourning resemblance! God strikes us in the same place, my poor friend; we can sympathise in grief. Let us unite at the foot of the cross: that will be better still, more Christian. Prayer is of greater value than tears: at least, those poor departed souls are helped thereby. I return to your sister what you did for my brother. I recommend her to God, though as for her we may indeed hope that she is already in heaven. She had suffered so much! Nevertheless, my friend, there can never be positive certainty; God ordains that these shadows should rest on the other life for the trial and exercise of our faith. Let it be ours to adore, to pray, to expect heaven for all. O the blessed day when we shall be reunited there, shall recover all we love, never to lose them again ! The happiness of heaven will be very different from that of earth, which is so short, so transitory. You know this, and better, perhaps, than I, my poor much-tried friend; but one likes to blend words and thoughts about sentiments shared and common sufferings.

By writing yourself on this sad occasion you have given me a very touching proof of your friendship—a friendship that you have always entertained for me. You have thus increased the value it already had, for which mine would fain repay you if it could. If I write to you less frequently than in time past, do not suppose that I am changed towards you. Oh, no ! it is *I* who am changed towards *myself*. If I can decide upon leaving my desert, I may perhaps come to l'Isle to prove that I love you. It would be a delight to me to see you again, as well as dear Antoinette, an angel who must sometimes be with you. The afflicted are her friends.

Adieu, my dear Irène ! You tell me nothing of your health, which I am anxious about, for so great a shock as this must have impaired it. I would say, "Take care of yourself," as the phrase runs, if that could in any way avail the body when the heart is suffering. The best restorative and support is God, is your own piety, which tears will but make to grow.

My father and all my family desire to express the share

they take in your grief, of which they assure both you and all your circle.

I embrace you, and always with my whole heart.

---

TO MDLLE. LOUISE DE BAYNE.

*15th January,* 1840.

Will this letter be more fortunate than the one written on St. Cecilia's day? Will it find any one of you at home, my friend? But this *heart-paper* is not selfish, and, without getting or expecting anything, wends its way towards you as often as it can. So was it in the past, so is it in the present, so will it be in the future, be always: friendship knows no change in its habits and feelings. Yes, my dear Louise, I hope that you think sometimes—nay, often—of your friend the recluse, that you would have written to her had you been able, had not the bell-ringer chanced to ring at the very moment when you were going to take pen in hand.

I return to that bell-ringer because he amused me, and I thought this strange excuse for not writing to me very droll indeed. Everything is allowable in the case of friendship, and all reasons are good between you and me. Nothing should ever offend us; and if ever I happen to weary you, just tell me, "You weary me." I should like it. Does not Fénélon somewhere say that we may tell God this? Oh, yes! perfect openness; let the soul be just what it is, both to God and to friends. This is why, Louise, I am under no restraints with you, and sing out to you all my tones. Do not you understand them all, enter into all? How I wish this could be nearer at hand, and otherwise than by letters! It is very sweet indeed to write, but still it is talking to each other from a distance, and there are so many things one does not want to speak out aloud. Low-voiced talk is best. This is the case even with God, who says to the pious soul, "I will lead thee into the wilderness, and there I will *speak comfortably to thee.*" Divine intimacy this, recovered in some measure in human intimacy, for whatever is good comes from above.

Send me, therefore, something or other down from your mountains; tell me whether or no you have set off for your enjoyments at Castres. There you will again meet charming acquaintance, those merry conversable young people you told me of. This relaxation cannot fail to do you good after the grave meditations of the retreat, which so absorbed you in serious subjects. Seriousness is useful: it is well for the soul to dwell upon the solemn thoughts of faith, but God permits some diversions even to saints, and St. John had his partridge. My dear friend, I rejoice at your journey to Castres. I look upon you as almost too earnest now, you whom I used formerly to think not earnest enough. But that *formerly*, where is it? All things change with time, and it is with rapture that I see you change *in God.*

But you have not all you want at Rayssac. Like me, you lack a guide, nay, even more than me, for I have one—not, indeed, the Abbé Legrand of l'Abbaye-aux-Bois, but still one, and near at hand too, while your

Father Amalrie can only give you advice from afar. This is very uncomfortable. What is to be done? The soul as well as the heart has its sacrifices, and God accepts and appreciates them all lovingly. This love it is which will supply all we lack, even our love, which is so small. Let us, however, try to increase it all we can.

I talk to you, my friend, as I do to that other friend, and indeed I care little for dwelling upon the things of this world; they are so slight, so transitory, so empty at last. She replies, "Speak to me incessantly of God." There is no soul that does not feel this want, and hers more than any other—sensitive, lofty, and suffering as it is. The kind creature! There came to me by coach a box, and in this box a valise, and in the valise some foulard silk for an apron, a gold medal, and a lovely statuette of the Virgin. These were my New Year's gifts from the Nivernais. Last year I had a gown, a watch, books, and I know not how many more pretty things; but what I liked best of all was that we were together. How many *togethers* lost since then! Is it not the case with you whom I have not seen again, and who no longer take your journeys in our direction? I had been depending so on your going to Toulouse! Why have not we got that little girl that attracts you? Always tell me about her as well as her happy mother; I imagine that you will end by going to embrace her. The month or May is a long way off, do you know, when one is waiting for it?

Yesterday we had tidings too from my poor Paris sister. The letter is full of details respecting Monsignor de Quélen, whom she went to see lying dead in Notre Dame, and of prognostics about the year '40. It had been foretold that Monsignor would not see it open, and also that the Faubourg St. Germain (ours, you know) is to sink into the Catacombs. Abyss of the future! who knows what it contains for us? Then Caroline adds: " I have no fear; God is with us." Oh, yes! with her, at all events. She has sent us a head of Maurice, drawn from her imagination. Poor young woman! Her aunt is still ill, her brother coughs a great deal; so that she is incessantly in tears, or on the brink of tears.

Now for a contrast. Marie, the happy Marie *—Marie the betrothed—has arrived from Toulouse with exquisitely tasteful and lovely dresses. The wedding takes place the end of the month. Poor child! with my whole soul I wish her all Heaven's best blessings, as much happiness as she deserves. Marie is full of good qualities of heart and mind. I shall pay her a visit after the gaieties, and even then it will be an effort to me to go away from here. No oyster clings so firmly to its rock as I to Cayla. In the same way, my heart clings to your heart, my cheek to your cheek. Adieu! Louise. Be sure to tell your sisters that I love them.

P.S.—My respectful regards to the pastor. He ought not to preach so loud or so long, if he wants to live; but he prefers converting.

* Mdlle. Marie de Thézac, cousin of Eugénie de Guérin, married to M. d'Assier de Tanus.

To Madame la Baronne de Maistre.

*My little room, 27th January,* 1840.

O woman of sorrows! poor sufferer: poor mother! I had no idea of the agony in which you had been plunged for a week beside your dying Valentine. My God, how rapidly illness comes on! But God cures it also rapidly. You will only have had a great shock, a terrible alarm. It is not for the little one that I am fearing now; but for you, who must have been so shaken by this attack. Tell me soon, and at great length, what have been, as regards yourself, the consequences of this distressing trial. Perhaps you have not left Nevers, perhaps you are in bed, perhaps your heart has relapsed into its bad ways, as it will do after excitement. In short, my friend, tell to your friend all that concerns your health.

It is true that the second page of your letter reassures me about you in reassuring me about Valentine. A mother and a child are so closely connected that everything, whether good or bad, passes from the one to the other; therefore, the amelioration in the dear little girl's state constitutes yours, I fancy. But how then was it she fell sick? Do not let her run about at will, whatever the weather, as I have seen her do at Les Coques. It is true that there is a difficulty in keeping a child indoors all day long, that it is even an excess of care to confine them to a hothouse; but Valentine is so fragile, so delicate, that what would be too much for another child is not so for her. I hope that the good God will spare her to you, since she is so patient, so pious. She will be a little model of sanctity to your whole house. The dear child! I embrace her for being so good while suffering, for praying as she does for her mother and her mother's friends. All you tell me on that head is really charming. Do not be uneasy; leave that hell of Dante, to which you compare your life. I don't know what this hell is; but, be it what it may, 'tis not for you: Christians should have none. It is heaven we should see underlying our life.

My poor friend, I oppose you. I am always running counter to your ideas and sensations, almost to your tears. What a wicked friend I must be! Can you love me? Nay, I really do not understand what it is you find in me; my reason gives it up. *But the heart has its reasons which reason does not comprehend*, to quote once more your friend Pascal.

How you make me love this Pascal! I have just parted from it with regret: I am always sorry to see a book go away, and feel almost as if it were a pleasant visitor. This is so much the more true that we only have books on a visit, and that rarely, so far are we from libraries. When this lack of reading gets painfully felt I take up my distaff, I come here and write, I do what I can to prevent *ennui* occupying the empty space—*ennui!* that most dire enemy of the soul, the demon of recluses! Oh! try hard to guard yourself from it, my companion in solitude. I wish I could be at hand to help you. Alas! we are so far. All I can do is to think for you at your piano, to accompany your music, to give you something to sing. This idea of working for you seems to have come to me from heaven, encourages me. I make it serve my purpose as well as amibition would : but, alas ! even it will sometimes desert me. I say to myself, " Pooh ! what can she do with this poetry? Will there be any possibility of arranging it for the piano? Will my inspirations accord with hers? We are sisters in heart far more than in talent." There I am ! when once I doubt, there is an end of me ; no support left. I must have hope in you, be able to associate your notes with my hymns.

But really and truly, my friend, I have a rage for being useful, for devoting myself to somebody or something. If it cannot be to you, I shall go off to the Arabs rather than continue good for nothing. I seem to myself a useless being, and the thought makes me sad. Perhaps, though, it is vanity to want to be something. If so, away with it, by all means ; I am content to be nothing. Is it not enough to have the working out of our salvation for life's long business? He who should reduce his wishes to this would be very wise and very happy. Let us make our desires concentrate in this desire.

That of seeing you, however, has somewhat akin to it, methinks ; 'twas something from heaven which first united us and will rejoin us, and always for our good. Oh, how grieved I should be to do you harm ! God knows how dear your soul is to me ! If you were to come here, we should talk a great deal ; there is no saying what we should not do. I look to this as to one of the chief joys that remain to me in life, but, as you say, I do not depend upon it; you have always so many hindrances. Nevertheless, let us hope and believe, spite of obstacles. Those who believe the impossible are the happiest.

Therefore nurse yourself for this journey—a useless thing to say, I know, but one likes to say useless things. What importance they assume when I connect them with you! Oh! you are right, quite right, to begin your letters by yourself. Set forth the good wine first, as at the marriage in Cana :* quench my thirst about you, my friend; what is there that can interest me more? You apologise for a fault that pleases me so well, I would have it occur at the beginning, middle, and end of your letters. Yes; always tell me of yourself, your sufferings, your interests. Am I not your *receptacle?* Oh! I no longer call myself useless if you can repose on me, if God grant me to be a moment's comfort to you. Write me long letters when it does not fatigue you too much. Think a little of the pleasure of her who is to read them, and who always finds they come to an end too soon. The last came to me at daybreak, before I was up, the day before yesterday. A charming surprise and sweet awaking! The postman had slept on the way, and came with the dawn like a rare and swift messenger of joy. It is seldom one has so good a thing in such good time. You sweetened one whole day for me; I spent it more pleasantly than I had done for a long time past. There is nothing equal to loving words for putting the heart into a good mood; after God, nothing is more potent.

* Sic.

P.S.—My father, my dear father, has expressly enjoined me to say something *very tender and affectionate* from him. I add a little song for Valentine, which you will sing to the piano for the poor invalid.

TO LITTLE VALENTINE (*when ill*).

Oh, when I see thee spend in pain
   Thy sweet child-years,—
See thee, instead of early flowers,
   Gathering tears,—
A bitter thought will sudden flit
   Across this heart of mine—
How, if thy mother's suff'ring lot,
   Dear child, be also thine?

When languor-bent as bends a reed
   Thy head I see
Droop like the tender youthful shoots
   From willow-tree;
Thy cradle turn to martyr's rack,
   Whereon to writhe and pine—
How, if thy mother's suff'ring lot,
   Dear child, be also thine?

When like a saint thou seem'st to me—
   No tears, no cries,
Through all thy weariness and pain,
   Seeking the skies,
Gazing, where dies on Calvary
   The Sacrifice Divine—
How, if thy mother's suff'ring lot,
   Dear child, be also thine?

---

TO MDLLE. ANTOINETTE DE BOISSET.

*3rd February*, 1840.

Thank you, my dear Antoinette, for writing to me and telling me of your affection. I never doubted it, but this renewed assurance has its charms. We like to see over and over again what pleases. Only your letter has been very long indeed on its way; it might have come from China in the time. The truth is, our post little regards the impatience of friendship. It was but the day before yesterday that I got your letter; and I answer immediately, hoping to find some messenger to Cahuzac who will not, I trust, travel tortoise pace.

I long, dear friend, that you should know how I participate in this fresh grief that Providence sends you. That poor Camille, how I pity her, and you through her! Misfortunes, then, positively rain in our families. May we not indeed say that we have a fellowship in grief? Let there be also fellowship in prayer. This is what I try to keep up on my side, dear friend, as you on yours. Each day I unite myself to the prayers of the Novena, thanking you before God for the intention towards me and my family combined with it. Oh! we are all most grateful for this, and I in particular am much affected by this sweet proof of Christian regard from my dear Antoinette. May the good God preserve your sister to you! I have great faith in the power of the Holy Intercessor. Alas! how poignant a remembrance this awakens. I too had written about Maurice, but too late. God had already taken him away when asked to spare him to us! I only received the answer after his death. Why were we so long before we thought of the miraculous? Poor human nature! first of all to have recourse to human aid, and then so to deceive oneself as not to see the danger under one's very eyes! One fancies that what one loves cannot die.

My dear Antoinette, tell me of your poor invalid, for this only brings me back to you and her. They had written me word from Gaillac that she was worse. My God, thy will be done! For a long time back this poor child has made you uneasy, but yet I did not know she had come to this point. Disease works swiftly. And that Saint Lisbine,* but for you should I ever have heard that she had left you? Happy child! called by God to the religious life. 'Tis far the safest as regards heaven, and perhaps it is the sweetest as well. Yes, I do indeed believe that the world's crosses are a hundred times heavier than those of the cloister. True, I hardly know either, save by hearsay; but one can easily discern the difference between them, and also that God helps us everywhere. Let us make no exceptions as to graces, means, or salvation. Is she with the Lisle sisters? If so, you can see her, and her family has not lost her as yet.

I had heard much that was good about Madame A.; canonised by you, this young woman seems to me still more saintly, quite worthy of the family she has entered. You are a community of saints at Lisle. Accordingly, my poor soul would much like to go and be edified there; but, my dear Antoinette, I can no longer drag myself hence, even to see you, my sweet magnet. My little life prefers to pass away in the smallest space possible,—here where I have my all, my beloved living ones and beloved dead.

* Sister of Mdlle. Augustine de Gélis, a member of the Sisterhood of St. Vincent de Paul, who died at Hing-Po in 1863.

Adieu! wherever I be, behold there one who loves you. My affectionate homage to the poor mother who is so afflicted in heart. Write to me, pray for me, love me.

---

TO MADAME LA BARONNE DE MAISTRE.

*17th February,* 1840.

Your letter reached me in church during vespers, and, as I had to keep it there unread, I gained some conception of waiting in purgatory. Oh, how much one must suffer, near to a happiness one may not possess, near to heaven! This, my friend, was what the little paradise of your letter, which I would not open, made me think and feel for two whole hours—hours of self-sacrifice; but should we not do as much for God? I was glad to have this to offer Him, and actually I chanced to be reading in the *Imitation* these words in the chapter on patience: "God will not leave unrewarded any pain, however slight, that we may have endured for His sake." " Courage!" said I, looking at my letter; "if I were one day called to greater sacrifices, I should have the more strength for them." One can practise oneself in willing. If I had to leave you! There are a hundred ways of separating on earth : not, indeed, that I have any one of them in view; but, sooner or later, have we not to leave everything, to part one from the other? We are only here below as in an inn on a journey. Let us, then, have the feelings of travellers. We should think a man very strange who attached himself much to his inn. The wise

Christian will not do this. Do you not consider that I have profited a good deal by the mountain mission, and that Saint Louise herself would hold no other language? It is true, indeed, that I do learn many things from her and from time, and especially that we ought to think of heaven, and, moreover, to think about it as we think of a fortune, in striving to gain it. Alas, my God! the greatest blessing is the only one for which we make no effort, which, it would seem, we expect to be ours by a miracle. The greatest miracle would be to arrive where we are not going, to reach the south in the direction of the north. Nothing is so irrational as conduct like this, as faith without practice, as a baptized heathen.

My friend, you must ascribe this singular page to a secret anxiety of mine, and bear with it; just as I allow you your ideas, your dreams, your griefs, so you too must allow me mine and the perfect spontaneity of my style when I talk to you. It is not with you, besides, that I should ever think of constraining myself; with no one, indeed, when I write. Without too closely calculating their range, needs must that my convictions explode. I am sure they will not wound you. My poor friend, I should be so grieved to do you harm! I repeat once more this expression which seems to have struck you so much, that must ever be mine about friendship, every relation of which should tend to good. For my part, I have no remorse on that head. God preserve me from yours; from what you would feel if you happened to do me harm! What a twofold calamity, and how ill we should fulfil the purposes of that Providence which brought us into contact; for, my friend, it was not pure chance which led to our meeting. I see in it some divine intention of Him who directs even the flight of birds, and who, it seems to me, has led us by the hand one to the other. Let us, then, make for ourselves a friendship agreeable to God, like two Sisters of Mercy. Let us take care of each other, dress our wounds, and reject what flows from them—the corruption of the human heart.

This is what I try to do in the case of my dear invalid. Accordingly, I do not think that you ought to charge yourself, as though it were caught from you, with that depressed mood you have thought you observed of late. Alas! you know it well, *sadness is the groundwork of human life.* 'Tis mine sometimes, but rarely; and then owing to my state of health, much more to the body than the soul. Sometimes I need the sun; if a fine day comes, I revive; I become once more not indeed gay, but serene. A fine creature though, one that a drop of rain can cast down! What nothings we are! I learn this ever more and more, and how great our need of strength from above.

Do not think of sending me books, kindest one: the carriage would make them too dear; and then I know how to do without. Nothing is essential to me; and, indeed, I have no lack of anything in my dear, peaceful, and much-loved Cayla. Some obliging neighbours throw open their libraries to us, and every now and then I take out whatever I like. I am now occupied—*re-occupied*, having read them before—with the works of Bernardin de Saint Pierre: sweet simple author, whom it is well to read in the country. I could fancy next *Notre Dame de Paris*, but I dare not. Those romances make such ravages that I dread their influence; merely to see the effects they have on certain hearts terrifies me. Mine is so calm, it would fain remain as it is. If that word "calm" surprises you, remember, my friend, that God gives peace. I am not deceiving you!

---

To M. LE BARON ALMAURY DE MAISTRE.

*Easter Tuesday,* 21*st April,* 1840.

Your letter, Monsieur, has given me too much pleasure not to be acknowledged at once. I was so uneasy! At length, then, our dear Henriette is better, and it is she herself who commissions you to tell me so! Amiable friend! amiable *you* too, her secretary, to tell me this in your own way, fraught with feeling, and interesting details, which I devoured with all the eagerness of a keen appetite. I was dying of hunger of Henriette; her last letter had left me in the greatest need of further tidings. What surmises, visions, apprehensions since that sad note! Alas! Monsieur, how much I love your wife! I have felt this very painfully. The feeling lasts, but 'tis much modified: there is a great difference between loving in tears and loving in hope. Thanks to you, 'tis this last I now experience. Yes, I hope everything from God, from your care, and the present improvement. I do not know that (as you suppose) my prayers have had anything to do with this favourable change; but one thing is certain, I implored the whole of heaven for her, poor dear sufferer! and was full of hope. The good God is so good! He is Love omnipotent. What may we not then expect from Him, even though our petitions be not always granted? But, then, do we always know what is best for us? Alas, that better tidings from Les Coques must be blent with such bad news from Saint-Martin and Nevers! There are special seasons of calamity for families; the whole of yours is a hospital. I believed your mother with Henriette; and there she was, all alone and suffering herself. No doubt, it was anxiety which gave her those dreadful headaches. Tell me of her, and her of me, I pray you, without omitting either to mention me to that good M. de Sainte-Marie, whom I pity much on account of his fever. Alas! alas! how sad for you all to be thus ill and scattered! Believe me, I too consider myself at far too great a distance; believe that I would fain replace, or rather second you in your care of Henriette. How full of anxiety and distress I picture you! No doubt you must have been terribly uneasy. At last the crisis is over! How I shall yearn to hear further! But I will not have the dear friend fatigue herself; in her weak condition the pen is heavy. I shall content myself with a direction as now. Tell her it was very kind to write it. She well knows what terror any other handwriting from Les Coques would have caused me at this juncture.

TO MADAME DE SAINTE-MARIE.

*7th May*, 1840.

It was only yesterday that I received your letter: that letter of yours, my dear adopted mother, which gave me so much pain and pleasure both. You say, Come, and I cannot come: not yet, at least. The nun has set out, and that so suddenly that I found her gone when I went over to see her and talk to her about my commissions. Always there are hindrances, and more than are supposed; for you must not think that this was an obstacle to my journey, or that travelling alone could terrify me. Were that all, you would soon see me in my dear Henriette's arms. But alas! 'tis not enough to wish it; I feel this too keenly just now, when a something stronger than myself keeps me back. Business, melancholy business, absolutely necessitates the presence of the whole family at Cayla.

But I shall come by and bye, let us hope! God will not forsake us; God will reunite us after so many trials, and we shall tell each other how we have borne and how we have profited by them. They are so many stepping-stones towards heaven.

Adieu, you whom I can only call Mother. My whole family desire to be remembered to you in the most affectionate manner. I embrace the dear little girls and their dear mamma. My best respects to M. de Sainte-Marie, whom I long to know to be well and with you all again. M. de Maistre will, no doubt, have received my letter. I add nothing but my regards to-day. Always and very lovingly your daughter in heart.

---

To the Same.

*31st May*, 1840.

Shall I arrive at Coques, my poor afflicted mother, in time not to console but to embrace you, to clasp you lovingly in my arms, to tell you, to *repeat* to you, as you say, that I have been painfully affected in reading the account of my friend's sufferings? Oh! I knew only too well, from the absence of her handwriting, that there was sad news inside. My God! how quickly I broke the seal to read, and how broken down I was myself by the reading! Poor friend, within an inch of her end! And what pain, anguish, terror, martyrdom for a whole week! I saw, felt, pitied, I hardly knew which most, the victim or her mother. Is it indeed possible to say which was the greatest sufferer? In short, you are fearfully tried, and no doubt there was danger, and extreme danger, in this unfortunate accident; but you give hope; you tell me, my mother, that this misfortune may do good, that through it our beloved invalid may be freed from a part of her complaint. May God listen to you and the doctors, whom I do not often hold to be true prophets.

But let us rely upon Providence, which acts by human means—very painful ones, sometimes; but pain constitutes one-half of all things under heaven. And after your tears, throes, terrors, to see your daughter better and perhaps eventually cured, oh! is this not enough to make up for all? enough to sing *Te Deum* over, both for you and me, and all who are interested in this dear Henriette? This idea, this dawning hope of health, filled me, as it were, with joy—I, who no longer have any joy of my own. Yes! call me your daughter: I am so, my mother. I am the sister of your Henriette. I cling to her as I do to no one else, in a way that only God knows, and that comes so close to my family affection that no one intervenes between my dear relations and Henriette. Louise is also dear to me, but in another way. Nothing so strong as what is born in tears.

And you, and M. de Sainte-Marie and M. Adrien, all of you, were round that bed of pain, and I was not! Your heart noticed this, and led you to mention it to me in a very touching manner. 'Tis balm poured on wounds to be spoken to thus; to see myself, without knowing why, so tenderly and truly loved by you and yours. How much my father feels it! Accordingly, he said, after I had read him your letter, " This dear family ! I must make a point of letting you return to them so soon as business permits."

God be thanked! God be praised for everything, and for the mercy He shows us in the midst of afflictions! Never did I know so sad an Easter in one respect, nor so blessed in another, in the matter of faith, life's most important matter, it is so full of benedictions for those I love! How my Henriette comforts me! I foresaw so many difficulties for her, so many material and spiritual embarrassments at Coques, that I was very uneasy about her. But God has given her an Ananias, that Abbé of Nevers, that holy, enlightened, and consoling young priest, who came, like the angels in the Garden of Olives, to sustain our Henriette in her agony. Poor friend! how much good she derived from it, as is ever the case with all who seek their support in God! and not only she, but you also shared the benefit by enjoying it through her. Happy they who, like you, my mother, and like M. de Sainte-Marie, draw down blessings on their family. God never fails, sooner or later, to grant their requests. This is the only support adequate for the soul's needs, and then, as you say, everything counts for eternity. It is with reference to this that we find written, " Blessed are they that mourn."

I am much delighted with what you tell me of the little girls. You will please to embrace them both on the part of their second little mamma. And as for their sick mamma, what am I to say to her? All that can proceed from a heart full of sorrow and affection for her, and that refers itself to yours.

Adieu, dear mamma! I am all your own, like another Henriette. I have no room for all the affectionate messages from my family to yours, and to yourself in particular.

Let me soon hear, if you please. Thanks for the flower of the Month of Mary: although faded, what a perfume of Coques it brought me!

To Madame la Baronne de Maistre.

*(No date.)*

Since you are able to write me two or three words, dear friend, you will also be able to read a few in answer to your infinite kindness and the infinity of proofs of it that you so frequently afford me. Thanks! thanks, a million times! I consider myself too unfortunate in not being able to profit by them at once. But insurmountable difficulties detain me : nothing less than these overpowering *cables* would suffice to prevent me from flying to you, to that bed of suffering whence your sad and tender voice cries, "Come! come!" Oh, how I wish I could, with my papers and everything that could interest you! We are expecting to hear from Paris; I shall press M. Raynaud to hurry on this business: meanwhile I implore you not to afflict yourself too much about a visit postponed. Everything arrives in the end, and especially friends. And I, who was depending upon seeing you at Cayla! Alas! how many disappointments!

Adieu! always adieu! nothing but adieu! But the meeting will come, depend upon it, my dear. Do not leave me without tidings. I am very grateful to all who write to me and to the hand that writes the address. Yours ever.

TO MDLLE. LOUISE DE BAYNE.

*St. John's Eve, 23rd June,* 1840.

Your precious missive has reached me, dear friend, by a messenger who is going to return immediately. Wearied as I am, I wish to give him these few lines of thanks for your friendly interest, your search for my sake, amongst melancholy documents.* Your letter—in short, everything that comes from you—is dear to me, as usual. It is well, my friend, to meet again, as you say, or rather for you to come and rejoin me; for you it was who were lost to me, and for far too long! If I did not complain then, or if you did not hear my complaints, 'tis that by dint of suffering one grows accustomed to suffer. My heart-sufferings are still very great, and at this moment all revived by a sad but sacred occupation—the revision of the letters and poems of that beloved one, for notices which they ask me for in Paris. Therefore your parcel could not have arrived more opportunely. Madame Sand has written a very high-toned, very eloquent article ;† but it is incomplete and even inaccurate in a religious point of view. Maurice is made to appear almost like a Werther or a Byron, and some friends are anxious to draw a truer and purer portrait of him : a homage this to his Christian memory which we receive with profoundest gratitude.

\* Mdlle. de Bayne had been sending her friend the letters of Maurice de Guérin found amidst her father's papers.

† Allusion is here made to the striking article published in the 'Revue des Deux Mondes' (May 15th, 1840), in which *The Centaur* appeared.

My dear friend, I am writing in too great a hurry to tell you all to-day; but just two words: your return to Rayssac and to the solitary Léontine rejoices me for her sake and mine, as now that we are nearer I shall hope to hear oftener from you. As to meeting, alas! 'tis the finale of all prospects with me just now. Erembert will, perhaps, go to the Waters; my sister-in-law will, perhaps, be coming here; perhaps . . . . Oh! these *perhaps!* there are so many of them, unfortunately, in my life and on the way to Rayssac!

Thanks for your kind recollection of my Baroness. Another letter!—alas! and a very sad one. I have had afflicting tidings, fatal tidings almost, on account of a little creature which chose to be prematurely born. This terrible casualty overwhelmed my poor friend with pain and depression. "It would have been a son," she wrote me word; "I had built so many hopes on his life!" It is only the last week that I have begun to see her dear handwriting again. I used to get bulletins of her health from her mother or M. de Maistre.

You tell me nothing of yours. I imagine it at its best on your return from that fine air of Castres, which so pleases and profits you. And now there is the pretty little niece, who will turn Rayssac into a paradise. for it will have an angel. Adieu, my dear one! May you be very happy in this family happiness. My remembrances to your Marie, love to Léontine and to the absent Countess. Pray for and love me; I have need of both.

P.S.—You ought to have some other poems of Maurice's: *The Storm* and *Sainte Pulchérie*. Once more, thanks for those you have sent.

Receive my father's paternal affection. Of necessity, adieu!

---

To Madame la Baronne de Maistre.

*8th July*, 1840.

Where are you? on land or sea? in bed or on a journey? In what place, in short, that I cannot discover, whence nothing comes to me from you, sweet friend? This silence torments me; it is now more than a month since you have written, and since then how much may have happened! Misfortune strides on fast, especially in your case. I am afraid you must be worse; for I so earnestly implored you to write to me, my heart being impatient and oppressed about you. Terrible distance! to see nothing and know nothing! Why are there not telegraphs in the service of friendship? I should not be now inquiring what can be going on at Les Coques. Are you there? are you not there? All these questions answered by fear! Wherever you may be, you must be suffering, and suffering so much that you are unable to tell me so. My friend, or whoever there may be about you—if it were merely Antoinette—take pity on your friend, who entreats for tidings. Let me have tidings of *you*, of *you*. If you are at Chambon, you have surely some of your family with you there; M. de Maistre or Madame de Sainte-Marie. I beg and entreat them to write to me, to recollect your friend, who is ill in and through you. Your last letter grieved me so! When I believed you on the way to recovery, you tell me the reverse. Poor friend! one would say that you have taken a vow of perpetual suffering, of suffering or dying, like St. Theresa. But at least let me know it, in the name of that intimate fellowship of ours in God and in everything. My father, who is very fond of you and your letters, was observing to me last night that your pleasant "causerie" was long in coming. From thence we went on to discuss a little my not always reading your letters aloud or only showing fragments of them; for my father, who delights in what is pretty, would like a share in all you write. He pretends that a daughter ought to read everything to her father, and that the contrary custom is quite wrong. I, on the other hand, declare it is quite right, justifying myself by that maxim of Fénélon, "Between friends there is no secret but the secret of others:" a sentence which at once makes your confidences exceptional, and your letters, which no one ever touches, sacred. They, with those of Louise, are the only ones thus privileged. That is why the subject got discussed, but so pleasantly that it was rather talking about you than anything else.

This would come under the head Friendship in that journal you ask me for. But, my friend, I shall not always have Sisters of Charity by whom to send you my *every day*, and it would cost too much by the post. And when I myself—a living, talking journal—am with you, what need shall we have of the other? But when will this meeting be? I cannot yet fix it; you know how slowly all business gets carried on. Nothing is further advanced than when I wrote last. Since then I have been sadly afraid of having to take another journey, much less to my taste than the one to Coques. It is the lot of almost all of us to have our life crossed to the very end. Has yours been anything else than a torrent of griefs? Oh, how often, my Henriette, I think of this, and how I wish I could offer you some remedy! But, instead of this, on account of your extreme sensitiveness, what you receive from me only afflicts you, and this rends my heart. I say to myself it might have been better that you should not have known me, since I add to your sufferings. But yet, my friend, do not let us part; let us place the cross between us as a support to both—a strong support, I assure you: the only one that bears up all and bears up ever. There is this of divine in religion,—it is gentle to those who suffer.

What would you say if I told you nothing about a publication that closely *concerns us*, one that Madame Sand has just brought out at the recommendation of M. Sainte-Beuve?—a publication that had given me some pleasure, changed just now into bitterness, alas! like everything else in the world. Not but that there is much charm and grace in this notice, but it is spoiled by philosophical views, and I am distressed by it and by the noise it will, they tell us, make in party journals. Contests such as these are little worthy of the occasion, and very distasteful to us respecting a sacred memory, which, moreover, never asked publicity. Perhaps you may have seen something of this in the *Gazette* and the *Quotidienne*, which both mention it, we are told. What do we know here in our desert?

Adieu, very dear one! What interests me above all is to know what you are doing, where you are, whether you love or forget me? To forget—impossible! Then you are ill: and of two such misfortunes which is one to choose?

Love and regards to all around you. I embrace the little girls. Write! write! Eternally yours.

P.S.—Will you ever tell me a word of *Sophie?*\* I forget nothing and no one that is dear to you. What a good effect the waters have had! May all your pains be drowned in them! You will tell me that this would require an ocean. If to-morrow you were to regain strength to walk, I should be very happy to hear and still more to see it. Oh, to see it!

---

To M. Hippolyte de La Morvonnais, Val de l'Arguenon.

*19th July (the day of his death)*, 1840.

God be praised, Monsieur! We have not then lost you either by death or by forgetfulness, but your silence had led me to fear and believe both the one and the other. Else do you suppose I should not have written you word of our sorrow? that I should have left it to a

\* Mdlle. Sophie de Rivières.

newspaper to apprize you of the loss of a friend? Alas! no! More than once in my tears I thought of you, for I knew you loved our poor Maurice; but no longer receiving any letters, any replies from you on any occasion, I was forced to conclude you were no longer in the world. When I was in Paris I saw Maurice announce his marriage to you; but neither then nor ever after had we a word from you! To whom at Val could I then announce his death? Your little girl is too young to ask her for anything but kisses, to inquire from her, "Where is your father?"

And so you are still there, widowed, solitary, and sad. God knows how I have desired consolation for you, the sweet and powerful consolation of heaven: for there is nothing else availing, nothing adequate to sustain the soul. Oh! I feel, I see, I know this in my own case, under crushing sorrow caused by the death of Maurice, my beloved brother, my heart's intimate friend. His loss is irreparable: there is, as it were, a void within me that God alone can fill. Formerly you used to speak to me of prayer, and I prayed for you. Oh, pray for me now! Pray for Maurice as I prayed for Marie and as I still pray, for I have forgotten nothing.

My greatest consolation is derived from his pious death, from sentiments of pristine faith expressed in prayer and the reception of the Last Sacrament, as well as in that last and ardent kiss given to the crucifix. I reveal this to your friendship, to that Christian interest that follows the soul into the other life. Let us hope— hope that it is a very happy one to our Maurice. His was such a beautiful spirit! Oh, God will surely have opened His paradise to him: God, who is only love, will have held this soul of Maurice dear. If you write a memorial of him—the thought of which deeply affects me—let it be impressed strongly with signs of faith, that *pure and Catholic* faith in which he died. This is wanting in the notice by Madame Sand, and the want has much grieved me. It is true that she did not know my brother, and only traced his portrait from scattered lineaments; but all of you, his friends—you who did know him—do better than this, and remove, I pray you, from this Christian figure all philosophical and irreligious clouds whatever. Will this funeral tribute appear in the *Université Catholique*, of which, I am told, you are one of the editors? We should be deeply interested in seeing it, and as a family we offer you the expression of our profound gratitude.

I equally thank you for the two publications that you have been good enough to send me, but which I have not received. Madame de Guérin will, I am sure, be much touched by this tribute. Send her, Monsieur, the *Thébaide des Grèves*,—full as it is of Maurice, whom she still mourns. You are right in believing that the wife he chose must be a remarkable woman. She is indeed an interesting creature as to beauty, endowments, and virtues —a charming Eve, come from the East for a paradise of a few days. Death parted them at the end of eight months. No child is left. This young woman was an Indian, brought up at Calcutta,—who came to Paris three years ago. She is still there, in the same house where I saw her so happy, for, as I have already told you, I was at the marriage. I remained eight months in Paris, and we returned hither last July with our dying Maurice. His widow left us soon after, but she writes to us. I have no doubt that your book and your visit both will give her great pleasure. You will find this dear sister at 36, Rue du Cherche-Midi.

And now let me embrace your dear little Marie: that child whom Maurice used to kiss and fondle in her cradle and on her mother's knees. Alas! alas! how much sorrow has come since then! The groundwork of life is all black and very sad; but God wills it thus, in order that we may look up to heaven.

Adieu, Monsieur! receive once more the assurance of feelings which have been necessarily silent, but have in no way changed.

---

To the Same.

Cayla, 6*th August*, 1840.

I have just received your two poetical communications, and now that I have looked over and partly read them I feel a thousand grateful acknowledgments that want to get themselves expressed; but what words can convey the speech of the heart? Hence, monsieur, I can only bless you. I bless God for your inspiration, and you too for having allowed me to enjoy it. It is very good and amiable to pass on to others whatever one possesses of sweet and soothing, and I owe you both pleasure and profit. In my hours of sadness I shall read you like a book of prayers, for your strains are full of God. With what a melancholy pleasure I contemplate this *Thebaid*, filled with celestial objects, with so many memories of Marie the mother, Marie the child, and of my much-loved Maurice: alas! almost all of them in heaven now who once were there! Thus it is that everything passes! thus fade away from this world those lives that made its happiness! Hence we can only bear to look up to heaven, where we recover them, where we know them to be with God.

The death of friends detaches the heart from all below, and makes us comprehend the need of an immortal affection, the necessity of loving God, the Friend who never dies. I am very sure that your soul becomes more and more religious since you are more and more alone, widowed and afflicted. Time only deepens grief, I fancy, at Val, as in other abodes of mourning. But courage! As we used to say formerly, "Courage and faith!"—these two strong supports of man. With them we do not, indeed, suffer less, but we suffer as Christians, in union with Jesus in His agony of sorrow even unto death—Jesus who entered heaven through Calvary. I know nothing more sustaining than the cross. One is comforted to see it planted in your Thebaid, and watered by prayers and tears. Your little Marie is the angel of that chapel: pious child, full of the love of God and her mother. It is thus you bring her up, no doubt; and your daughter will be your most pure and celestial poetry, your crown of glory before God. Unfortunately, we have no child at Cayla, and in this our desert is still sadder than yours. My eldest brother is not yet married, and the other is wholly dead. Thus divine Providence has willed it. It is afflicting, but the bright side of things is the one we do not see in this world, but for all that it exists.

Adieu, Monsieur! and once more permit the expression of a gratitude less expressed than felt. What can I give you in return for your touching gift? Will you accept a lock of Maurice's hair? The sister of your friend has nothing more precious to offer.

---

To M. LE BARON A. DE MAISTRE.

*31st August,* 1840.

Alas! Monsieur, how much I thank you for your letter, and how much it grieves me! Poor friend, in what a state you paint her for me! She must be very ill, not to write to me herself, for she knows how sad any other handwriting on these bulletins makes me; but continue, I pray you, continue to send me them; you will thus gratify my tenderest interest, and you minister to it so well! Your letters are dated from her bedside; through you I have all the pangs of our dear sufferer sent me from the fountain-head—all at least that can be witnessed of them transmitted to me,—and I deeply value this mournful satisfaction. I live in what I suffer. When, then, shall we see some assuagement to her trials? May God be our helper! I hope much more from Him than from human aids and appliances: those of science are enough to terrify one. What a state she has been plunged into

by so many doctors, and latterly by that fatal M. ——!
I say fatal and doubly fatal, for he seems to have been
imposed upon our dear invalid by ill luck. You were all
unanimously against her in this matter, as I should probably have been had I found myself amongst you. There
is regret enough, I assure you! she reproaches herself as
well as you for having wished to do right. To deceive
oneself or to be deceived is sometimes terrible.

I do not tell you how I participate in this fresh misfortune: a friendship like ours has no need to speak.
Why cannot I act in reality and in person, as I do in
sympathy and heart?—that *nursing* heart of mine, which
nevertheless cannot divide with you the care of our invalid.
But I have a hope, a possibility of travelling to you.
Repeat this to our Henriette, for I have already told it
her. May this hope be sweet to her! may our meeting
bring her the pure pleasure that God has attached to
friendship! Poor friend! tell her I shall not scold her.
I have been rather severe lately, but I love her so much
that I tell her everything—perhaps too much so—that
occurs to me about her. Just then I had a grudge
against her imagination, *that mad member of the household*, as St. Theresa has it. But I see that it is not
merely her imagination that runs mad, and that she really
has frantic and too real pains, alas!

When is the Lyons pilgrimage to take place? I long
to know that she has set off: first of all, because that
will prove her better, and also because I hope better
results from this journey than from medical treatment.
Send me word always of what is doing and to be done.

I answer you immediately, that I may the sooner have tidings, which, nevertheless, will be a full fortnight on their way. This is long for one who waits patiently for patience. Here we, like you, are broiling beneath the most fiery heat the skies ever sent down. However, our healths keep up. I am going to take great care of mine, now I have this prospect of travelling. May God preserve us all. I commit affections and afflictions to Him. Tell me soon that she is better. Tell her I love her. Tell her I would fain cure her; tell her I would do impossibilities for her; tell her that I embrace her, all that is *her*, soul and body, *the other and the animal*,—a pretty animal, indeed, and more to my taste than any spirit in the world. Very cordially yours.

---

To MDLLE. LOUISE DE BAYNE.

*4th September,* 1840.

Would it be disturbing you, my friend, to present you with a token of loving and constant remembrance— a remembrance of long date and always full of trust, like those old friends who return again and again to visit you? I cannot forget your love or your heart, and, whatever the silence within, I shall knock outside: my little knocks will surely make themselves heard. You will answer me, Louise, at last; very tardily,—but never mind.

I do not fancy that you are away from home, as I know that Gabrielle de Paulo is gone to see you. I should like to have done so too, for you know whether or not I love the mountains, but so many things keep me back. I have told you some of them. Since then we have been expecting Caroline, who now informs us by Charles de Thézac that she will not come; but, however, I have written to her all the same for a final decision, knowing that plans may change when they depend upon health or other varying circumstances. Hence I do not yet despair of seeing this poor sister again, and I cannot leave when she comes, or till I know something definite. This of itself would prevent my paying any rather long visit, such as one to Rayssac would be; for you may well imagine I should not come to you merely for two or three days. Have we not so much to say to each other, so much of the past to recover?

My friend, this will get done some day, when I can, when God vouchsafes to bring us once more together on earth. Meanwhile I should like to know something of what you are doing, whether you did write me that announced letter which never arrived. For several months past I have heard nothing of you. I have received nothing since that most interesting packet full of Maurice's things. I instantly sat down to thank you for it, but I choose my messengers very ill, since they never bring me back an answer. I am vexed with them for it. I love all that you would send me of loving and pleasant, which I listen to in spirit. I must no longer hear it in words,— a sacrifice added to others, alas! that you lay upon me.

By way of news, I have to tell you that Marie, my sister, is on the point of returning from Montauban, whither Gabrielle* carried her off. We expect her to-morrow. I am impatient to see her again, although I have Euphrasie Mathieu here to relieve my solitude. Madame de Tonnac is much better; Charles is arrived from Paris, this is all I know of Gaillac.

Adieu, my dear silent one! I love you always and embrace you as usual. Keep, keep as long as you can the good and loveable Gabrielle,† who gives you so much pleasure. See, I always wish you happiness.

My best love to your sisters far and near, and believe me all your own.

---

To MADAME LA BARONNE DE MAISTRE.

Cabanes, near Cordes, 26*th September*, 1840.

Friend! friend! your life on earth is then to be nothing but a perpetual conflict, an endless trial! Oh, I believe it, I feel it! but, without going on with this Job's lament—which is only too well suited to your case—I have to reply to your letter—dear letter, so long expected! How I yearned to see your handwriting again. I had had lugubrious dreams, which, added to what I knew and what I did not know, alarmed me. Thank God! you live, you love me! What more do I need?—more, that is, just now? for I do not limit myself to this alone for you or myself. Alas! we need so many things besides, and I, for my part, shall only cease to wish when you cease to suffer.

* Mdlle. Gabrielle de Bellerive, cousin of E. de Guérin.
† Mdlle. Gabrielle de Paulo, now Mme. de Labroquère.

My dear friend—my dear other self, so near and dear are you to me—you seem to me better. Your letter has been a balm to me, so much was I suffering mentally through you. The last tidings of you were so heart-breaking!—I allude to M. de Maistre's bulletin—a detail of agony. On arriving at Cordes, where I still am, I recommended you to the prayers of a holy priest, the Abbé de Rivières, whose very name should do you good. God knows how much benefit I expect you to derive from his influence with God, from his Saturday's mass!

My poor friend, this shall not be a sermon. I am distressed to have been a source of something like bitterness, and I ask myself how it could be—I who would only be sweetness to you? But if I failed in this, pardon me; 'twas that I was speaking to the disease, not to the sufferer—to that disease which I saw torture, destroy you so atrociously. And then, my friend . . . . But no, I will say no more on that head. You suffer, I suffer; that is all. This powerlessness, this new form of pain, oh, how I share it, believe this, my friend. I should wish really to suffer what those I love are suffering.

This entirely human sentiment helps me to understand in a measure why God took our griefs on Himself. It was because He loved us, and willed to be as one of us. Oh, how I recommend you to His divine tenderness! You will experience it, you will suffer less; you will be consoled, I hope, by a hope which is not like so many others, all of which, as you truly say, get annihilated. Life is nothing but a deception—except, indeed, that portion of it which leans on faith. I see this more as I advance; hence this train of thought, too grave, perhaps, for a poor invalid, whom I would fain divert from her pains. My friend, can it be that I have poured you out all my honey, and can now only prove an empty vase? Oh, no! no! As much as I desire to be of some use to you, so much do I dread not being so, and, nevertheless, I feel my heart full of tenderness for you. Are you content with it? if so, I am contented too. Come back to me soon, to tell me of that poor dear health of yours. *They have killed you.* Did I not write word that the doctors were killing you? And now another of them! May he repair the mischief done, and cure you, at all events, of some one ailment, and he will be dear to me as the apple of my eye. Send me information on this point at once, I am impatient for it.

It is strange, too, that I should not have touched on that hope about my journey I wanted to impart to you, and in which you will come to believe one of these days, my dear unbeliever. You are, as always, too kind to your poor friend on this subject. You say things that are enough to make me take flight at once, in order to fall into arms that give such tender embraces. Why am I not in them already? We have discussed this journey a good deal in the family conclave: my father is going to write you a few lines about it—my kind father, who bids me tell you that he loves you very warmly, and greatly regrets his small chance of ever becoming acquainted with you. *That poor young woman, I shall never see her so long as I live!* He would, if he could, accompany me : this would be an inexpressible pleasure to him, but his health alone, were it only that, precludes from such a journey, and there are many other obstacles. Hence I should come alone : but it has been pointed out to me that you may probably be going this winter to Paris. Tell me, my friend, what do you wish to do? Will you stay or go? Shall it be Les Coques, or elsewhere? I am ready to follow you everywhere, but I should not like to be a travelling encumbrance. Talk this over with your mother. I should like to know that she was with you. Write to her poor mother, she will be so delighted to see something in your hand. Send her word that you are expecting me; oh! how I regret being unable to say, " I am setting off." Why are not events as prompt as hearts ? Why are there always so many things to be considered? Why? All these *whys* would never come to an end. Shall we at length exhaust all those that separate us? Try, see, arrange. On my side I have nothing to influence me but my devoted attachment. Unfortunately, though, everything does not depend upon that.

This will not suit your notions. This will seem to you an excuse. Oh! nothing of the kind, believe me. I am unfortunate. I give you pain. There is some comfort, however : it is to know you are looking well, hardly at all thinned. What delight! I had been picturing to myself thinness and hollow cheeks like mine, and that saddened me. I like all my friends to be prettier than I. . . . .

Cayla.

Here are three great, large pages : three fatigues, perhaps, for your delicate eyes. Oh! tell me too about those eyes, it is so long since I have heard anything about them. Are they less spared? Erembert has seen how much interested you are, now and always, in his health, and prays you to accept his most ardent wishes for yours. I must now finish this medley, begun yesterday at Cabanes but written everywhere alike under the inspiration of the heart, my familiar—which is quite as good as the demon of Socrates—Papa takes the pen out of my hand.

*After all that has just been said to you by my angel, my Eugénie, my second self, and much more,—what remains for me to say, madame? I will also say my very dear and excellent friend, if you do not consider the expression too familiar. But however that may be, and though I would on no account displease you (which can hardly be the case since I know you appreciate genuine feeling), I will tell you that I love you, both you and yours; and in proof of this assertion I consent, so soon as it is possible, to let you have my Eugénie, without whom I am but a poor creature, however great the support I find in her sister and Erembert. Why cannot I accompany her, to tell you much more than I write, to see, and know you? This is what I dare not hope, unless you can come and visit your friends at Cayla.*

DE GUÉRIN.

Again I, always I who follow you like your shadow, my inseparable. Pray, say many affectionate things to M. de Maistre, so good, so excellent to you that I must needs love him were it only for that! The paper fails me here; no room for all I feel.

---

### To the Same.

My kind, dear friend, I am packing up; and knowing the pleasure you would have in seeing me do so, I write you word of it. Can I too soon give you the assurance that at last we are about to meet again? Dear meeting! has it not been delayed, hindered, like everything in the world that has any semblance of happiness? But at length I am setting off. God brings me back to you, my perfect friend—back to your sufferings, to soothe them if I am able, to associate myself with them in that intimate and present way which makes them half one's own. Oh, my friend, how this thought consoles, supports me in thinking of my departure! It will be on Monday the 16th that we shall reach Toulouse; Erembert accompanies me so far, my cousin not being ready for the journey. I shall wait no longer for any one. I suffer too much from your suspense. I realise too much your palpitations at the opening of every door. I know all, I know to what an incredible degree you love me. How happy should I be if you did not suffer so much from it, poor friend, in whom everything turns to sorrow! I am going to pray God that those pains may be eased, that your heart may grow calm, your face animated, that I may find you better, as you lead me to hope, as

I so ardently desire. You know how bent I am on miracles.

The letters of M. de Maistre and Madame Sainte-Marie have done nothing but increase my depression about your health: no progress, nothing about you that is not heartbreaking. My friend, how shall I find you? This is what I shall keep thinking of the whole way. Never did any interview so completely occupy a heart. Once away from here, I declare to you that no place will have any charms for me nor be able to detain me. Nevers! Nevers! will be my only goal, my only aspiration: just as the Crusaders used to cry, "Holy Land! Holy Land!" Adieu! you will soon welcome your pilgrim. I embrace and quit, without quitting you.

---

### To the Same.

Toulouse, 19*th November*, 1840.

Your friend, my friend, is galloping on. Here I am at Toulouse, and now about to set off again. I write, as I promised to do; but I do not yet know the morning or evening of my arrival at Nevers. I shall inform myself on this head, if possible, at the diligence-office. All that I do know is, that at Châteauroux I shall change into another diligence, and from that into yet another at Bourges, which last will take me to Nevers. All these changes will occasion some delay, but at last I shall get to you, as I believe, on Saturday. We have been a day here, exploring the city, visiting the museum and the antiquities of the place. A charming town this Toulouse of ours, our Troubadour town.

But adieu, very dear one! I cannot discourse longer. I write standing up, my hand on the icy marble slab of a commode: anything serves for desk and leaning place to travellers. I have just come from La Dalbade, a church two steps from hence, in which I remembered you.

In every place all your own.

P.S.—It will be Friday evening that we shall reach Châteauroux; there we sleep, and from thence to La Charité, where I shall take the Clermont conveyance. My itinerary being traced, adieu once again, and off I set. My respects to your family.

The weather is radiant; the sun will, I think, be my pleasantest travelling companion.

Erembert, who is here, presents his homage.

---

To M. HIPPOLYTE DE LA MORVONNAIS.

Nevers, *Hôtel Sainte-Marie, 4th December*, 1840.

It is by the bedside of a *gentle sufferer*, of another dear Marie, that I reply to your most kind and touching letter, which reached me at the moment of setting out, in the midst of the cares and anxieties of a parting; but I did not part with it, nor with anything that had reached me at Cayla. Wherever it may go, the heart carries with it what it loves, and lives on its own stores. I feed on memories, books, on that remnant of the past in which you so largely share. What you now add affects me no less than its forerunners, and I shall never be able adequately to express the feelings excited by each new notice of Maurice. I even prefer your article in the *Université Catholique* to anything that has yet appeared: doubtless because it corresponds with my own ideas and to what is due in a Christian sense to that beloved memory. Art had already made our Maurice very beautiful, but the heavenly side was wanting. Madame Sand could not attain to that, however exalted her intellect, because she lacked the wings of faith. For you, poet and Christian friend both, this task was reserved, and you have accomplished it perfectly. You speak so well on sacred subjects!

I garner in my heart your beautiful poem,* those celestial aspirations, those songs on tombs, which make one weep, but make óne hope also. It is thus you will sing of our Maurice, and we will bless you—we who love him as angels are loved—I, his sister, and she, his friend, that Marie of whom I spoke just now, who like yours, only somewhat later, received and comforted him in days of misfortune; amiable as she is to all the world, and to him a source of happiness, which now reverts to me, but alas! in tears: for my friend is a martyr, her life but one long agony. I am come here to see and seek to soothe her, to love her near at hand. How sadly sweet my post beside her, my dear and loveable invalid! In speaking

* 'La Thébaide des Grèves.'

to her of Brittany I have told her of Val, which she slightly knew, and of your poems, which she did not know. She has been charmed with them, and this, Monsieur, is true praise, believe me. Never could a finer intellect admire yours, never could a woman's voice discuss a poet better. . . . . But of all your poems the one she heard with most pleasure was *The Voice of the Wind*—most beautiful indeed, to be ranked with the loftiest hymns of Lamartine, if poets allow of comparisons, but we may compare glories. Madame de Maistre charges me to transmit to you her admiration as an artist and her thanks as a friend, both of which have been called forth by your poems and your papers on Maurice.

I have heard nothing as yet of your communications to Madame Sand. This subject remains a mystery to me, but I know some one who plans publishing all that remains of Maurice. You tell me that you possess some of the sweetest expressions of his remarkable talent, and this delights me. We shall have many beautiful things. If these last may be seen, will you entrust them to me? This is, perhaps, asking a great deal; I feel the secrecy of your intimate correspondence, but mine would be the only eyes to look into it, and there was no great distance between the brother and sister, you know. Nevertheless, I do not desire the impossible and refer it entirely to you.

Perhaps my sister-in-law has now returned to Paris, and will have found your parcel there. She has said nothing about it to me. With much superiority of every kind, it is possible that, owing to difference of nature, she may not enjoy your works as we do.

Adieu! although we plan going to Paris this winter I shall hope to receive what I ask you for here, and in any case one of your letters. I embrace our little Marie, and am always and everywhere your devoted friend.

---

To Madame la Baronne de Maistre.

Saint Martin, *Friday*, 17*th December*, 1840.

Dear friend, here I am far from you, but near in heart! *Souls never part.* You have experienced this, and I want to prove it to you again. Unfortunately, it will not be at any length this time; the bearer is waiting, and I, who did not expect him, write these few words in haste to add them to those our mother is writing you. I may well say OUR, for she has welcomed and embraced and treated me as her daughter's sister. We have talked of you a great deal, and shall not cease to do so while we are together, then when we are with you we shall talk on all the same. Titine is charming and enchanted.

Your mother's letter is gone without waiting for mine, for which I am glad and sorry both. The bit written to-day goes for nothing, indeed, but to-morrow I shall send a budget. I shall tell you everything that occurs, my very dear one. In the first place, know that this morning it snows, which clothes Saint Martin with a fine white robe, by no means unbecoming. It changes the melancholy, barren aspect of the country in winter. The snow, and the trees which fling their great black arms across the whiteness, form a contrast that I much like.

A transition! I pass from the white snow to the white sheets that cover my poor invalid's bed. . . . . That sad bed that never changes: I have very often approached it since I went away. Each evening I embrace you; each morning I say to myself, "Has she had any sleep?" Oh! how one feels the want of a spiritual messenger in the heart's service! I learned, on my way from Cayla, that it was a lover parted from the one he loved who had invented the telegraph, as I had always thought. There are things one guesses when one has not found them. Why cannot I, too, find something? It should neither be gold nor silver (though this is an urgent want, too), but a thing most precious to you and me: that which made a king exclaim, "Alas! without health what care I for a kingdom?" Am I not to have some tidings of that dear health which you have not got? A word about yourself, please. 'Tis too long to be kept a week in ignorance. The bell is ringing for breakfast! Tiresome bell! which obliges me to put down my pen.

No one has come here as yet, and, indeed, who is there that thinks of travelling just now unless it be the crows? And yet this morning, soon after daybreak, I heard under my window a little song of a little bird, which pleased me. I was sorry not to be a musician to note down this music amidst snow, and to take back with me a voice from Saint Martin—a place which tells me so much! Your home, your Cayla, your solitude, where I am so surprised to find myself! My friend, I see more and more that God has given us to each other. Your father and mother are infinitely kind to their daughter's friend, and I am deeply sensible of it. All that is wanting is to be here with you. We shall soon be together again, I hope.

The little girls are too happy: they never cease laughing and playing. This morning they were chirping away like larks on the snow. It required a prohibition from grandpapa to prevent a cold being caught.

---

To M. H. DE LA MORVONNAIS.

Nevers, 13*th January*, 1841.

First of all, monsieur, let me thank you for your letter, which would have been a great pleasure to me but for the news it brought. You have been ill! Alas! I have seen so much suffering, I still see so much, that I should have learnt to sympathise, even if compassion were not natural. This feeling, however, is inherent from our birth, like so many others that God gives us, and when we exercise them it seems as though it was then they first came. I pity you as much as a poor solitary sufferer can be pitied, and, if wishes could confer health, you would already have recovered yours. The state of my sweet friend has made me very uneasy for the last three weeks, and though there is some improvement, it is still so far from being satisfactory that we are not yet free from alarm. I tell you this in return for the kind interest with which Madame la Baronne de Maistre inspires you—an interest to which she responds with equal cordiality, but which can only express itself through me. That correspondence you appear to desire —and which could not have been refused to so gentle an entreaty—that correspondence, alas! is an impossibility to the feeble hand which for more than three months has never been raised from a bed of pain. "Tell M. de La Morvonnais," my amiable invalid said to me, "that I shall receive with much pleasure whatever he is good enough to send me; but that as to writing to him, I can hold no correspondence in my present state except with heaven." These are her own words, too sadly true.

And yet, in spite of all, she feels herself equal to going to Paris. The change of air, we hope, will do her good. With my watch over this dear friend I shall combine watching over our dear publication, and give you all information as to its progress. I accept the share you wish to take in it—a tribute of affection, of which I can never have too many like yours offered to that beloved Maurice. I am very sorry for what you tell me on this head of Madame ——. If I read aright, she *proceeds* against you! Unhappy misled spirit! Alas! how much one pities this woman who came forth so gifted from God's hands! What a painful admiration she inspires! She seems, moreover, to have thrown herself now into politics of an abominable kind. Thus deep calls unto deep, and this is what comes of forsaking the faith. O let us hold fast to it! we, poor human beings, let us hold to the sure anchor! It breaks my heart that there should be so many lost souls; I seem to see an ocean covered with dismasted, sailless ships, with leaks sprung in all parts of them. 'Tis thus the world appears to me:

enough to make one say, "Happy they who have left it; who on some fair day landed on the heavenly shore!" If you, in your depression, picture to yourself a lovely country with a sweet friend, and find consolation in so doing, so much at least we may always possess in our guardian angel, that celestial friend : a somewhat spiritual consolation, if you will, but is not this best? Alas! others are so often imperfect.

At last M. Quemper is returned from America. He little knows how I have been calling out for him in order to ask him for that dear, precious green manuscript book. I hope we shall see both the book and M. Quemper in Paris. You might also give him the manuscripts you promise to send me, or else (if they have not already set out) have the goodness to address the whole to M. Jules Barbey d'Aurevilly, Hôtel de Neustrie, 9, Rue *Port Mahon*. He is the friend who undertakes the publication. I much fear our short stay at Nevers would hardly give us time to receive your papers, and therefore I hasten to write to you in a hurried moment and wish you an abrupt Good-bye, that I may not lose the post.

I shall try, when in Paris, to procure *l'Université Catholique*, which will interest me for its own sake.

---

To M. DE GUÉRIN, Cayla.

Nevers, 18*th January*, 1841.

Saint Petersbourg, Odessa, Pera, Milan, Rome, the Isle of France, and other places,—all this I have seen since the departure of my last journal. I begin this one on my return from a voyage round the world that I have just been making on the ducal 'Place' of Nevers at the *Temple d'Illusion*—an illusion so perfect that one really does get a sight of the places and objects represented in their own natural size and colours. Accordingly, I am now acquainted with Russia, its pale sky and snow-covered ground, its sledges and reindeer, as well as with the fiery soil of Africa. With what interest I contemplated l'Isle de France, and that Port Louis, so full of memories for us! and then Milan, where there was a different kind of interest in that magnificent cathedral, of which Papa has told us, and which was exactly as he saw it, with the shrine of San Carlo Borromeo on the high altar. But nothing came up to St. Peter's in Rome, represented at the time of the Pope's consecration. One never wearied of gazing at it, and fancying oneself amidst the cardinals at the foot of the pontifical throne. Poor hermits of Cayla, what were you doing at the time? At every moment, in every place, I find myself reverting to you.

19*th*.—I have just been paying my farewell visit to that pious Breton priest of whom I have told you, and taking him back quantities of books that he had lent me. He is the kindest man in the world, one who would give his life's blood to serve and save a fellow-creature. We had a long conversation, all about our invalid, in whom he takes an indescribable interest, something akin to the ineffable tenderness of the Saviour for the afflicted. We set out the day after to-morrow.

*Sunday, 24th* (Paris).—Perhaps you are returning from vespers at Andillac; perhaps on your way you are thinking of Paris and your absent one, who also on her way was thinking of you as she returned from stately St. Roch. Alas! yes; I thought of my own place in this place so distant from mine; of all of you, from whom I am removed so far by a singular fate. It seems like a dream to find myself once more in Paris. Poor Paris! In crossing a bridge on arriving, I saw Caroline; but without being able to speak to her. I shall go and see her one of these fine days. Her aunt is in a very suffering state. Meanwhile I have written to her.

When shall I have news from Cayla? Ever since I have been here, I begin each day and night with this intense longing. It includes you all, my dear Papa, my dear Mimin, my dear Eran. Affections accompany the heart, go where it will, and nothing can divert me from constant thought of you all, especially as it will soon be a month since I have had letters from you. Happily, however, Auguste tells me he has heard lately, which somewhat comforts me. Perhaps you have written to me at Nevers; and, although I left my address, the letters may possibly be delayed or get lost. At all events, write to give me pleasure, if not to relieve me from anxiety.

I should already have finished my letter, but that I wait to see Caroline, that I may tell you about her. To-morrow, at latest, I shall post this, which will perhaps cross yours; for you cannot be long without writing to me, can you, my dear Papa? you, who think so much of your daughter while others enjoy her, according to the expression of Louise, who knows your tenderness well. That dear Louise! you will be having a letter from her. She promised me this, and quite of her own accord: for I don't go begging favours, which are sure to come to you naturally. But I am glad of it, knowing how pleasant her correspondence is, and that you have not very often pleasant things coming to you, my poor recluses.

Not having been able to go and see Caroline after all, I throw my letter into the post without further waiting. Cadars, who has just written, does not say a word of Cayla or any of you; can it be that he has not seen you then? Can any of you be ill? I torment myself with conjectures, and hasten to write them down on returning this evening to my little solitary room—solitary, though surrounded by people, and lit all night by neighbouring lights. From time to time I look out, and see pretty things to describe: for instance, some one who is reading behind a white curtain, and only shows her book and her hand; but I am not in the vein to write any more. Adieu! I am going to bed, after praying God that no misfortune may have happened to you.

To MDLLE. MARIE DE GUÉRIN.

Paris, 16*th February*, 1841.

Nothing could come quicker than your letter this time, posted only three days ago. The interval is so short that the paper still retains all the perfume of Cayla. Thanks, my dear, for having, in the midst of your occupations, found leisure to write me so many details of your feelings and of our country both. I imagine you quite overdone, unable even to go to mass the following morning.

At that same hour I was at St. Roch, listening to M. l'Abbé Cœur, who gave us a fine discourse upon waiting for Jesus Christ. Oh! there is no lack of sermons in Paris; nor indeed of anything for all needs and all tastes, whether of earth or heaven. If only we might enjoy health! I allude to our dear invalid, who continues in very much the same state. Your good wishes and love are always acceptable to her, and she responds to them with all her heart. We very often speak of my sister Mary, my dear *Mimi*. This last appellation, anti-Parisian as it is, made her laugh.

But let us come back to Cayla and your letter, line by line. Is Paul * come? Is Papa gone to Alby? Are the disturbances in the commune quelled? Interesting matters all. I should especially rejoice to hear that these eternal electoral debates had come to an end: I fear that they will make Papa ill. Last night I dreamed of dis-

* M. Paul Mathieu, judge of the Civil Tribunal at Albi.

asters, not political but physical ones: of inundations like those at Lyons, of a sea rolling mountains high, and nevertheless I saw you saved. O power of the imagination! It was the narrative of the floods which recurred to me in my sleep, amalgamated, in dramatic fashion, with—I know not why—recollections of Cayla, although generally that dear train of thought is carried on very naturally and very sweetly.

Now, then, I am at ease about your letters. The one from Nevers is come at last; I answered it immediately by a private hand to Toulouse, and wrote at the same time to Elise and to Antoinette. I do not wish to neglect any one, and consequently I have a great deal to get through in the way of correspondence. One of these last days I wrote to M. Lacordaire, whom my dear invalid wished to see. We expect him this afternoon. I have already heard him at Notre Dame: he is admirable. Unfortunately, I could not catch all he said, for we were very ill placed, although M. de Maistre and I went there three hours before the service began.

I should like to do something for our church. But for that I need the help of the good General. No one has heard anything of him for the last six months, not even Caroline. The rest of our acquaintance are well: I want to see them all. One of these days I shall write word to M. Augier to come and take me out to Montrouge, to embrace little Billy.

Of all our cousins Paul is the most cordial: I wrote in his envelope to Gabrielle. Cadars, you tell me, is bringing me a letter from Marie. This poor Marie principally occupies me. I am very glad that you should have passed some days at Gaillac, where they are so fond of you. Those Thézacs are so kind! That *minet* has been given you most opportunely for your cold experiences on the Andillac road, if you have had the same cold we have. Adieu, my dear Mimin! for every one of your lines I give you a kiss.

And you, my dear Papa, what shall I do to you? What shall I say to you, in return for all of tender affection I receive from you, both for myself and those who love me. This dear friend is most grateful, and never speaks of you except as that *good M. de Guérin* that she always so much wants to know.

Since I began this letter M. Lacordaire has been here in his Dominican garb, which suits his ascetic, humble, and inspired face to perfection. I know nothing comparable to his expression, radiant with intellect; but the most beautiful thing of all is his holy and consoling conversation. Our invalid has had an hour's conference, with which she is enchanted. He is to return and to bring her some of his writings. On hearing my name he was reminded of poor Maurice—a young man, he told me, of so much promise. This reminiscence touched me. It is in the neighbourhood of Bordeaux that M. Lacordaire has founded his monastery, which already consists of twelve fellow-workers. As for him, he is going back to Rome.

And you, my dear Papa, are you too going to become

a founder? From the way in which things get carried on, it would really show a noble devotedness to public affairs;* I am always afraid you should be made ill by them, either through travelling or other worries. Do take care of yourself; attend to Mimin, the wise counsellor of your health. Alas! once lost, it is often for ever! Another thing that you are not to torment yourself about—the falls and accidents that the newspapers tell you of, and which generally befal only the awkward, the absent-minded, or the dead-drunk. Now, as I find myself included in none of these catagories, I may, with perfect confidence, defy all the impediments of Paris; I walk about the streets with as much safety as in the Andillac roads. So do not be uneasy, my dear Papa. Thanks for having thought of sending me the letters; but they are too confidential to be exposed to the chances of a journey: keep them. Good night, dear papa! when shall we say this face to face?

There will surely be room for an embrace in this corner, dear Eran, as well as for the remembrances of all your acquaintance. No such a small matter, either; but a sign will represent them. Adieu, my dear! Take more than these two or three lines; my letter is also for you, *for all*.

* There was a prospect of M. de Guérin being made Mayor of Andillac.

To M. H. DE LA MORVONNAIS.

Paris, *Hôtel Sully, Rue du Dauphin,*
*20th February,* 1841.

Here I am in Paris! that Paris where I no longer have Maurice, but where I am still occupied about him. On arriving I informed myself about the publication, and am collecting materials for it. This is the time, monsieur, for you to send us the precious manuscripts and the green book which came from America. M. d'Aurevilly has not received anything, which makes me anxious as to the fate of the parcel that I begged you to direct to him just as I was leaving Nevers. Can it be that you did not get my letter, or are you ill? Alas! one may well fear misfortune when it strikes on every side! My friend is more and more suffering. I have nothing but sad presentiments, in which you are sometimes included, and which the past state of your health too much justifies. If, then, you are indisposed, be kind enough to tell me so, that I may, at least, get rid of suspense—suspense, which is often worse than reality.

I have seen my sister, but not yet sufficiently to say all I have to say to her, or to ascertain whether she has received your poems. As for that, she has been absent from Paris for six months, which accounts for her silence respecting a tribute which could but affect her deeply. But perhaps ere now you have received her reply and thanks. How much gratitude have I not in my heart for all you have done for Maurice! But when will it be given me to enjoy it? To read *l'Université Catholique* and to possess those copies that you are giving yourself the trouble to make? This is, indeed, a great undertaking, too laborious; and, if it fatigue you, you had much better send me the originals, which, as soon as transcribed, shall be faithfully returned to you. An idea this that occurs to me owing to your delicate health and my wish to abridge your labours.

I am to tell you what I do in Paris? Alas! nothing but remain quiet in my poor invalid's room: a sweet, sad life, which gives scope for so much thought and so much suffering. I know not when I shall regain my peaceful Cayla,—that cloister in the desert; better for the soul, I think, than being cloistered in the noisy world. But all places to which God leads us are good; from each and all of them we may go to heaven. This thought is my gentle consoling companion on this poor earth of ours. I would I could bestow it on all the afflicted. I imagine it yours, too, in your Thebaid. And you also carry on your poetic studies there: spiritual enchantresses these; and then the little Marie is ever there to smile at you. You have suffered much, but God has still left you some happiness—enough to make you bless Him as we all do:—

> "Yes, in the bitter cup from which we drink our life,
> Some drop of honey ever intermingles,"

as our Lamartine has sung.

M—— does not appear to have received your papers, or else she keeps them. Be so good as to tell me how the case stands, in order that I may recover those dear relics, wherever they be. Caress for me the *white and pink child*, and receive the renewed assurances of my regard.

---

To M. DE GUÉRIN, Cayla.

Paris, 23rd February, 1841.

This morning I was in the Carmes sacristy, having a talk with that good M. Buquet. What a man of God, and how he loved Maurice! We recalled the past, the Stanislaus time. He promised me some curious papers belonging to that period; and what is more, we may get others by means of his intervention. Nor was Cayla forgotten; he several times spoke of you, my dear Papa, and of all. In short, I left him quite delighted with our meeting, and carrying with me a permission to spend a day out for young Belmont, who will come to us to-morrow, as well as all Auguste's little ones. We shall take them to see the *Bœuf Gras* and other wonders of the Paris Carnival, well fitted to gratify childish curiosity.

Eleven o'clock. I have just returned from Auguste's, where we were a family party at dinner and talked of our own neighbourhood; we only wanted the inmates of Cayla to complete our party. Auguste asked me what you were doing on your Shrove Tuesday? I assured him that you had the pastor with you and were eating pancakes! Was this true? Good night! Oh, how far away we are!

25*th*.—Another visit from Father Lacordaire: the last, unfortunately! He sets out for Rome sooner than he had expected, and therefore he could only carry on a little general conversation with our invalid, in which I shared. He speaks but little, but his glance says so much! I see in him the inspired and radiant brow of Saint Dominique. God grant that he may revive the Order with equal benefit to society! It needs it now as much as did that of the middle ages: but M. Lacordaire is very hopeful about it, and especially about France.

*March.*—Since I left off I have dined with Caroline. She wrote me a very affectionate note and received me, too, most graciously, and so did her aunt. Kind M. Augier drove with me there. Here I am, as usual, by my friend's side. A very singular kind of practitioner has presented himself, a prince, a king, the Dauphin risen up from the Temple, that Baron de Richemont, fellow-prisoner of Pellico, chief of a savage tribe in America, physician in India, and I know not what in Paris. *He goes everywhere, can do everything, hears everything*, like the 'Solitaire'; and above all, he amuses us by his narratives, all inlaid with anecdotes. We have had three long visits, during which my time for believing in the royal visitor never came! What is striking enough, however, is a decided resemblance to the profile of Louis XVI.

13*th.*—How much has arrived to-day from Cayla, Port Mahon, and Brittany—things to fill the soul in the first place, and next a thousand reams of paper! M. d'Aurevilly has brought me compositions in the style of the *Centaur* and enchanting letters. Nothing is wanted but to strike out private allusions. The packet from Brittany also contains treasures, that good M. de la Morvonnais has given himself much trouble in copying out. His notice has appeared in *l'Université Catholique*, —a good and beautiful notice that I shall try to send you. Oh! thanks, thanks, Papa, for the long letter that you have sent me by M. de Rivière. To-day has been quite too fortunate! But let us not complain of happiness, even when it is sad. 'Tis thus I designate all these papers of Maurice; your letters, too, gave me all the pleasure in the world, showing me that you are all well, and as contented as I can wish you to be.

This page replies, my dear Papa, to the first part of your letter. I shall add in conclusion that I have not seen M. Charles, having been out when he called, but that I am to dine with him to-morrow at Auguste's. There I shall find the remainder of the papers sent me. This publication is certain to appear, and is anxiously expected. Friends vie with each other in offering to see it through the press. Ten copies are ordered in Brittany. You will be pleased with this, dear Papa, sufficiently so not to desire any more fame: a desire besides that I cannot indulge with any hope. Publications are no easy matter, and even if they were, my name will never appear in the literary world.

Oh, *pater bonus* that you are! How return you your infinite tenderness, save by assuring you that I love you as much as it is possible to love! Adieu, and thirty-six thousand embraces!

To MDLLE. LOUISE DE BAYNE.

Paris, *Hôtel Sully, Rue du Dauphin,*
23rd *February,* 1841.

You told me, dear Louise, to write to you so soon as my heart moved me. You must have thought this movement was very tardy, for it is a long time now since your letter came—long, that is, for a friend's letter. But, my dear, I am obliged to suspend the greater part of my correspondence, and you will not be angry with me for a momentary silence, the result of my present position. Once out of Paris, and back again at Cayla, my life and my thoughts will resume their accustomed course and my letters their way to the mountains as often, and oftener, if possible, than in the past. Why have we not our black messengers * here? I should load them with Parisian trifles, those little nothings that have only the charm of the moment about them, with a journal of every day, which would, I am sure, please you far more than this rough sketch of a month.

It is a month exactly since we left the Nivernais, to find ourselves here, alas ! as elsewhere, shut up in a sick-room with medicaments and medical men. Such is our life! very sad, both for the one who suffers and those who have to witness it. My poor friend will, I fear, be amongst the number of incurables and martyrs, and yet, as she is young and strong and prayed for by all the Saints, one may hope for a miracle, and I do hope.

* The mountain charcoal-burners.

Meanwhile I remain at her bedside, assisting in his ministrations that perfect and indefatigable nurse M. de Maistre, the model of devoted husbands.

These last days we have had in addition a sister of *Bon Secours*, charming and cheerful, full of the love of God and of interesting anecdotes. She goes here, there, and everywhere; to the Tuileries, to a duchess, to poor people. Nothing can be more varied than the life of these good Sisters, watching by night all kinds of sickbeds, young and old. I am going to tell you a dreadful story of a young Sister who was in charge of a sick man who died. After having remained three hours alone with him she prepared to wrap him up in the windingsheet, and, as she drew near for that purpose, the two arms of the corpse suddenly closed upon the Sister with a horrible pressure. The monster had counterfeited death! The poor girl dropped down dead from terror. "'Tis thus," said Sister Isabella to us, "that we are sometimes recompensed here below; but our reward is above." Such devotedness, indeed, can never find its price on earth.

I know another story of hers, but it would be too long to send you now. I will reserve it to tell you, I must write of other than these conventual matters, else you would not believe me in Paris; and, in fact, it is very much the same as though I were not there: all walls resemble each other. We are every day waiting for an improvement that never comes, to take our poor invalid out. A drive in the outer air would do her so much good, and she has to languish and suffer in bed: a singularly unfortunate destiny, of which we can only say, "It is God's will." That was the last word of comfort from Father Lacordaire to our invalid, while promising to pray for her recovery for a whole year in Rome, where he is just gone. With how much interest I used to see this young saint, for a short period intimate with Maurice, at the school of La Chenaie! But, what was still better than seeing him, I heard him preach, and have read some of his works: the *Life of Saint Dominic* and the *History of the Preaching Friars*, an Order that he is going to revive. A certain set in Paris is much taken up about this: for there is a set for everything here. No orator addresses himself to the present epoch more successfully, or expresses religious and social truths in a manner so consonant to its taste.

M. de Ravignan, another eloquent apostle, is also preaching at Notre Dame; we had him lately at St. Roch. Oh! there is no lack of sermons: assure M. Massol of this, in return for the interest he takes in my soul and its conversion. Tell him it requires it less than he supposes, and that I have reason to be anxious about his, since he is deficient in charity. This message is to be accompanied by respectful remembrances.

How I enjoy myself at St. Roch, at the end of a dimly-lit, out-of-the-way chapel, where one might believe oneself in the Catacombs! It is in a confessional there that dwells a seraph who directs me gently and sublimely towards heaven. I have blessed God for giving me this holy consolation, which I need: for alas! I often have to cry Alas! in the world. Paris has no longer any charm for me, or very little, after what I have lost there.

This brings me to my sister-in-law, ever more and more celestial. She wanted to become a nun, but I believe her strength was not thought sufficient; and then how can she leave her aunt and her young brother, who have but her in the world? I am a long way from the Rue Cherche Midi, which renders my visits rare, and besides I do not leave my dear invalid much. There is a crowd of acquaintances that I am neglecting: Sister d'Yversen, Lisbine, and others belonging to Paris, that I no longer see because I have left off going out.

I should require nothing less than you, my dear Louise, to draw me out of my solitude, and you would do so irresistibly. How Paris would delight you! This stir, this brilliancy, this society, this intellectuality—all that one sees nowhere else—the distinguished men, the elegant women; in a word, Paris would charm you, and every now and then I find myself wishing you were in my place, for I am unworthy of it—I, who am more touched by the song of a thrush on the juniper trees of Cayla than by the Valentin concerts. Judge if this be not thought strange, if I do not cause a laugh, and nevertheless they are all very fond of me—spoiled child of the heart that I am! This, amongst other things I tell you will give you pleasure to hear, you who first taught me the sweetness of friendship!

My dear Louise, will my letter give you this time the same little thrill of pleasure the other did? No doubt it will as you open it; but while reading it I am not so sure, for I feel very stupid and somewhat akin to the sky that is above our heads—dull and morose. It is scarcely worth while to send you such a letter from so far, but the heart prompts it and wafts it to you. Look upon it as an evidence of my strong and unvarying affection.

Why have you not written to Marie, my poor solitary sister, to whom your letter would give a sweet moment of pleasure. I should be tempted to scold you, did I not know that your silence is not forgetfulness, did I not see that you neglect all your affections, even society, even Gaillac, where you used to laugh so much formerly. But now, oh! how time changes us! Should we know each other again, you and I? No doubt we should by our tenderness, that side of *ourselves* which is not touched by time.

Adieu! I scribble too badly on this transparent paper to go on writing; hold the page singly when you read it. All sorts of things to your three sisters: things that I feel for them wherever I may be. Have you, then, been weaned from your little niece? Oh, I can enter into your regrets and into the charm that child had for you! But you will see her again: absence is not death, and then— make a little sacrifice for the good God who accepts it so graciously! Dear Louise, adieu! I have not yet been able to enquire for your Abbé Caire. I go no more out than a Carmelite; but if a charming Sophie de Rivières, whom we expect, arrives, I shall do so a little with her, as she knows Paris as well as her own room, and loves to run about like a lark.

To M. H. DE LA MORVONNAIS.

Paris, 10*th March*, 1841.

The sweetest words would fail, monsieur, to give you back the sweetness I find in yours when you speak of spiritual things and, as in your last, of Maurice. On receiving your letter I ran off to the office of *l' Université*, and I now possess and treasure in my heart your precious notice, so beautiful as to feeling, expression, and truth. Thanks to you, our Maurice is seen there in his life of poetry and faith, and beneath the heavenly aureola which until now he had been deprived of. However highly they had exalted his talent, it was not up to heaven, its native place. Praise be to you, who, like a friendly angel, have raised him on your wings before the eyes of those who did not discern that he could soar so high! And then how much I delight in those unknown beauties of his mind that you reveal, those divine reveries in Brittany by the side of the ocean, in the great forests, in that beloved Val: treasures these that I owe to you! May God bless you, my kind poet! It is to Him I remit the proof of my gratitude, which neither my soul nor anything else can sufficiently testify to you. What can my weak woman's language express? Nothing, I feel, or very little, although you flatter it by calling it very poetical. To make it so, you must hear it through the medium of kindness, through Maurice, its brother. Yes, that dear object invests me with its own charms in the eyes of his friends, and I am proud and happy it should be so; as also there is on my side a return of affectionate and enduring sympathy towards them.

And yet does this correspond with your devotedness and your most kind letters? If I have not sooner told you how much they touched me, 'tis that I have been unable to write. I do so at my first leisure. I say leisure, because this is a quiet moment, in which one may dwell on what pleases, as a weary man will throw himself on moss in some retired spot. You who take solitary walks have, I dare say, done this before now. As for me, a few steps knock me up in Paris, this world of fatigue to the mind, where nevertheless I find a sad enjoyment in life and death. For me Paris encloses so much that is dear, so many joys, so many pains! It is paradise in mourning!

M. Quemper came to see me with an amiable alacrity, which I keenly appreciate. This good young man at first sight justifies your praise of him, and deserves the title of friend from all who confer it upon intellectual superiority and goodness of heart. Madame de Maistre, who is eminently correct in her appreciation of character, passed the most favourable opinion on M. Quemper, and he is one of the men with whom she would like to grace her drawing-room. But alas! her drawing-room is a bed of pain, at the foot of which M. Quemper has once been seated. On another occasion I received him alone in a 'salon,' without fire or external charms of any sort; but for all that there was a charm for me in conversing about the past, about Maurice, Brittany, friends in those regions, the sea, your little Marie, and much besides. The streams of the soul are not easily checked.

You have quoted charming things in your notice, fraught with a nameless perfume! What a rich hope this excites as to the promised collection, the dear treasure that the diligence is rolling towards us! M. d'Aurevilly is going to occupy himself incessantly with the work, with this monument for France and ourselves to which you have so largely contributed by the labour of heart and mind. I should much like to be here at the time of publication, but there is little likelihood of that, although our departure is still uncertain. I shall be sure to speak about your ten copies; and do not be uneasy about the course of our poet; his channel is already hewn out in slopes where flow streams of gold, and he has but to burst forth. Indeed, this book is devoutly expected. There are still many things to be collected, which I discover here and there. He was wont to scatter himself abroad with an unjust carelessness, was my poor Maurice; he valued nothing of his own, and went away without enjoying any of the gifts with which he was so richly endowed. It is we who are to enjoy them, but there is in this a profound sadness that nothing can console.

I had got so far in my letter to you when the parcel arrived by the diligence. Beloved relics of my beloved Maurice! Oh, thanks! thanks! a thousand times, my kind friend! I have hardly seen or read anything as yet, but I have them all in my heart, and I must at once express its feelings to yours, which has done so much for me; almost too much, if I dared to complain of seeing my name by the side of Maurice's, beneath the aureola that you so piously place on his brow in *l' Université Catholique*.

Adieu, and infinite gratitude.

P.S.—I find another letter from you in the parcel. Will you take this as a reply to all, oh! too kind friend? Madame de Maistre accepts with the graciousness of her grace all your graceful homage. Now as always, I kiss the child.

---

To M. DE GUÉRIN, Cayla.

Paris, *Holy Thursday, 8th April,* 1841.

I have just come from St. Roch, from the midst of crowds, sermons, music, and prayers, too; for in all this there is surely something that tends God-wards. In general, however, there is but little devotion in these comings and goings. To preserve myself from distraction, I took refuge at the bottom of the dark and silent Calvary. It was sweet as Paradise, and I kept thinking there of the Andillac chapel, where you, my dear far-away ones, doubtless were, thinking of Paris, I believe. There are times and places where hearts are sure to meet. To-day we shall most certainly have prayed for each other on this holy festival of Holy Thursday that for some years past I have so seldom spent at Cayla. Three years ago I was at Albi, with that poor Lili; the year after I was here; and this year here again. A singular destiny mine! connected with so many unexpected things, according to a providential purpose, no doubt! We have all a mission in this world: mine is to go far to witness suffering...

*Good Friday.*—I shall not say much this evening, being tired with my day in church. Once in St. Roch, there is no getting out, such is the succession of sermons and services. This morning, meditations at six o'clock; then the Passion, by M. le Curé, who spoke divinely; at nine the office, the Adoration of the Cross by from two to three thousand souls; at twelve until three o'clock, the words of the Agony alternating with the music, which was in perfect keeping this time: finally, the darkness and the *Stabat* at seven o'clock. Was that not a day after *Rousou's* * heart? Oh, how radiant she would have been during it! I saw her very image at the Calvary: a girl with the same headdress as hers, devout as she is, always kneeling like her. Had it been right, I should have asked her where she came from—from the South, I am very sure, from her costume. Tell this to our Rousou, and how a thought of her occasioned both interruption and edification. Good night! after this holy day. Do not go and fancy that I passed the whole of it in church; I left it both for breakfast and dinner, but the priests, I imagine, sustained themselves on holy water.

Since I left off then some days have passed; your letters and the fearful affliction of the De Thézacs have reached me. What a thunderbolt! I cannot get over

* *Rousou, Rose la Marguillière,* see Journal.

it. Hippolyte, who was so young, so healthy! What is the strongest life! I spent part of yesterday with Charles, after announcing the terrible tidings to him. M. Cadars came to fetch me for this purpose, as he was commissioned to do by the family. The worthy man and his home circle were as much affected as if they had lost a relative. Gabrielle de Paulo wrote to me in perfect consternation; she told me that he died of croup, —a singular complaint at his age! In short, he is gone, that powerful young Hyppolyte; and God alone, and the pious sentiments he evinced, can console his mother. He died with the resignation of an angel, Gabrielle told me. God be praised that in so brief an interval this poor young man was able to think of his soul!

Let us turn to something else: from death to life, to the important announcement of a drive taken yesterday with our invalid to the Bois de Boulogne, an excusion which will be followed up by going to the sea, provided this improvement continue.

And so *our prince* appears to you a very suspicious character, and you do not like to think of my being with him, in-doors or out, and nevertheless we shake hands like good friends. He has such a frank, kind, sincere look, that one believes him all he likes to be thought, perhaps though not exactly what he is. However that may be, he asks for nothing, and moreover he is received by all the most distinguished royalists, amongst others by MM. de N—— and De la Rochejacquelein. M. de Sainte M—— considers him very remarkable as to political tone and information.

The book has not been found as the Sibyl foretold; I rather begin to mistrust the oracle. And yet I am as sure of the existence of the manuscript as of having two hands, but where can it be? M. Quemper made over to me one that had traversed America from north to south. I can tell you nothing but what you already know about this publication, and, besides, it is some time since I have seen M. d'Aurevilly.

The other day I went to a party to hear Lablache, who never came, and I got very weary listening for three hours to other singers; Auguste was with me. He took me on almost all the Sundays in Lent to hear M. de Ravignan at Notre Dame. Sermons have been my great delight; God grant that they may have been my salvation as well. Adieu, dear Papa; in spite of myself I have to leave you.

P.S.—Another acquaintance made! that of Maurice's copyist;[*] that devoted young man, who for the last six months has given up all his time to this writing out. I made over to him a remarkable heart out-pouring to M. Buquet, which M. Buquet had made over to me.

---

To MDLLE. LOUISE DE BAYNE.

Paris, 29*th April*, 1841.

Why not scold me, dear Louise, as you were inclined to do? It would have amused me; nothing prettier than affectionate reproaches, passing through your bright mind, more particularly when lost in air, for they find in me

[*] Charles-Auguste Chopin, a devoted friend of Maurice de Guérin.

nothing on which to alight, do these little black butterflies. I offer them neither forgetfulness nor indifference; only a little of that dilatoriness which somewhat belongs to my character and to Paris life. The time passes here in the most unoccupied way; in trifling visits, conversations, and then, and then ... a thousand details, which slip away like sand, and, nevertheless, fill up the space of a day. This morning I spent three hours in church for nothing.: my seraph was confessing a legion of angels, who left no room for my poor soul; so I shall have to try again this evening, which will give me six hours of waiting. What time shall I have for anything with the company that we are expecting to dinner? Therefore, my friend, I begin by writing to you, even though I should have to break off and resume.

And, first of all, thanks for your two letters, dear tokens of your dear friendship. I was going to reply to the first when the second arrived, that second one written in the beginning of a vexation which I should not have found out. Everything inspires you pleasantly, my pleasant one. I had also had tidings of you from my father, who wrote to me about his journey to Rayssac. For his own pleasure's sake I wish he may have carried it out, but I fear he has not; so many causes—business or health—detain him at Cayla, that my father seldom has his time at his own disposal. But, if in any degree he has, it will be disposed of in your favour: we give to those we love, and my good father loves you deeply and constantly; he will, therefore, go and see you as soon as possible. You will renew those *tête-à-tête* conversations of the olden times, that both were so fond of; you that you might talk, he that he might listen to you. But I would have you know that your confidential communication soon reached me, and that the seal of secrecy is not kept with your friend the *angel*, who is rather spoiled by her father, both in name and everything else.

I cannot tell when I shall rejoin this dear father; nothing gets said on this subject by our invalid, and I know not how to talk to her of departure. And yet a good opportunity presents itself of returning to our part of the world with M. Charles de Rivières, but he will go away with nothing more of me than my letters! We talked for a moment of you all in the parlour of Saint-Nicolas-du-Chardonnet, with Lisbine, who I was at length able to go and see. She gave me a truly saintly reception, was enchantingly beautiful and gracious. What innocence! what a smile! what a peaceful soul under that white head-dress. I said to her "How happy you must be!" "How should I not be so? I have done God's will." Indeed this is the only thing that can ensure happiness, *the doing God's will* in whatever position we may be, whether in the cloister or the world, but in the world it seems to be more difficult, and yet there is no lack of grace, or merit either, there; as, for instance, when we meet temptations in order to conquer them—open St. Jerome in a drawing-room when we might read a romance; but St. Jerome has grave and profound beauties that please thoughtful souls, and looking at your present mood I doubt not that you have great delight in this said St. Jerome. It is the beginning of a serious vocation. And yet, see the strength of early impressions; I cannot picture you to myself other than laughing, chatting, diverting, dancing; I only see my Louise of former days, and not very remote ones either, for we cannot go back quite a hundred years like the Sleeping Princess.

Sleep reminds one of death—I shall not attempt to tell you how thunderstruck I was by that of poor Hippolyte. My God! what then is the strongest and youngest life? In two days, in no time, there he is—gone, poor young man! I had to go and break the terrible tidings to Charles, who was in Paris recovering from a cold in the chest. Heaven grant that he may not have had a relapse on his way home! His mother could not do without seeing him at once. Marie and Gabrielle de P. gave me the details of the peaceful, happy end; for which I have heartily blessed God, and that in so few hours the poor young man was able to think of his soul. He did so, and in the most Christian manner possible. M. Louis de Combette was the one to recommend his soul to God, and he too showed himself full of faith and devotion. Oh! a Christian education is sure to save sooner or later.

As to that poor General ———, I doubly regretted him because of his Protestant death. May God have taken pity on his soul and his sincerity! A few days before, he had been to see me; after that I wrote to him, and the answer was his death. Nothing else is spoken of in life just now. A lady of our acquaintance has just lost four grown-up lovely daughters in an appalling way; one fell from a precipice in the Pyrenees, another was crushed by a carriage, the third died of brain fever, the fourth in her confinement. The poor mother is stunned with grief. Beautiful Saint Roch, where I daily, go is always hung with black, and so is my soul sometimes. And, indeed, there is nothing to enliven one in this perpetual sick-room, not even the splendid marriage that my friend's brother is about to make. The bride is an angel in face, mind, and piety, and has an income of forty thousand francs. The festivities are to take place in the country, and we shall be here on our bed of suffering. Here I am installed as Sister of Mercy for the spring, perhaps for the summer too. The favourite plan is to take me back to Cayla.

We shall not have my sister-in-law, whose aunt is setting out for India. The young woman remains in Paris, in order not to leave her brother of eighteen alone there. I sometimes see her, but we are a long way off, besides which I go out but little, and soon get tired in this great Paris. One of my sadnesses is going out alone, finding myself isolated in the midst of crowds. M. de Maistre never leaves his wife, so that I have not an arm to take here, where, alas! I once had one.

Amongst the singular acquaintances one makes in this singular Paris I must tell you of the most striking of all, that of the Duke of Normandy, the pretended Dauphin, an astonishing man as to wit, information, and political acumen, in profile resembling Louis XVI., and charmingly genial in manner. It is curious to hear him speak of the Temple, the King, the Queen, and his own abduction, as though he were really the Dauphin. I don't believe in him much, but he amuses me like one of the Arabian Nights. I do not mean Landorff, but the Baron de Richemont, the fellow-prisoner of Pellico. Adieu; I am in dreamland, except when I think of you, and tell you that I love you.

P.S.—My respects to the good pastor; tell him that I ask him for prayers, without saying why—for one of the converted if he likes.

---

To M. DE GUÉRIN, Cayla.

Paris, 29*th April*, 1841.

What a beautiful place the Palais Royal is at nine o'clock in the evening, with its lights, its walks, its verdure. O! if there were a continuance of days like this, the dead would arise out of their graves; the air has resurrection in it. All the birds of Paris, caged and free, sing their loudest. The Tuileries are resplendent in verdure, and send us wafts of perfumery, blended odours of lilacs, jonquils, pinks, and I know not how many flowers besides, full blown in that great royal garden. As I followed St. Mark's procession to Saint Roch, I thought how beautiful it would have been in those magnificent avenues. And you, Mimi, you were taking the path to Andillac, and wondering perhaps where I was. Let me, in the retirement of my cell, tell you all about my day.

Sleep cut me short the day before yesterday. Since

then I have had your letter, and the terrible news of the affliction at Cayla. Can it really be true? I seem to be under the influence of a night-mare, dreaming only of deaths. That poor Adolphe, that poor Misy, how I grieve for them! Here is a presentiment fulfilled! She said to me the last time I saw her, "I am too happy, I tremble lest something should befal me." Poor young woman, who was so fond of her Adolphe, what will become of her? I am going to pray God to sustain her, and I shall even write to her. However painful it may be to write such letters, we owe this to each other. You did well, Mimi, to go and see these dear afflicted friends. So, then, you only pay mourning visits, while I remain with an invalid, which is somewhat the same thing; and thus we continue sisters in matters of friendship and Christian charity.

Twenty-eight degrees of heat, this is excessive for Paris on the 1st of May, but everything runs to extremes in this Paris. This evening we shall, perhaps, have rain, together with the fire-works that celebrate the King's birthday. I saw the preparations as I passed by the Tuileries, which, probably are all I shall see of St. Philip. I am not fond of these crowds, and, besides, I am in no mood for gaiety, thinking of those poor vanished friends. Adolphe had always a tendency to blood in the head, and a sun-stroke, out shooting, may probably have brought on brain fever.

That meeting of the De Rivières made us laugh, and gives me reason to regret that I cannot enjoy the two. The Duke of Normandy is in the drawing-room, which will make you laugh, especially if I add that we like him as Cagliostro was liked, that cleverest of all jugglers. What an interesting and incomprehensible man! Adieu for the present. I shall go on writing, but you will get the letter by the Alby or the Gaillac post. I do not know whether I have duly answered everything: at all events, this will not be the short letter that Papa complains of, though without cause I think; his reproach, therefore, strikes me as a compliment. Dear Mimi and dear Eran, take your share of it. I write to you collectively, but I offer especial congratulations to Mimi about the chickens and *Pituit*,* whose flourishing condition assures me how well he is cared for. I embrace you all. Adieu.

To the Same.

Paris, *Hôtel des Bains de Rivoli, 8th June,* 1841.

At last you are free from your perplexities, my dear Papa, and thoroughly convinced that I am alive, and very much alive, to our mutual satisfaction; for it would be a pang to me to pass from this world to the other, far from you, dear Papa, and all those I love at Cayla : God will rejoin us, I hope, before this final separation. As to my departure hence, it is always in my thoughts, but not yet upon my lips. The time for actually settling it is not yet come ; and where would be the use of saddening this poor friend beforehand? I content myself

* Her goldfinch.

by acquainting her with the strong wish you feel to see her, which I fear will not be gratified for a long time to come, certainly not this year. We had, as I mentioned, planned going into Brittany; M. Quemper had told us of a delightful station in a village near Val. It sounded very pleasant and promising; but now good-bye to all travelling, owing to the impossibility of bearing the movement of a carriage : I am speaking of our invalid. How you would love and pity her, dear Papa! You love her without seeing her ; what would you feel could you but see her! We are in the midst of great wedding preparations for the little girls, who are not going to be married, but going to their uncle's marriage. To-day the contract was signed. My friend and I remain here during the festivities, which M. de Maistre is to attend. Mdme. de Sainte Marie is come in spite of her sufferings. We have had a great deal of family talk; have talked a little of Cayla too ; this whole family is perfect in its feeling for us : the misfortune is to be so far off; but are we not far from heaven also ? It is always so with what we love best.

 Have you been to Rayssac? I am much touched by Louise's remembrances and fears. You may assure her that I do not forget her; I wrote to her by M. de Rivières, begging him to execute a commission about books which she had given me. She has letter and books both by this time, I imagine. And *apropos* of books, M. d'Aurevilly brought me one to-day in which is a beautiful poem to Maurice's memory, and also the announcement of the early publication of his manuscripts.

This pleased me. My chief happiness in Paris is constantly hearing Maurice spoken of with tender admiration.

Adieu, my dear Papa. You are not maltreating the brook, which, inconstant by nature, was possibly weary of its old channel. But let me once more compliment Erembert about that vine, so speedily planted, under the terrace. It is one of the most perfect improvements of Cayla; I am delighted with it.

You are leading a patriarchal life, digging wells and planting vines. Oh, what a beautiful existence is that of an agriculturist! Can Cecile draw water from the well? That would be as good and pleasant for her as is the basin in the Tuileries, which for the last two days I have had under my eyes, for me; I am constantly plunging into it as it were, indulging myself freely in gazing at it, and inhaling the fine fresh air. Our invalid determined to bestow upon herself the pleasure of a new apartment and the sight of green trees. From her very bed we have the finest prospect imaginable: opposite us the Invalides, to our left the Tuileries, and everywhere the immense garden and its world of promenaders. It is delightful, and our rooms magnificent. Last week we had frantic heat. To-day is fresh and pure: you know the variations of a Parisian atmosphere; but it matters little to me, now that I can see a wide expanse of sky from my window. Adieu, dear; go on planting and embellishing. How delighted I shall be to see it all!

And you, Mimin, you too are making chicks and ducklings grow for your part. It is only I who am useless as regards Cayla; but, alas! what can one do in absence? If I had the gift of doing whatever I liked, I would make Cayla perfectly resplendent for you on my arrival, like *Peau-d'Ane*, when she used to put on her sun-coloured gown. What beautiful things there are in this Paris! Sophie was saying to me: "What a torment scarcity of money is in Paris!" Very true, my dear; but scarcity of bread is much worse. This wretchednesss that, in the midst of luxury, one sees and meets at every step, prevents one complaining; and besides, I have so many enjoyments that I have nothing to complain of. Adieu, dear; assure the pastor of my respects, and Marie of my remembrance. I embrace you all.

---

To M. H. DE LA MORVONNAIS.

*24, Rue de Rivoli, 12th July,* 1841.

What have you thought of my silence, and what shall I say to you about it, monsieur? An embarrassing question, yet only as regards the first clause; and then I have sufficient reliance upon your kind, gentle way of judging to presume upon indulgence. At all events, grant it now to a rather serious indisposition—to a stitch in the side that has kept me in enforced and absolute repose beneath the curtains of my bed; and go on granting this same indulgence to a little cough and a great lassitude, my habitual companions for some time back— to the *far niente* of a life that can no more for anything whatever. My will would fain have it otherwise—would wish for the mind a little possibility of action; but however it may strive, the spirit sinks with the sinking of the body. And this is profoundly sad; and it is this perhaps which made St. Paul exclaim, "Who shall deliver me . . . ?" Which of us is not familiar with that passage—which of us has not suffered? To ask this is to address you, my brother in sorrow; it is appealing to your sympathy, and expressing mine. Receive it, and believe in it in spite of its rare proofs. The little that is shown sufficiently attests the sentiments of the heart, as a few footprints do a passer-by. It is thus I would have you think of me; and thus I think of you when you are long without writing.

Your last letter is very kind, and makes full amends for past silence. At the same time it reassures me about your health, which had made us anxious. M. Quemper told you this, as I had begged him to do; but he did so with a charm all his own. Your friend has an infinity of talent and feeling. We much like seeing him and talking with him of Brittany, the sea, Val,—those known and unknown scenes that have so much interest for the sister of Maurice. Mdme. de Maistre, my sister in heart, also delights in these fancied excursions, keenly regretting her inability to take any others. Her health is still in a deplorable state, no hopes of travelling; and thus adieu, without having seen them, to the banks of L'Arguenon, the shore of the ocean, whence so many sweet things come to us. Adieu to the poetic solitudes we pilgrims were to traverse! My friend will remain in Paris, and I shall regain my Cayla.

And further, if I leave soon, I shall not carry away with me what I came so lovingly to seek for, the dear works of Maurice, which I expected to have. They will not appear till the beginning of winter. M. d'Aurevilly found it impossible to get the publisher's consent to a shorter delay; but, however, he is very promising as to all besides. I do not forget the interest you take in this publication, nor the ten copies you ordered. We shall have a satisfactory work, both as regards Maurice and ourselves. You have enriched us with admirable treasures. M. Quemper, too, has brought his offering in a very touching manner. Thanks, friends, to you all. Accept, too, my very lively gratitude for that *name* incrusted in *La Ville des Mers*, and for the feeling that placed it there. Sweetest thanks, oh, my poet!—but when are we to have your poetry? M. Quemper, who is always talking of you, makes us long much for it, and you increase this longing by your letters.

Adieu, my good hermit. Always tell me of your angel, and accept, in order to give her, an image of my patron saint. Children are fond of images, which makes me find pleasure in what may please Marie, to whom it would be nothing but for that.

Mdme. de Maistre begs to renew the assurance of her most cordial feelings; to which I add the affectionate expression of my own.

To MDLLE. MARIE DE GUÉRIN, Cayla.

Paris, *August*, (1841 ?).

It is you, my dear Mimin, to whom I mean to write to-day. Every one in their turn; and Papa has had his so often that he will consent to yours coming round. Besides, Papa will be no loser, since the substance of my letter is for all. If I have not answered yours before now, 'tis that I depended upon mine reaching you about this time. I emphatically charged Raymond to send them off immediately from Alby: he himself will visit you later. His intention was to go in the first instance to M. Robert, and thence to make a descent upon Cayla. This delay will give our fruit and our grapes time to gild themselves, and our pigeons and poultry to grow. All these matters occupy me; a thousand times a day I look in at Cayla; and soon I shall be there in reality; the next month will, I trust, see us reunited. Auguste has told you, or will tell, how difficult I find it to tear myself away from hence; but, however, we must all leave each other some day or other: God permits no eternal union here below.

I have seen Caroline several times since her return from Bordeaux. She spoke to me regretfully of not having written to you; but I told her that since she had done so to Papa that was enough. Everything goes on as usual with her. Her life is spent in prayers and good works: one may call her a saint. Nothing short of such conduct would suffice to screen her from the dangers and the gossip of the world, all alone, young and pretty as she is.

So at last Lucie has been to see you as well as her cousin. This visit pleased me on your account. I shall go and return it on my return; but first of all I shall take a long rest at Cayla, dear Cayla! What does Mdme. P. call her little girl? The names of the newly born interest me.

I shall soon belong to you again, dear Papa. Compose yourself, I beseech you; you worry yourself too much about your children. After having done all you can, leave the rest to Providence. I was very sure that you would be much pleased by the article of M. Morvonnais. That good recluse sends us kind words from time to time, both by letters and by M. Quemper. He has even introduced my name in a work about to appear—*La Ville des Mers*. I hear it highly spoken of. If I pass through Bordeaux, I shall endeavour to see Elisa; I do not think, though, that one stops there. I wish I could travel to you by steam: where could I pause with any pleasure?—only beside you, my dear Papa; on that sofa where my fancy so often reclines. Mimi, Mimi, what happiness to be together again! Adieu, I embrace you all.

---

To M. H. DE LA MORVONNAIS.

Cayla, 14*th October*, 1841.

*Poets never die*—nor friends either, I assure you, monsieur. Neither death nor silence in reality change the soul. Maurice is still Maurice, and to you I am always his sister. If I have delayed replying to all that your two letters to M—— informed me of, 'twas for only too good reasons, which, however, would take up this paper to no purpose; and I want it all for you—not for myself —for you and *him*, for him who loved you here on earth, for you whose friendship follows him into heaven. Holy affection, that I have so often blessed in evil days of his that you rendered sweet—those days of charming hospitality spent under your roof, in *that room*, that retains for you so touching a memory of Maurice. Alas! must everything pertaining to him be no more than *a memory!* Oh, what are we, what are the noblest and dearest of created beings? What anguish this blank would cause if the soul did not emerge from it! But it does emerge, but it sees the heavens opened; but one weeps, but one hopes! How sweet is faith to sorrow!

This sentiment that sustains me is one you have the happiness of sharing, and you express it exquisitely in your pictures of Brittany; the *Petit Pâtour* is fragrant with that pure and simple piety which one might call natural faith. This put into poetry is very beautiful. If I only quote this piece, 'tis because others charmed me equally, and I should be only repeating myself. I much applaud you in my heart, you poet, who consecrate your voice to God, and fulfil the mission he has assigned to poets—a mission of religious harmony. It is thus they do good to men, and perform, after the manner of angels, that duty of love and charity we owe to our brethren.

Once more I say this is very beautiful, and I delight in seeing you thus befriend Maurice; and how much too I delight in his being sung by you. For really it is a song upon him that you pour out in your letters to G. Sand—a hymn to his memory which will have echoed far and wide, I hope, as well as within my own soul; for I am ignorant of what goes on without. I have not been able to discover what became of those papers you so religiously preserved, and sent as an offering to his tomb. Oh, how much that affected me, and how you have won my pious gratitude by producing these pious writings of my brother! Sooner or later they will be seen, and will cover the errors of that first notice—a rehabilitation which we all, relations and friends, owe to this Christian memory. Happy they who can contribute to it; and this happiness I shall owe to you. I, on my side, occupy myself in collecting what I know to be scattered here and there, and which ought to form part of the publication. Alas! to me nothing is more sad and sweet than collecting these remains. This work concluded, I shall have hardly anything of an attractive nature left to do on earth: all my thoughts are turned towards heaven, that other world where God and all our hopes await us. It is very consoling, very sustaining in this poor life, to believe in the next, to enter it already in heart—to say to oneself, "Behold the price of my sufferings, my trials of a few days." These are your thoughts too, pious recluse, in your Thebaid. I observe this with comfort, and that you endure your griefs, your great desolation, in a godly manner. In olden times 'twas thus your hermit brothers bore themselves under afflictions, valiant men by faith that they were.

Adieu. Embrace for me your dear little Marie, whom I love without seeing or knowing; but 'tis thus we love the angels. I pray you once more to receive the expression of my feelings in return for your touching communications. Your books, and the two journals, will be religiously preserved by a family who owed you much before, and are attached to you by a sacred tie, the pure memory of Maurice. In him and for ever your devoted friend.

P. S.—You have a sister, Mdlle. Adèle, whose kind message of remembrance I retain; and, encouraged thereby, would have her accept mine! All my family unite in thanks and feelings of affection.

---

To Mdlle. Antoinette de Boisset.

Cayla, 11*th November*, 1841.

When your last letter reached me, my dear Antoinette, I was on the point of leaving Paris, and I waited to reply from a shorter distance. To reply in writing, that is, for the heart does so at once, and nothing is so instantly appreciated as your touching kindness. Receive, dear friend, the tender assurance of my feelings for you; feelings which follow me everywhere, from the world to the desert. In the delights of my home, amongst my much-loved family, my thoughts turn to you. I come to seek you out at Lisle, whither, no doubt, you have returned,—to say, "Here I am again! let us resume our neighbourly correspondence, the bulletins of our two districts. What is going on at Lisle? What is going on at Cayla?"

For the present we have nothing to think of here but the joy and rapture of my return, endless accounts exchanged of travel and local news. Then to see everything over and over again, to retake possession, as it were, with inexpressible delight, of one's home: this lasts at least a fortnight. And then I receive so many visits and curtseys from the good women of Andillac, as much out of affection as curiosity, to see that wonderful *doumarsélo dé Paris*. Can you picture me holding my court and receiving more compliments than the Queen, or at least more sincere ones? But the great, the ineffable happiness, is the inexpressible tenderness of my father, of Marie, and of Erembert. Oh! this is enough to make one forget a thousand years of anxiety and absence.

At last the good God has reunited us and preserved us all: a great mercy, when so many sorrows have fallen upon others. I left Madame de Maistre mourning her father, the amiable and excellent M. de Sainte Marie. She herself is still very suffering. My sister Caroline is better than when I first arrived in Paris, but still stronger in soul than in body. The advanced season prevented her following me and coming to pray over the tomb of her dear Maurice. She charged me with this pious duty, as well as to express her regard for all who feel an interest in her; and you were specially named, dear Antoinette.

I have a thousand messages for you from the good Yversen sister, whom I left nearly recovered from her accident. I only got a note from Sister Marie de Gélis, having been prevented seeing her by a cold, which almost always interfered with my going out. I was often vexed at this, on account of visits I had it at heart to pay, as, for instance, to the holy, gentle, pretty Sister Marie. When I saw her she was flourishing, and had the radiant look of Paradise. Pray tell all this to her friends (to whom I should else have written), and add my warm regards. Adieu, my dear one! Love and respects to your family. I do not forget Irène.

Adieu! I embrace you very tenderly.

---

To Mdlle. Louise de Bayne.

Cayla, 31*st December*, 1841.

My unending affection comes to end the year with you, my dear Louise, and with you only; for I am quite alone at Cayla, which ensures to you exclusively loving words, such as I have not sent you for a long time, at least not outwardly. You know, however, the place you occupy within, and how my heart reverts to you, or rather dwells there, like a fish in water. Nothing has drawn me away thence, my pretty one, for others may have surrounded Louise's dear niche, not entered in. Some think that the world has a good deal changed me. They, however, know nothing about me; and I should be sorry that such an error were shared by you, especially as regards feelings of mine too well established, too profound, to be susceptible of any influence. Do believe this, Louise; believe that your Paris friend is the same as your Cayla one, who at this moment would be far more enchanted to see you again than to see the capital. Yes, if Paris came to me on one side and you on the other, it is most certainly you whom I should embrace.

But in all simplicity, without compliment or ceremony, I love you, and nothing equals the delight of seeing what one loves. When will this delight be mine, dear friend? You have led me to hope for it, and I do hope, hoping fervently that Time—that old deceiver!—will not pass away at Cayla this winter without you. Yes, at Cayla, as I declared to you before. I shall come and fetch you at Gaillac, but I positively will have you here. It is only here that I shall be able to possess you; at Gaillac you will belong to everybody rather than to me. We shall neither be able to meet nor chat. Follow me, then, into my country freedom. "I know nothing sweeter," said a lady, "than a beautiful sorrow in a beautiful meadow." I quite agree with her, changing *sorrow* into 'causerie.' Sorrows, in my opinion, are always ugly, place them where you will; and I am not acquainted with any of the bucolic order, unless they be those of some shepherd about his lambs. Accordingly, I please myself with the thought of walking with you in my woods, my nymph; or, if the outer air be too keen or too cold, we will establish ourselves over the fire, and prattle away, in the warmth of the hearth, like two Trilbys.

How many conversations have the ashes of our chimney corner covered over since my return from Paris! My father especially is never weary of listening to and questioning me. The moment we are alone we fall into a confidential mood. This good father,—I speak to him as openly as to a confessor, and he knows my whole life. He left me two hours ago, to go and confess in his turn at Andillac. At present my soul is tranquil and well directed by M. Rieunand. One of these last days I came across this note amongst my papers: "To-day, October 19th, 1841, I confessed to the new curé of Andillac, a man of great faith and sound judgment. Perhaps it may be he who will commend my spirit into God's hands. Who knows? who knows?"

That which is always the most certain of all things is death. How many I have seen die during this year! How many graves, and those the most unexpected! Poor Hippolyte; poor Adolphe; the brother of M. Verdun; Olympe; and that amiable, holy M. de Sainte Marie, with whom I was staying this time last year! To-morrow year I left; I said adieu, apparently for ever, to Saint-Martin; but how little I thought the master of the house would leave it so soon! He was so vigorous, so strong, mind and body! But there is no resisting that mighty stroke of death that strikes us all at our appointed hour. My poor friend, the Baroness, is almost as dead as her father; she no longer writes; I only hear of her through her mother, another incurable. Thus lives and ties die out, and this world is, after all, nothing but a great grave!

My poor sister-in-law has recently lost one of her brothers, a young man of twenty-three. This loss has replunged the young woman into deep affliction, out of which, indeed, she has never entirely emerged since the great sorrow. But she mourns and comforts herself with God. I know no piety more deep and fervent. Oh! how well she has done to choose for the portion of her lacerated heart that religion which has sustained martyrs! Caroline is saintly in her whole life. At the age of two-and-twenty, pretty and bewitching as she is, to be dead to the world, to go only from her house to church and to live all alone too in Paris, is a very rare example. I do not know whether we shall see her next year; she leads me to hope it, but I have lost so many hopes that I no longer believe in any but those of heaven.

Do not you, too, say the same, dear friend? Have not many bright prospects come to break against those Rayssac rocks? Poor Louise, how often I have thought of your sufferings! In my Cayla calm I am able to offer you some alleviations, and they consist in piety, the true life of women. I say in my Cayla calm, because amidst the agitations of the world one does not so well perceive what is necessary to the soul and to true happiness. Send me, dear friend, your thoughts and feelings: send me your *self*. Mine can intimately unite itself therewith; mine has suffered, mine knows how to sympathise. They tell me that you are rather sad. Is it the mature appearance you pretend to wear, or sorrows that bring this about? Whatever their nature, I make these sorrows mine, and, as though for my own self, I put up prayers, some against these very sorrows, and others for all sorts of happinesses during the next year—all in submission, however, to the gracious will of God.

Assure the Countess and Léontine that I include them in my wishes for those I love, and embrace them by way of New Year's gift. How goes on the little love, about whose health you were uneasy? And his mother, is she beside the cradle? Tell me all about your family, for anything and everything interests me. I told you that Marie had taken flight to Caylux; Erembert, too, is away; so here I am keeping house with my father, and much disposed to continue in retreat until the spring, when I shall go and see my relations. I have not yet been out, and find great difficulty in stirring, so absorbed am I in Cayla. Antoinette wants me at Lisle. She writes me all manner of sweet things, by which I am greatly touched. Antoinette is a pearl of a soul, and a soul of pearl. Adieu, my friend! I know a heart of gold, which I preserve most sacredly in mine.

---

To M. H. DE LA MORVONNAIS.

*Cayla, 2nd July,* 1842.

I have been waiting for the letter you led me to expect from M. Quemper, and therefore delaying to answer yours, kind, perfect friend of Maurice. But that letter does not come, and I will no longer put off thanking you for your devoted zeal in the matter of these dear manuscripts. I relied upon it, and therefore took the liberty of appealing to it in my need, and I did so with all the confidence of our mutual interest as brother and sister in this legacy of Maurice and the efforts required to realise it; but shall we succeed, after all? I very much fear not, and that the whole of it will be for ever lost. What a regret! a second loss of Maurice to me who felt a nameless delight in the prospect of, as it were, again seeing him in his genius, in the works of his mind brought to the light of day! This we seemed about to enjoy; the copies were made; I saw them; nothing was wanted for the publication, except a notice requested by M. ——, some anecdotes, recollections of childhood, account of our family, and these I sent off in January and never received any reply. Nothing can explain this silence except the death of M. ——, who was ill at the time. I say this, because I know for certain that he was about to publish. I had another conversation with him on the subject just before my departure, and he answered me in a way that left no doubt as to his intentions. This was some time after his meeting with M. Quemper, and, though certain of M. ——'s ways of thinking pleased me as little as they did him, I had confidence in his promises. I could not doubt a friend of Maurice's. As I told you, I could more easily believe in his death; and this is what I want to ascertain, that we may reclaim our papers. My father is determined to write to his family. Everything will be attempted rather than lose and leave in oblivion the most precious portion that remains to us of our Maurice, of the *dear and beautiful soul*, according to your expression, my gentle poet. Oh! how you sing this soul; make it, as it were, your own, by memory and contemplation! How I love your admiration and your still remembering the day when Maurice wrote beside your hearth in that blue book! Days and books both lost! This gives us too much to regret! I can only reconcile myself to so many sacrifices by reflecting that from this world, where *everything dies, everything passes away*, I shall go to heaven to rejoin Maurice and all that I have lost; *for where eternity resides even the past is recovered.* Happy hope!

Meanwhile, here is a sweet joy I want to tell you of: a melancholy yet delightful surprise; an album that I opened by chance in a neighbouring house, and in which I found the death of Maurice. How touched I was to meet there, on those secret pages in a young girl's journal, a record made and kept in the depths of a heart—an unknown and very delicate tribute to the memory of Maurice! I read in it these words, "*he was their life*," alluding to our family. All those who knew us would say the same. There are some of those beings, those loving natures, who afford so much to others it seems as though others lived on them. And such was Maurice to us. From him there flowed to me affection, sympathy, counsel; life was made sweet by his sweet intercourse and intellectual aid; in short, he was the sustenance of my soul. This great friend lost, I need nothing less than God to replace him. Or rather, God was already there, but He now comes forward more prominently in the empty space. There you have the whole of my life: smitten, but sustained; and, in addition, family tenderness, domestic consolations, a church to pray in; all this gives one enough to thank God for, and to make one pass serenely the days that remain.

You asked me about my health, my kind recluse, which is why I have spoken to you of my soul; of the balm instead of the vase, which is not worth talking of. Nevertheless, since you take an interest in it, I may inform you that my poor little health goes on well. No more cough, thanks to the healthy country air and to the milk that I drink so freely. May you be able to send me an equally good bulletin of yourself—too often invalided! The influenza, I trust, has taken its departure, and will not prevent your writing at rather greater length than the last time.

Send me some of your literary and other news, and, above all, never doubt the interest I take in it. There are too many ties between you and me, between Val and Cayla, for us not to live a good deal in each other. Accordingly, your publications will have a very warm reception. I am in continual expectation of *Le Mal du Pays*. Farewell, poet! may God and poetry console you! They are potent aids: God especially, who lifts the soul up to Himself and communicates His own life thereto, while poetry sheds it abroad in magnificent streams. Flow, then! flow, sacred poetry, over this arid earth!

I put Marie's white arms around my neck, and very tenderly kiss her pink cheeks. Dear child! tell her that far, very far away from Val, little Marie is tenderly loved, that we wish for her all childhood's joys, and that she may always be a joy to her father.

If you are writing to M. Quemper, or if he be with you, pray recall me to his remembrance, and thank him for the steps which he has no doubt taken, whatever may be their result.

Again adieu, after much writing, which pray accept as a token of still more affection.

---

### TO THE SAME.

*Cayla, 20th October, 1842.*

A traveller bound for your part of the country will carry you, my good hermit, these greetings from Cayla—these kind thoughts and tidings sent from my Thebaid to yours. Thus, in former days, the Cenobites in their desert used to correspond when a rare opportunity offered. But I shall not imitate that one of their number who kept his friend's letters unopened—an admirable instance of self-denial, but above my strength. To have and to read are one and the same with me when a loved handwriting appears. So is it with yours, which, however, costs me some effort to decipher, unskilful as I am in matters of any difficulty, and in too great a hurry to see what gives me pleasure. But let not these impediments in the way of my reading prevent you from writing to me whenever your numerous occupations permit. Steal from the Muses a few moments to give to friendship, which will be truly grateful.

Nor is it I only, but my whole family who thank you for your kind thoughts of us, and expressly charge me to tell you so. I set about doing this by thanking you, in the first place, for your last letter, because it is ever with the heart that I begin. My good father is greatly touched by your affection for our much-loved Maurice and your devotion to his memory and his talents. They were very, very great, very high. To collect and publish their achievements is a holy work; a homage to the dear, true poet, and to God, the Father of intelligence. Blessed, then, be all those who take part in this design; and blessed more than any other be you, Maurice's devoted friend. Thanks to that devotedness and to the trouble you are willing to encounter, I still hope for this publication, my heart's one ardent desire. Whether or not we recover the copies, we still have the autographs: not all of them, it is true, which is very grievous, because, after all, our edition will be incomplete; but never mind, better fragments of such a treasure than nothing at all.

And besides, I depend a good deal upon certain negotiations that I have begged one of my relatives to enter into with M. ——, who is not dead, as I had concluded from his silence. Incomprehensible conduct! I will not judge it, but I suffer from it. I had relied upon the loftiest promises. I looked for that publication as certainly as for the rising of the sun. And there everything remains standing still, without my knowing why. This becomes unbearable; accordingly, we are determined to bring it to an end and relieve ourselves from suspense. We should have done so already, had we known the direction of M. ———, but neither M. Quemper nor any one else can give it me. But my cousin has undertaken to find it out; and then he will instantly go and ascertain what the obstacles are, or reclaim our manuscripts. In the latter case you will procure them from him in Paris, and I shall make them over to your care and to the interest of the friends of genius. You advise me to come to terms with a publisher; but how manage this, or who apply to? I have not any idea of my own on this head, and got no information when in Paris, depending as I did entirely on M. ———.

And now what is it I must do about my poor dear relics? Whatever it be, I will save them from oblivion: we will save them, for I reckon on your pious assistance. I shall have something very precious to give you, wherewith to enrich Maurice's works: 'tis a portrait of him, a drawing of his fine head, which we owe to an artist friend, who did it in secret for himself, and who showed and gave it to me when he knew I was in Paris. What a treasure! Maurice is there, very like, in a calm thoughtful attitude, suffering marked on the brow, the eyes closed, the expression of a lakist. This drawing will, I am sure, please you; as for me, I rejoice in it: the shadow even of what one has loved is so dear! And yet all this is not he: 'tis but his image, his thoughts that remain to us! The reality is elsewhere. This it is that raises the soul above the poor sad world, so profoundly imperfect in its happiness, where what might have made it happy dies or fails us. In this we see a divine purpose, which we should adore while contemplating for our consolation the joys that faith presents, and saluting them *from afar*.

I am delighted at the ushering into the world of *La Famille des Ames*, and above all at the prospect of seeing it arrive at Cayla. I promise it a loving reception, as to whatever may come to me from Brittany—noble country that I love. Your literary gifts will be to me like those wondrous fruits of a distant island, sent by a prince to his friends in a gold box, which preserved them for ever. I shall bequeath your books to my nephews, if I have any.

This brings me to my family joys, in which you will, I know, share. What can I tell you but that we live here in the love and concord of angels, in the sweet peace of Vallambrosa? Nothing is wanting to us but a little child, a young life in ours, such as you have in Marie. That dear little girl must be the sweetest charm of your solitude. But I can conceive that when a little older she will be a still greater source of happiness; she will then be able to understand you, to share your thoughts and feelings, to be your intellectual companion. One day Marie will become this to her father, and then your isolation will be less; then you will say, less bitterly than you do, *Woe to all loving hearts!* Yours has suffered much, and still suffers, I see, from the state of things around it. But how meet that state except by bearing it as a Christian, and in hope of that better world where every one will be in his right place? May God always console you for all things! I often pray to Him for you, my gentle poet. Adieu! may your health continue to improve. I very tenderly embrace Marie.

To the Same.

Gaillac, 27*th January*, 1843.

Here I am, very dilatory indeed, my good recluse, but not oblivious. That is an impossibility between us, as you know and I like to repeat. Occupations, absence from Cayla, and then the expectation of those dear manuscripts, are all reasons that will plead for me with you. Certainly, friends are sufficiently rare not to be neglected; they are life's best comforters. Nothing is sweeter than sincere and sympathetic relations, and you may easily judge, therefore, how dear mine with you are to me. I often regret, and so do my family with me, that Languedoc and Brittany are so far from each other. Our deserts ought to touch, as our souls do. But is anything here below exactly as we would have it? Distance separates, destiny divides; the whole world is a place of exile and valley of tears, which would be overwhelmingly sad indeed did not heaven cover earth. Oh. the glorious mysteries veiled there that await us for our bliss! When I raise my eyes above, I know not what kind of joy I derive from it; but it is joy indeed and supernatural life which makes me forget the present, or at all events support it easily. What are brief sufferings in prospect of eternal felicity? What is a bitter drop, compared to an ocean of delights? And then this is not like one of our deceitful human hopes: it is a divine promise. Oh! God is a good friend indeed, and good friends somewhat resemble and flow from Him, as do all our blessings.

You were very kind in sending me the G——'s direction. I at once availed myself of it to write to M. ——, but with no more success than before. It is true that things turned out unfortunately, and that the person I desired to take measures has not yet done so nor delivered my note. I am not sure whether M. —— is to be found at the offices of the G——, or whether his address is to be had there; but the fact is that he has not been got at, which exceedingly annoys us. If I were not afraid of troubling M. Quemper, I should beg him to be so kind as to call at the G——, but you yourself have often told him of this unsuccessful search, and that keeps me back. This is why I have not replied to you sooner, nor inquired whether you have been a sick-nurse long. I hope soon to be a *baby's nurse*, which is a much pleasanter post. My gentle sister-in-law has announced this happiness to me. Alas! I had promised it myself long before from another marriage, that was also rich in hopes as regarded my heart, and that bequeathed it nothing but tears. Since then the world and life are changed to me, and whatever happy event may occur it bears this sad impress. My family is still a centre of affection, but its keen interest is wanting. You understand me, you who have lost, you who mourn. But yet I speak of this only to God and to you who knew Maurice intimately. My gentle poet, sing me this death in your pious strains. How are your publications getting on? I put up hearty wishes for their success, and at the same time for their arrival at Cayla. Should you have anything for me from Paris, you might have it left at M. Raynaud, 27, Rue de l'Arcade, as he has frequent opportunities of sending to our part of the world.

Adieu! Always give my love to little Marie, the angel of your solitude, and accept for yourself the old, yet ever new, expression of my friendship.

P.S.—I have been absent for some weeks from my loved solitude, but I can assure you that you are affectionately remembered by its inhabitants.

---

To MADAME D'ASSIER DE TANUS, Vèze (Aveyron).

Cayla, 27*th April*, 1843.

I know that you are well, my dear Marie, and that Ninette continues pretty and uproarious. I have just heard all this from your mother, and I come to tell you how much pleasure it gives me. I had been longing for news of you, for it is already a considerable time since you left Gaillac, and, above all, since I have seen you, my good Marie. I had got so accustomed to the pleasure of being together when we were staying with your mother that I can hardly reconcile myself to the idea of your being no longer there and to my having to go all the way to your mountains to seek you out. But however, here I am, seeking you out: for were you at the antipodes my friendship would follow you there.

It will not be my fault, I can assure you, if I fail to do this some day in a less spiritual fashion than now. To meet in imagination is pretty much like dining in imagination, and I like the one as little as the other. I intend, therefore, to come and see you in good earnest, and my plan is as follows: to avail myself of the first spring day to go as far as Madame de Faramond; when there, in the course of conversation we shall naturally get upon Madame de Tanus, and the pleasure it would give me to see her again and to have a seat in Madame de Faramond's carriage, when she goes to Valence. Here I am, you see, at Vèze. But, really, what delight it would be to spend a few days with you under your own roof, to become acquainted with your country, your woods, your mountains.

I am very fond of mountains, probably because I have had friends among them. But how far away some of them now are! Poor Louise * is pretty nearly lost to this country. I deeply regretted seeing her depart for Africa, where Heaven knows what her fate may be! But just now everything smiles, everything pleases her. Max renders her perfectly happy! it is only the yataghan of Abd-el-Kader which can cut short their bliss. Those Arabs frighten me. There was a pretty sharp encounter with them a little time ago; I believe that Adrien's regiment was engaged, but nothing has happened to him this time. Louise writes me a very long letter, very Oriental and very affectionate, which is still better. The most brilliant descriptions are not worth one heart-word. To my mind, the especial charm of Louise lies there, over

* Mdlle. Louise de Bayne, married to M. de Tonnac.

and above all the other charms she possesses. She inquires for all her friends, sending a message to one and all, and you are to have a share in the cake.

At last, then, your health is good, and you have left off suffering from that horrible pain. May it be a long, a perpetual respite! It is too dreadful to have it to endure. and I pray the good God not to rank you amongst the holy martyrs, if such be His will.

---

To Mdlle. Antoinette de Boisset.

*18th August,* 1843.

I am writing to you, my dear Antoinette, beside a cradle, in which sleeps a blue-eyed angel, which is tantamount to telling you that I am an aunt. I had no idea that this delight, with which you are familiar, could be so sweet, or that the heart could rejoice so much at the birth of such a little creature. This child was, it is true, ardently desired by our whole family, and we never cease blessing God for one another's joy. May our darling live and grow and resemble its mother in charming qualities! For some days past I live only in the future and in my little Marie. We have given her this name of celestial augury, and I hope infinite good from it. Already the little one promises first to remain in the world, next to have good health in it. I know not what else this little life may contain, but I accredit it with many blessings.

I also depend with perfect assurance upon your participating in my happiness, dear Antoinette. I associate you with all my feelings, and your friendship never fails to share them. Would to God you could do so in person as well as heart! The pleasure of mutual relations is doubled by presence, and to see you would be a sweet privilege to me, my celestial friend. A visit to Gaillac has got put off till winter, though if I listened to my cousins and to my own desire of seeing them, it ought not to be so late. But a thousand causes bind one to home, and hinder one when one wishes to leave it. 'Tis ever this, that, or the other : for me, it is often my father's suffering state. May you, dear Antoinette, have no more alarms on the subject of health! I am very anxious that this charming holiday time should pass over with you free from all bitterness, except that of the departure, which must always be bitter. Speaking of departures, we have had one which was very painful to me : I allude to that of my beloved Paris sister for India. She has returned to her own country, whither she was summoned by her aunt and a brother whom she fondly cherishes. The farewell was full of affection and regret, and leads us to hope that we may see her again. But will that ever be? May God grant it, and preserve this angel !

Adieu, my dear Antoinette ! pray for her and for me.

To M. PAUL QUEMPER, Paris.

SIR,                       Cayla, 22*nd September*, 1843.

Kind M. Morvonnais writes me word that you are in Paris, that you met M. —— there, and that I need not hesitate to beg you to recover from him my brother's manuscripts. Accordingly, I do not hesitate to charge you with this commission, which, moreover, seems naturally to belong to you because of the friendship you entertained for Maurice and the regard you still have for his memory. To gather together all that remains to us of him, the beautiful thoughts of his soul, is a pious task that the friends of the poet should delight to share. In this character you were one of the first to undertake your part of the task, and I saw you evince a very affecting interest in occupying yourself with it. It is to this interest I now appeal, and rely on its recovering the treasure possessed by M. ——. He has doubtless forgotten all about it. I cannot understand this conduct, nor will I express myself further about this *friend of my brother*. All I would say is, that I positively insist on claiming the dear manuscripts. This determination transmitted by you would, no doubt, suffice; but I support it by the accompanying letter from my father, which will serve you as credentials in case of need.

And now I have to make a thousand apologies for the liberty I take and the trouble I am about to give you; but you struck me as being benevolence and kindness itself, even during the few moments which I had the pleasure of spending with you in Paris. I have retained a very agreeable recollection of those interviews, with sentiments of interest and esteem for you personally, which I am delighted to have the opportunity of expressing to-day.

Be pleased to accept them with the assurance of my perfect regard.

P.S.—In order fully to succeed in the steps you are about to take, it will be necessary not only to obtain the manuscripts but the copies taken. These I saw a few days before I left Paris. M. —— will surely not refuse them. The journal which came from America, and was delivered to me by you is also there; I place the highest value upon it, upon everything, in short, that remains of that beloved brother.

When once you have the papers, M. Morvonnais tells me you will set about their publication; he depends a good deal upon the co-operation of a M. Pitre* (if I read the name correctly), who lives at 34, Rue de Verneuil.

I might also perhaps get another coadjutor to associate with you, the Comte de Beaufort, who made us most flattering offers of publication. This was two years ago, but I then declined, having but few materials. Since then we have made many discoveries, thanks to you and M. Morvonnais. This M. de Beaufort used to write in the *Revue de Paris*: he offered to publish without any

---

* M. Pitre-Chevalier.

expense on our part. If you think it advisable, I will write to him; he used to live at 50, Rue St. Nicolas d'Antin.

Once more adieu! You see how I rely upon your kindness.

---

TO THE SAME.

SIR,        Cayla, 20*th September*, 1844.

I come again to occupy your attention with a matter that is always occupying mine, and in which you have not ceased to feel an interest: those dear papers of Maurice. I know how much trouble you have taken to collect them, and what researches you have made. If success necessarily followed zeal, I should long ago have had nothing to do but to thank you for the possession of my treasure. But, although it be still undiscovered, I am none the less full of gratitude for your pious endeavours. Pray accept the liveliest expression of my feelings, and permit me to commend to you those papers that I have recovered, and which may perhaps compensate in a measure for the losses we deplore.

Do not you think that with these and the *Centaur*, which is found entire in the *Revue des Deux Mondes*, we might venture to publish? I would also point out an article of Maurice's in the *Revue Européenne* (January 15th, 1832), entitled *Life of the Blessed Nicolas de Flue*; and another in *La France Catholique* on the *Chapelle expiatoire* of Louis XVI. I do not exactly know when it appeared, but it must have been between 1830 and 1834

I make this suggestion very timidly, without venturing to build too much on it; but the least hope on this subject is too dear to me not to be grasped at and shared with the kind friends who are ever ready to receive with pleasure any fragments of the work.

My cousin Raynaud will give you the packet of papers to which I allude, and gladly talk over its contents with you.

I do not know whether M. Morvonnais has returned to Paris or not; but if he is still there, pray assure him of my affectionate remembrance, and tell him that I regret not having received those volumes of his works which he had kindly intended to send me on arriving in Paris. It was with reference to them that I gave him M. Raynaud's address, of which I would again remind him if it be in that good M. Morvonnais's power to let me have the books.

I seem to be always charging you with commissions, but I know your indefatigable zeal, and moreover, you may depend upon my gratitude.

---

To M. H. DE LA MORVONNAIS.

Château du Cayla, 3rd *January*, 1845.

As I was expecting to hear from you, my dear poet, I did not write; but here is the season of good wishes round again, and I come to offer you mine, or rather to tell you of those I address on your behalf to Heaven; for it is from above that happiness comes. I would fain see all that God can bestow descend upon you—that is infinite happiness. Indeed it would be no more than I desire for you; but in this the heart's petition is not often granted, not at least in the course of earthly life. God has never promised to render that happy since we lost Paradise. My wishes therefore do not limit themselves to time; they claim celestial blessings for you: these last are the only ones which seem to me worthy of belonging to you, or in harmony with your poetical and Christian soul whose voice I know, and it seems to me one raised far above our lower world: it is a bird that soars while it sings.

And speaking of your songs brings me to my regret at not having received the works you so kindly promised me. 'Tis now a long while ago, I always remember dates connected with the heart. My fear is, not of any forgetfulness on your part (between Brittany and Cayla there can be no such thing); my fear then is that there may have been some unfortunate hindrances to this intention of yours. You led me to hope the work would be sent from Paris last June. Perhaps your journey thither was prevented by illness; your health is sufficiently fragile to lead to melancholy interpretations of your silence; and in me the thought of death readily occurs ever since I have seen a loved one die. Deliver me then from anxiety, my gentle poet; write me one of those kind Breton letters that I love, and that my friendship for the friend of my dear Maurice craves for. O, my dear Maurice! he could have made me love a serpent; judge then of the feelings he bequeathed me for you who were so tender and kind to him.

I do not know why M. Quemper does not notice a parcel I sent him containing a portion of our dear Maurice's works. Despairing of ever having the complete collection of them, it struck me that these might make a small volume of very choice things; amongst them were all his poems, his letters to you, and several written to different persons during his stay at La Chênaie. I requested M. Quemper to lay these papers before M. Pitre, and to take counsel with that gentleman and with you about their publication. If there were no way of accomplishing this, I should have to resign myself to silence, to locking up for evermore these precious writings, this soul of the poet's soul, in a funeral urn beside his tomb. But I still look for a letter from M. Quemper. I am so sure of his kind readiness to oblige and his devotion to Maurice's memory, that his silence surprises me much.

I have already told you how I felt about yours, and that will give you to understand the welcome your letter will receive. Tell me of your dear little Marie, whom I love; nor is this love any new thing. Not long ago, in looking over a journal that I used to write for Maurice, I came upon a long page about that child of Val. ——. With what a sad pleasure I paused over that pretty image, and pretty passage!

The days pass by, but time will never efface the charm of dear and holy memories to me.

Adieu, my gentle poet. Believe me, at the beginning as at the end of the year, your friend.

P.S.—What of the health of that brother of yours about whom you were anxious?

---

To the Same.

*Cayla, 15th June, 1845.*

I entirely excuse you, my gentle poet, for your delay in writing to me; for not only are the reasons you allege excellent ones, but I never accuse your silence; nor, however long it may last, does the thought of your forgetting me ever come to trouble me. We are too sacredly and too closely bound to each other for that, I think. What belongs to the soul can know no end.

Therefore, as far as that goes, be at rest, dear poet, as to the consequences of your silence. May I not myself be rather to blame this time? But you told me that your health was not good, that your correspondence increased, and your strength grew less. That made me feel timid about writing to you, lest I should add to your fatigues. Why cannot I see my thoughts wing their way to you like those little flights of birds that pass from one hemisphere to another? You would then but need to raise your eyes, while as it is you are wearied perhaps by any effort. I should be very glad to be reassured about your health. I am sure that such solitude is bad for you, and much regret that your charming Marie should not be living with you; she would make a sweet diversion in your life of study and solitude. But I can also understand how dear this child must be to her grandmother, and that for this reason you should often leave your angel with her. And, besides, a regard for her education may have much to do with this sacrifice of separation, which Heaven will no doubt bless; for it blesses all sacrifices made by the paternal heart. I feel full confidence in the delight you will have in your dear Marie. Her future interests me exceedingly. I have always felt for this child a peculiar affection, transmitted to me by Maurice.

Well, then, how do we stand now as to those blessed manuscripts? Do not you tell me that M. Quemper is really upon their track, and that the plan is to come to an understanding with M. ———. A thousand thanks, my excellent friend, for this good news! At last we shall be able to get hold again of these dear papers And yet M. Quemper has not written to me, as you led me to hope. Who knows what may have happened There are still many chances. I have been told that these manuscripts have lain for a long time past at the publisher of M. ———, who could not get them away again without a lawsuit. This would explain the delay in the publication; but nothing can explain the silence of the one who took such exclusive charge of it. Oh, how full the world is of inexplicable things! . . . .

Again you are in mourning, have had a loss that I have felt much for you! I allude to the death of your poor brother. Alas! what is this life but a continual separation? But we have heaven for meeting-place! It is there that we shall have neither mourning nor tears—there that the society of the saints will console us for what we have suffered in the society of men. You consider that the latter is in a sad state. What would you have? Perhaps it will yet improve. Meanwhile is there anything for us to do but to humble ourselves, as the Apostle says, "*under the mighty hand of God that he may exalt us in due time, casting all our care upon him, for he careth for us.*"

Adieu. I pray Him to take care of you.

P.S.—In expectation of your works, I send to invoke them *Saint Theresa's Brother*, a melancholy inspiration that visited me four years ago, over a grave.

---

To M. PAUL QUEMPER, Paris.

*Cayla, 22nd August,* 1845.

Be at ease, my dear sir; I am not hurt at your silence. There were only too good reasons for it; and some of them seem to me so painful, that I have nothing but feelings of sympathising sorrow to express. You have lost your mother! Alas, what a loss! How crushed you must have been by the blow, and dead to all interest, all business in the world! In less than four-and-twenty hours of illness to have her taken away—that good mother whom you loved so tenderly, to whom you were united both in thought and feeling, which is, as you say, so rare a union, and so fraught with happiness. Accordingly, what affliction when one comes to lose it!—what isolation on earth where the soul keeps continually seeking its other soul! This is the state in which you now are: it is one that I perfectly understand, into which I enter very *fraternally*, I assure you, praying God, the only comforter, to comfort you. Yes, that is the office of Heaven; and I will not therefore say any more on this head, but just express my heartfelt gratitude to you for not having, in the midst of such sad preoccupations, lost sight of the pious mission entrusted to you by me. Blessed be your affection for my beloved brother! I shall owe it much. I already owe it a hope to which my whole heart clings—we shall recover those dear manuscripts, that precious *green book* that I hardly read, but where I glanced at much that was admirable. Thanks to your efforts, I shall be able to enjoy it. Blessings on your pious zeal, and that of our excellent friend in Brittany. I am not the only one whose thanks you have to receive; my family, who all know you; my father, long an invalid, who now, in the retirement of his sick-room, rejoices to anticipate the precious collection of his son's thoughts,—thank you as I do.

At length you have discovered M. ——! You have perhaps even met him ere this! Is it possible that he can have refused us our papers? At all events, you will not fail to occupy yourself with those now in your possession, and to arrange about having them published. It was a good inspiration, then, of mine, the sending you those treasures. I confess to you I felt rather shy about doing so; but there is a happiness in laying oneself open to noble minds, and confiding secret thoughts to one who receives them so graciously. This tells me in a very touching manner how dear to you is the memory of Maurice.

Receive, my dear sir, in return the assurance of his sister's most true regard.

To Mdlle. Antoinette de Boisset.

*4th January,* 1846.

Your letter of the year's last day gave me much pleasure, my dear Antoinette. It told me that your friendship had not departed with the flight of time. Alas! as it is, he takes away enough from us without our letting him rob us of what is sweetest in life, our affections. Ours for each other is so deeply rooted, we need not fear to lose it in any other way than by the breaking of the vase that holds it; but even after death this celestial flower of friendship goes to blossom in heaven. This is what reassures me in our intervals of silence, makes me wait quietly for a letter from you. I have one at length! I hasten to reply, and to renew those dear conversations interrupted, I hardly know how, which you so gracefully recall to me.

Well, then, let us converse, dear friend; and first of all, let us speak of you, my poor afflicted one, so often in mourning now. I had heard a part of your griefs, but I was not aware of the fresh loss your family had sustained in your mother's only sister. All these deaths make us think of our own, and prepare our souls for the summons God may send them when we least expect it. Who knows if it will not be this year? And indeed I think the best wish that Christians can exchange is that of dying well. This is the true happiness; and of what use is it to wish each other that of this life, which never gets fulfilled? Accordingly, I have left off forming vain aspirations after felicity for any one, even for you, my dear. My wishes reduce themselves to prayers; and I have full trust in these being accomplished. There is no doubt of your loving the good God, and adorning your soul ever more and more in His sight with those virtues that make saints.

You on your side, I am sure, desire the same happiness for me, for which I thank you, as well as for all your other good new-year wishes. If it pleased God, I could desire the new year to bring better health to my father. He is a great invalid, as you know. There are three years now that his nights have been spent without going to bed, except for a few hours, and then he does not undress. So that on all sides I see nothing but suffering; for how long a time this has been the case! This brings me to my Indian sister, about whom you are kind enough to inquire. We are expecting letters from her; and I heard lately that the dear sister herself was well, but that her aunt—her mother by adoption—was very much out of health. This would be another irreparable loss for the poor young woman. I do not know if we shall ever see her again—Calcutta is very far from France. To do so would be one of the sweetest joys left on earth for me;

but we ought to have none other than in sacrificing everything to God.

Adieu, my dear and kind Antoinette. I should much like to see you, but I leave home seldom, and for a short time only. If, however, the *melancholy charm* that retains me here were ever broken, perhaps I might be able to get as far as you.

---

To THE SAME.

*23rd April*, 1846.

In your last letter, dear Antoinette, you express the wish to see me in so kind a manner that I am really much touched and much tempted too to comply with it; but you know my hindrances and will judge me with charitable equity. The eyes of your heart at once saw straight into mine, and recognised that nothing less important than the precious healths which bound me to Cayla could prevent my sometimes reaching you. During the few days I spent at Gaillac shortly before Easter, I too, on my side, was watching for some opportunity of meeting. The eloquence of the worthy Gélis would not have had much difficulty in deciding me to make an expedition to Lisle, but that dear spot is become a land of promise for me.

And in truth I am always promising myself a return thither, for I was so happy there, and shall always preserve a sweet and grateful memory of the kindly welcome I met from every one, and more particularly from you and your amiable family. I should much like a renewal of that week I spent with you there, dear Antoinette; but there are things that do not repeat themselves in life, and I much fear that the Lisle retreat, and Father Verrès and the delight of being with you for some days together, have passed by for ever. What would you have? Everything passes by in this world: our sweetest enjoyments —those flowers of life—first of all. We must offer them up in sacrifice to God.

And speaking of sacrifices, what it has cost me to lose that dear, loveable Louise! You keenly regret her, dear Antoinette—you, to whom she was only an acquaintance; but I, who loved her, can find no consolation except in God for the death of so cherished a friend. I have had the most comforting details of her last moments, which were full of piety, faith, trust in God, and sublime courage. Poor, dear Louise! I cannot realise that it is all over with our hope of meeting. We were widely parted indeed, but I did not think it was for ever. So Providence had ordered it! God had numbered my friend's days, and was throwing heaven open to her just when I calculated upon embracing her once more. She was to have come in March. . . . . The meeting must now be above with my dear Louise, as well as with other loved souls whom we have also seen go away from us very early.

I could go on indefinitely on this subject, but I must say Good-bye, not, however, without congratulating you on your father having won his lawsuit. You are right in believing that I take a friend's part in that as well as in all else that interests you. Accordingly, I *love for you* that charming little niece, your delight, and wish her a happy arrival of a brother or sister. We think our Caroline a gem. Some one who has seen your angel told us that ours resembles her. Upon which pretty speeches adieu, my friend!

To M. DE GUÉRIN, Cayla.

Cauteres (Hautets-Pyrenées), 11*th July*, 1846.

Here I am, my dear Papa, in those Pyrenees which seemed to us to be so far from Cayla, and through the mercy of God I have reached them without any drawback or accident whatsoever. All my travelling companions are perfectly satisfied. Marie is writing to her mother. Louise * is there, holding a conversation with the excellent and attractive Mademoiselle Pons, and I sit down as soon as possible to give you an account of my journey.

We have only just arrived and found lodgings, which is no easy matter. After an hour of going in and coming out of houses, we are very tolerably settled. My room has a charming view towards one of the finest mountains in the Pyrenees. There is something magnificent in the aspect of this gigantic range, all covered with firs and furrowed with torrents which, owing to the height they fall from, look like mere threads of water. We have had this superb spectacle the whole of this day, which began at Tarbes.

Tarbes is a very pretty town. In order to become

* Mdlle. Louise de Thézac, now Madame Brémont d'Ars.

somewhat acquainted with it, I went out early, and while these ladies were making their arrangements, paid a visit to the cathedral. A good woman who served as *cicerone* having placed me within sight of the church proceeded to say, "There, madame, is the Church, opposite you have the Prefecture, further off the Hospital, and down yonder the Barracks." You may judge how I laughed as I dismissed and thanked her. I had no wish indeed to be shown everything, and therefore walked off to the market-place to buy some fruit, but the hail which had fallen a few days before had ruined it all. On our way we saw nothing for three leagues but devastation. This threw a melancholy over the fine road which ran through a plain as rich and more varied than that of Gaillac, full of the productions of mountain and valley both; vines spreading from tree to tree, fields of corn and fields of millet, chestnut and fruit-trees: a blending of riches which seemed like a corner of a terrestrial paradise. What would you say, Papa, to tall millet two or three feet high, the rows planted very close, with potatoes flourishing in the furrows? How I should have enjoyed pointing this out to you, and much besides. It was the most agreeable journey I ever took.

These Pyrenees are an infinitely more beautiful sight than Paris, which, however, is very beautiful too. But there is the difference between the works of man there and those of God here. This indescribable architecture of mountains and valleys without end gives a very lively impression of Divine power. I intensely enjoyed the whole of the journey, begun at Tarbes amid vines and flowers, and continued along the sides of pyramidal rocks and above a torrent which rushes and leaps under one's eyes as far as Cauterets. The road is cut perpendicularly up this fabulous Gave, and would have done honour to the Romans: it is marvellously steep. I kept saying, "If from Cayla they could see us ascending this path for eagles, great would be their astonishment; and Papa, who is afraid of seeing me mount a donkey, would call out to me to stop." But how is that to be done? And besides, one must needs reach those marvellous waters to which you were so anxious to send me. May I find health in them! . . . .

Adieu! we needs must part. It is late, and I have no paper.* My first visit was to the Cauterets Church, to thank God for my prosperous journey. The population seems a pious one. We have priests in quantities and a few bishops, amongst others Monseigneur of Paris. M. Vergnes is expected one of these days, and finally, Mdlle. d'Hautpoul and her brother the Abbé are also among the bathers. I shall go and see her.

I embrace you all on this triangle of paper, which will remind you that I live by borrowing and that our trunks are still closed. Our room is a chaos, but there is room in it for Cayla, including you Papa, Mimi, Eran, Anais, and little *Caro*. I long to have news of you all. May it be good, *miraculous*. In short, God alone knows all that occupies me about you all, you dear absent ones,

---

* What follows is written on a flap of paper in the form of a triangle or *peak*, which explains the last words of the letter.

and especially about you, Papa. Send me a faithful account of everything that goes on. 'Tis to you, dear Mimin, that I apply for news of whatever happens at Cayla; and I, on my part, will tell you what happens at Cauterets. The company here seems to me a strange medley, but I had a mere flying glance at it. My remembrances to the pastor and the whole parish. Once more good-bye to you all. This peak terminates in a kiss.

TO THE SAME.

DEAR PAPA,— Cauterets, 13*th July*, 1846.

Being unable to write to you by the post as often as I should like, I mean, by way of compensating myself, to put down for you my *every-day* in this little book, which will reach you in the form of letters. This is a continuation of the one I despatched on my arrival. That was Saturday. The next morning we began by hearing mass to your intention. It was in a pretty little chapel to the Virgin, at nine o'clock, exactly at the hour when a saint was praying for you in Bavaria. Cauterets is a long way from thence, but from all places alike we may meet in God.

The mass being over, we went to pay a visit to the baths. There are several establishments, but it was to La Raillère that we mounted: a pretty steep ascent of twenty minutes, accomplished by some on horse or donkey back, by some in *chaises à porteurs*, and by great numbers in all ways. There is a whole world of invalids, crippled, catarrhal, &c., crowding around these baths, as the paralytic around the miraculous piscina. But, for my part, it is not there I make my plunge. I I have been taken down to a far more comfortable establishment, two steps from this house, called the *Grand Cesar*. This triumphal name seems of happy augury; at least I shall be able to say, "I came, I *drank*," and perhaps too, "I conquered." These baths are admirably managed, and the building magnificent—all marble; I fancied myself looking at one of those Italian palaces that used to delight you so much. As to that, however, marble is very common here, and almost all the better class of houses are fronted with it, which gives the town a certain air of elegance and distinction rather rare in France; and, above all, it is the perfection of cleanliness; but then, to be sure, it may be washed without any trouble. Water springs and flows everywhere, limpid as a crystal, with this only difference—that here it is boiling instead of congealed.

We have had a visit from the d'Yversens and Antoinette.* I went to see Mdlle. d'Hautpoul. They are all in this neighbourhood, and we have the church, too, quite at hand. It is not otherwise than prettyish, but too small, especially for the priests who crowd the choir, the famous Père de Place among their number. He is said to be remarkably agreeable, and, as he is much at the d'Yversens, I hope to meet him. This evening the

* Mdlle. Antoinette de Boisset.

Duke de Nemours arrived, his entry being quite as quiet as that of any common bather.

*14th.*—A storm has brought on rain. Wet weather is very tiresome here, but I must add that it does not last long. The temperature is most variable; and therefore when we have anything to complain of we may comfort ourselves with expecting a sudden improvement. And so it has been in this case, for the unpromising morning has been succeeded by a very beautiful day: it was quite hot till evening. We paid some visits. I have made acquaintance with a lady from Rio Janeiro, who is come here that her daughter may take the waters. Poor mother! It seems very doubtful that the result of her voyage will be a happy one. We lodge in the same house with her, and her daughter comes to play with little Albert. There are not many people immediately around; it is a rather out-of-the-way quarter, but suited to us because of its proximity to the church.

I have a very small room, with a few chairs and the table at which I am writing to you. The window looks upon one of the most wooded mountains of the Pyrenees. In the morning I hear the birds sing and the bathers summoned. We are a good deal scattered. Henri is sent off miles away, my cousins not quite so far. When shall we all be united at Gaillac, or better still, at Cayla?

The Duke de Nemours passed under our windows on his return from hunting, bowing with all the grace he could get out of his grey felt hat. Very little was displayed on returning his bows. They say that the country people detest him, because he is the cause of the high nobility going away to avoid meeting him. A singular reception to be given in Béarn to a descendant of Henri IV.!

15*th*.—St. Henri to-day. A few persons celebrated this festival quite quietly in their hearts and in the church. I was one of them. And now I am thinking that you too may have had hail; the storm of which we saw such sad traces at Tarbes extended as far as Cordes. A man and some sheep were killed by lightning at Cabanes. I am longing to know how you fared at Cayla—longing, above all, to have news of yourselves. Anaïs and Eran will set out very late from Gaillac: I should almost be afraid of the *loup-garou*. Here there is a good deal of talk of a white bear, who seems to require the baths of La Raillère, for he has been prowling about them for the last two years. The Prince's hunting expedition was directed against him, and it is said that an under-prefect and a tailor hit him, but he fled into the mountain gorges. But whether or no, don't go and be alarmed about me. Our baths are down below, and the bear is high above, miles off: we have nothing in common.

16*th*.—Picture to yourselves a snow-white and sky-blue torrent, rolling, leaping, foaming along from the top of an inaccessible mountain, which it cleaves in two. It is the cascade of *Mahourat*. Never did I see anything comparable to this horribly beautiful fall. We contemplated it in admiring wonder, but without venturing too near its edge. An Englishman who was fishing there fell in, but by singular good fortune was saved; the water in its rebound flung him out like a straw on the rocks that form the basin of the torrent, and thence the fisher was fished up : that happened last year. On our way I visited one of the springs, a hollow in the rock, with a little canal, and underneath it an orifice, whence comes insufferably hot air : it is all one can do to endure it, even through one's boots. After having drunk, ascended, and descended, gathered flowers and strawberries, here we are back at our hotel, enjoying a delicious rest.

17*th*.—Rain, no walk; we take to our work to while away the time. The Brazilian has been down with her daughter. She is an excellent woman, with the Creole tone and manners. There are people from all parts of the world here; but this crowd of company is only to be seen at parties, ball-rooms, and other places that we leave to the lovers of noise and pleasure. We constantly see Mademoiselle Pons, and not unfrequently Antoinette, who, however, in her character of bather, is less at liberty than our friend from Brittany. We have just had a visit from M. the Curé of Cauterets, accompanied by his vicar and the mayor. These gentlemen were collecting for the poor. I liked the Curé's look; I had heard him say mass, and knew him again. He is an angel at the altar.

18*th*.—At last, then, I have got this Cayla letter that I

was so longing for! Thanks, my good Mimi, for your promptitude in writing. I had hardly ventured to hope for a letter so soon as to-day, and am made quite happy by it. I have read and re-read it, and found only good news, and I do indeed believe that you would not deceive me. It is only the disasters made by the storm that I grieve over, though we ourselves were spared.

You want a bulletin of my health, here it is: My appetite has rather decreased, and I feel the effect of the waters a little, which is the case with every one. The doctor has told me not to take mountain excursions, has limited my walks to the park, a pretty spot quite near at hand, well wooded, laid out in avenues, with chairs to rest on, and filled with gay company, who walk, sit, read, sleep, and work at will. All this may be done for the sum of one penny, if one takes a chair. It is pleasant enough; but mountain excursions amidst torrents, flowers, pines, and heather would be far more to my taste. I hope to obtain leave to undertake some, but meanwhile I punctually obey the stern prescriptions of the doctor.

He is a worthy man, exceedingly polite in manner, with a high reputation; a visit to him is looked upon as indispensable, in order to learn which of the waters one should take,—this depending, of course, on disease and temperament. An American has come here merely to bathe his eyes in an unctuous stream that flows like honey. Antoinette goes up to the skies to drink, and descends to the centre of the earth to bathe. How often I think of Papa, with such a longing! But the temperature is so variable it would be almost impossible for Papa to endure it. There are hours of the day when one has to clothe oneself as in winter, a few moments later one is stifled; but this is out of doors,—the houses are always cool.

I had intended to hear Monseigneur Affre's mass, but he no longer says it. He is reported to be much out of health, and moreover he is everywhere quite the churchman and student. The day the Prince arrived it was noticed that his shutters remained closed. Marie means to go and see him, as being a country woman, and Henri as the school-fellow of one of Monseigneur's relatives. If this visit does take place I shall be of the party, though I hardly know by what title my presentation can be justified.

As to priests they abound more and more. This morning an additional altar was improvised in a side aisle of the church. I have, however, seen no acquaintance of mine, nor have I made any acquaintance. I was aiming at Father de Place, and, as ill luck will have it, he is ill in bed. But, as for that, here one may put in practice St. François de Salis' maxim, and choose among a thousand. Therefore do not let Papa be uneasy on this head any more than on that of railroads. Why, dear me! where would you have them run if not in mid-air? Picture to yourself mountains and nothing else, immeasurable mountains with narrow valleys at their base. This town alone nearly fills one of these last, and thence the roads wind along perpendicular rocks. Cauterets is a pretty place, about the size of Rabastens, and during the whole bathing season quite Parisian as to elégance. The dresses are really dazzling. Mine are, as you observe, most simple, but not ridiculous, which is all I want.

To-morrow, my dear Papa, ends the Novena for your health. Let us hope that it will not remain without some happy effect; it is not in vain that saints pray to the good God. A holy soul of these parts has taken a fervent part in our devotions. Madame Facieu, too, was to join them, and she is another friend of Heaven's. In short, my dear Papa, I wish you all manner of blessings and diversions too.

I embrace Eran, and Nicette, and Caro. There are some children at the baths, but I have not seen any so pretty as our little treasure.

---

TO THE SAME.

Cauterets, 20*th* *July*, 1846.

I had depended upon having something to tell you about preachers at the Baths. We had been led to hope for an orator among so many priests; but no sermon at all, not even a lecture! These gentlemen are ill, or taking their holiday. Poor Father de Place has no voice, Monseigneur Affre no strength, we have not even had his benediction. Here, as in the desert, we are reduced to preaching to ourselves. Happily I brought with me Fénelon, with whom I spend a few moments of pious meditation. And then that holy Madlle. Pons comes from time to time to edify us with her conversation and her example. She is excellent to us all, and I in particular have had sweet tokens of her affection. Oh, what a beautiful spirit is hers! The d'Yversens are very happy to have found so admirable a person to direct the education of their daughters. Antoinette is living with the d'Yversens, and Mademoiselle d'Hautpoul lodging in the same house, so that we are able to see the whole party of friends at once, nay, we can even, without going out, look at each other from our balconies, which almost touch. Monseigneur's apartments occupy the corner of our block, so that it is impossible to be nearer neighbours. Our visit has still to be made, and will probably continue in prospect, which I shall prefer. I do not fancy that Monseigneur receives women; in which case it would be awkward to present ourselves.

21st.—What shall I tell you to-day, my dear Papa? I really do not know; what is there to be said now I no longer explore the mountains? They are the features of the place most interesting to see and describe; the people are much the same as everywhere else, only, perhaps, there are more marked and numerous varieties among them. But the mountains, the chalets, the outline of the peaks, are what one only sees here. All the Yversen colony made an ascent to Queen Hortense's grange, one of those little dwellings I told you of, hanging from the mountain-side like eagles' nests. This one, belonging to the Queen of Holland, is much visited, and gives rise to all manner of opinions regarding that princess; some finding in it a taste for extravagance, others for lofty things. As to me, I deduce from it that the princess had good legs of her own, and also that small things survive great; this poor grange has lasted longer than the throne of Holland.

*24th.*—A letter from Humbeline has brought us good news of Gaillac and Cayla. Mimi had written to her on the Friday, and said all was going on well. Such assurances are needful for our tranquillity, and even for the efficacy of the waters; as we are told that mental uneasiness negatives their effects. The doctor even recommends one not to move about in one's bath, accordingly I lie there in perfect repose as if in my bed. I will not have to reproach myself with the least departure from rule. It shall not be my fault if I do not return to you in better looks.

As the event of our day we have had a magnificent thunderstorm. Those who like the sound may enjoy it in perfection here without any dread, for the thunderbolts only strike the mountains, procuring abundance of rain for the valleys. But may it not have been hailing elsewhere? Toulouse was ravaged on Sunday last by a terrible storm. I am always afraid of hearing of some disaster to our vines. Arsène has had a sad loss, the lightning killed four of his oxen in their stable.

*25th.*—This morning between two and three o'clock I woke up from a nightmare. I had dreamed that you were ill. Without having any faith in dreams, this particular one has harassed me, and I crave for news of you to tell me that dreams are false. This is Friday, I cannot have a letter before Monday or Tuesday next. I am longing much to know how you are, and whether Heaven has granted our prayer for your recovery.

We have had a visit to-day from M. Barthey, the Curé of Villefranche, a frequenter of the baths. Father de Place had been dining with him; I could have envied him that guest, who is said to be charming in mind and everything else. Now, however, he is gone, and consequently I betook myself to knock at the ear of the Cauterets Curé, who, without being a Jesuit, has a value of his own, he is very pious, and much devoted to the Church, where he passes half his life.

The people here are very fond of going to confession, the processions to the confessional sometimes continuing till ten at night. They are a race apart in manners and costume: the women's dress is remarkable for a large mantilla, black, white, or red, which they wear in all weathers, it is called a *capulet*, and being made of wool, when it is hot the unfortunate creatures must be smothered under it. But it resembles the veil of the Orientals: to go out without a *capulet* would be a disgrace.

*Sunday*, 26*th*.—Two eminences in church to-day, and accordingly the offices were pompous. There was such a crowd at vespers that we could hardly make our way in, and I could not get a chair. But I had not time to feel tired; there were neither complines nor sermon, but a great many benedictions by the officiating bishop. It was not Monseigneur Affre; he completely effaces himself. Here I am in my room after a little visit from Antoinette.

We talked Lisle and Cayla over, and often agreed that we longed to return thither.

*27th.*—Here is the much-expected letter, thy dear letter, dear Mimin. You can have no idea what fits of impatience come over the heart in these mountains. In vain they enchant, amaze eyes and mind—mind and eyes keep reverting to one's own dear home, to those one has left who are expecting one back. However, Papa is not worse; my dream was only a dream, thank God. I see you wrote on that very Friday morning. I depend upon your word; and then Papa writes to me as well, which sets me quite at ease.

Yesterday I was low; these mountains weighed on me with all their weight; but to-day your letter and splendid weather have quite set me up.

Mdlle. d'Hautpoul leaves on Thursday. I shall give her a letter; but that you may not be kept too long waiting, this shall go by the post. It will give you something to read at all events, though nothing interesting, since I have seen nothing. I defy M. the Curé to discern anything of Chateaubriand this time, unless he can find a mountain in a grain of sand. By the way, my affectionate compliments to the good pastor.

---

To the Same.

Cauterets, *Sunday, 2nd August.*

You will no doubt, my dear Papa, receive my Wednesday's letter to-morrow. Mdlle. d'Hautpoul tells me she will go over herself and deliver it to you. This attention pleases me, for you will be charmed to see and talk over the baths with her. Let us have a few more words about this place that I am to leave in a few days. I have no great things to say about it: we have had detestable weather; fogs like London, and, by way of change, storms and floods. One does not know what to do when there is no going out, or even breathing the air on the balconies; and so one gets dull and weary, and falls sick.

As to me, I still find the waters agree with me; the only tiresome part is the taking them. Picture me to yourself, at six o'clock in the morning, carried up by two men, in a chair, to the mountains, where almost all the world goes to drink. This road reminds me of the streets of Paris, there is such a crowd going up and down— ladies, priests, women in various costumes, Spaniards in their draperies, and chairs, which are the carriages of this street of the Pyrenees. As soon as I get there, I drink one glass; twenty minutes later another; and then I slowly walk down the mountain, sometimes with Antoinette, sometimes alone, as to-day, for instance. The mass that I heard before going up made me late in setting out.

But with all this I have never been able to go to high mass, and shall go off without knowing what sort of sermons they give in this country. As to that though, a poor curé, from the neighbourhood of Bayonne, preached to us very solemnly one of these last days. He died almost in a moment. Unlike the silent interment prescribed for strangers in general, he was buried with great pomp. All the priests, and many of the inhabitants of the town, accompanied him: this no doubt was owing to his profession. It poured with rain, so I did not follow the procession. I was made melancholy enough by hearing the dirges which went on long at the house door of the departed, close to which was too striking a contrast, a display of ball wreaths! The world is everywhere the same. Here the offices are Roman in style. Funerals are profoundly solemn; they sing much more at them than with us. One might fancy oneself at a Good Friday service.

*Monday, August 3rd.*—I was just waking from my second sleep this morning when Henri came into my room with your letter in his hand. You may judge of the reception he got! These tidings from dear Cayla almost surprised me. I was not expecting them so soon —not till to-morrow, or even the day after. But the sooner the better when the news is good. I am enchanted with your report of the state of all. One could hardly expect anything more satisfactory, though Papa's health is not perfect. But then it has been so much worse, that his present condition seems almost a recovery. I was afraid that the election journey would have checked the improvement; that was almost sure to be the result; accordingly I am pleased to find from the end of the letter that Papa remained at home.

Here we are indeed occupied with affairs of state, but much less than with those of the *waters*. Our doctor is the only person who has talked with any animation of elections, having come back from Tarbes, where some disturbances took place. People collared and *becudgelled* each other, and a poor elector, upon crutches, was disarmed and thrown down for dead by his antagonist. But we are going far away from all such tumults; our horses are waiting to take us an excursion to the Blue Lake. They say it is magnificent. We shall see.

Before all, however, let us return to Cayla, and to the first page of your letter. And so Mdme. Facieu complimented you upon Papa's good looks. I expect to find him flourishing, and quite well by day if not by night. We must not be surprised at the effect of the heat, which always disagreed with him. Here it is the cold we are complaining of. I have hardly ever been out without my shawl. The mountains are glorious, the country a very interesting one to see, but the climate is the worst in the world—a mixture of rain, fogs, and heat (which is the least lasting of the three), very prejudicial to delicate constitutions. Many precautions are necessary to avert ill effects.

On Sunday we had lovely weather. A bright sun shone out to embellish the prettiest popular festival I ever saw. It is an annual custom for the young bathers on a certain day to give a ball, and go to the expense of a '*fête champêtre*,' which consists of races to the mountains, pitcher-races, donkey-races, running in sacks, and the dances of the district, all which are pretty and amusing, and conducted with perfect order. The dancers are all young men. Monseigneur of Paris was looking on as well as we. We were admirably placed for the enjoyment of the spectacle, which went on under the windows of the d'Yversens. Picture to yourself a broad, brawling torrent, then a small meadow, then a mountain, and in this framework a gathering of several thousands arranged around a rope barrier, the actors occupying the central space. In the first place women, with their pitchers on their heads, run to a certain spot, which they must reach without letting them get broken. Very few carry off the prize; and at every fall of a pitcher you may imagine the shouts of laughter among the crowd. Next the runners set off to carry off flags placed some way up the mountain; and I can assure you the contest is a rude one. A flourish of trumpets greets the winners. The donkey-race succeeds to the flag-race. In this country the donkeys follow the conquerors, but they throw over a good many of the competitors. They appeared to me very indifferent to glory, and at least quite as obstinate as Bécaire, who moreover would have carried off the palm for beauty. I saw very few as handsome as he. The overturns accomplished, and the *asinine* victors crowned, the next thing is the breaking of some dangling bottles, which does not sound very difficult; but one has to hit with bandaged eyes, and many a blow is wasted on air.

The bottles broken, the dance began. This was the prettiest feature of the fête. Handsome young men (the bathers), in white trousers, white jackets, and red floating scarves, arrange themselves in line all round the circle. Suddenly they turn and face each other, and each couple carries on a characteristic dance, which they accompany by a play of white sticks, the noise of which blends in perfect time with the sound of the instruments that accompany the dance. This goes on for a while in the meadow, and continues through the streets of the town till night. In the evening a magnificent ball gathered together eighty women, among whom you may guess who was not. The amusement is kept up as long as possible, then comes the fatigue.

I have still to tell you of the excursion to the lake; but that is not a thing to be described, it should be seen; you must pass over those roads in the air to have any idea of them. Imagine ropes hanging down the mountain sides; that is their appearance from below. Even though they had been improved a little for the Duchesse de Nemours to traverse them, I am astonished to have my neck unbroken; but all do bring theirs safely back. The fact is, one is mounted on hinds; the horses here are marvellous, they thread those paths, ascend and descend those perpendicular stairs without a stumble. At the end of it all I saw beautiful beauties indeed, amongst others a waterfall with three rainbows. The effect of this, and the strange charm of the situation, are inexpressible. Next came the Pont d'Espagne, an immense cataract. There we found some fourteen or fifteen equestrians, ladies and gentlemen, and we went on together to the lake. A profound solitude, an immense sheet of water amidst mountains, bare, precipitous, and gloomy as death; and, to complete the picture, a funereal monument on the borders of the lake, put up in memory of an English lady and her husband who were drowned when boating here about ten years ago. The waters are icy cold, so that whatever falls in dies almost immediately. This lake has its source in the Vignemale, the glaciers of which one sees. This is one of the highest peaks of the Pyrenees, and on its other side lies Spain.

We saw a hunt, too. I touched a wild goat or a hind. And after that, from the edge of the lake rose a little bird, who went on flying before us as if to court our admiration. He was indeed the gem of the desert, a flying flower, offering himself to our sight as though to console us for so much desolation. But for all that a very cheerful woman lives there in a kind of wooden tent. We carried our luncheon with us, and ate it during a storm—rain, hail, and thunder, and all on a grand scale. This weather was gracious enough to accompany us a short way on our return; but the fir-trees sheltered us. I observed one with these words carved on it—" Fear God;" and the inscription is well placed amidst those glorious divine works—those mighty trees which bid you fear the hand that planted them. We had a very beautiful and successful expedition; but now I am thinking of another, and leave you to prepare for my departure. I shall post this letter from Toulouse the day after to-morrow. Adieu, dear, far away ones. I do not yet know the day I leave for Gaillac. Elisa is to go to Cabanes before long; and it is possible that she may detain me to travel with her.

*Toulouse, 9th.*—Here I am with Elisa, resting myself after two sleepless nights. In other respects I had a good journey. We set out after dinner for the country, shall return here on the Eve of the Assumption, and on Monday, the 17th, hope to find ourselves at Gaillac. My aunt's carriage will meet us, and put me down at Cahuzac, where I shall wait for *Blidah.*\* Adieu.

---

To Mdlle. Antoinette de Boisset.

Cayla, 17th *September,* 1846.

I remember, my dear Antoinette, and have pleasure in remembering, that you most affectionately expressed a wish to hear from me when I bade you good-bye at Cauterets. Here I am therefore writing to you to satisfy your friendship as well as my own; for I have as much pleasure in giving as you in receiving. But what will you have to receive, my dear? Nothing pretty, nor interesting, nor profitable, except that I think myself in Paradise ever since my return to the midst of my own family circle.

The Pyrenees are indeed the most magnificent Bastille in which one can possibly be shut up, but time hangs very heavily there, in my opinion. With what rapture did I find myself outside them again! And yet I have nothing but good to say of that district, except as regards the cutting wind and the fogs, which gave me cold so liberally. And indeed I will not say much harm even of that cold of mine, for several reasons, and principally because it is going away. Thanks be to God, and to the inexpressibly

\* The Cayla horse.

good nursing of my incomparable sister, my tender, loving Marie, here I am nearly convalescent, with no other remnant of my troubles except weakness. I begin to hope we may meet again in this world, my dear Antoinette; where, I know not—perhaps in the most unlikely of places, as of late in the Pyrenees.

Meanwhile I begin by writing to you, and also by saying good-bye. My head is not yet very strong; although my heart would fain aid it, it totters still. I will not, however, leave you without inquiring whether your health continues in the flourishing condition in which I left it? This is my warmest wish; for experience teaches me how much enjoyment there is in health.

I embrace you as tenderly as usual. Many kind messages to your dear parents, who must have been as rejoiced at your return as you at rejoining them. One must allow that these bitter separations end very sweetly. I have come to the bitter just now, since I have to leave you.

Infinite love to Irène and your dear Augustine. Give me a letter, if you please, and give me your prayers as well.

---

TO THE SAME.

*23rd November*, 1846.

I hope, my dear Antoinette, that you are not too angry with me, and that at all events my letter will meet with pardon and kindness from your kind heart. My silence, it is true, is almost unpardonable. This I meekly confess, and yield it up to your clemency, only humbly imploring you to make allowance for a poor creature dead to the world, even to the finger ends, so much so, that since the month of August I have hardly written to any one. But beware of supposing yourself forgotten, my dear Antoinette; on the contrary, the less I say the more I think, which will give you an idea how much I must have thought of you.

But to-day I emerge from my affectionate silence to ask how you are—how fares it with that flourishing health brought back from the waters? I should have great pleasure in hearing that it continues, and that you are careful of it; it is such a blessing to be well. Assuredly you are well acquainted with both health and sickness, those two widely different modes of life. But this is the trying season for delicate chests; and this *sour* temperature, as your mother calls it, makes me dread some attack of cold for you, for I do not imagine that you spare yourself overmuch, or that anything interferes with your going out to visit the good God and your friends. It is very tedious no doubt to have to calculate one's every step; and I can well understand braving frost and snow so long as one is not firmly chained to the walls of one's room—I was going to say, of one's prison.

Between my father and my sister, mine is very sweet to me; but my two guardian angels are extreme in their vigilance, and I cannot escape them even to have a look at the sky, which for the last fortnight I only peep at through the window of my room. I have not been to mass for these three last Sundays. Happy they who have the church nearer to them! I should not be able to comfort myself about this distance, so full of disadvantages to the soul, did I not know that God disposes of health and roads, and places churches where He sees best; and after all I appropriate the proverb, "*Lèn dé la gleyso, prep d' el cel*," which was originally said by some pious peasant-woman far from her parish church.

As I no longer leave home, I have only local news to give you. You probably know as well as I that Louise de Thézac is still with Gabrielle. I fancy that the announcement of a new arrival will take her away before long. Methinks I see from here your dear Blanche's little angels smiling upon your knee; Marie must be very pretty. My little niece, too, is coming on nicely, and her small rays of intelligence charm me.

Adieu, dear Antoinette, adieu. Between this and the new year I shall hardly write again; therefore receive now the same wishes that I ever address to Heaven for you and your excellent family. Pray, tell dear Augustine also of her share in my good wishes and my affection.

I embrace you as tenderly as I possibly can, as a perpetual friend.

---

To THE SAME.

*27th February,* 1847.

Here is my sister, who will convey my letter, dear Antoinette—not indeed to you, but to your neighbourhood, to Gaillac, her first Lent station. A second one to

Lisle would much delight her; but one cannot go everywhere one likes in this holy season, or any other. It is only a Sainte Lisbine,* to whom God gives both power and leave to traverse the world and the sea to follow her inclinations. And what inclinations! O heavens! how sublime it is and how happy for China to see such angels come to speak to it of God! It is a very evident token of mercy and conversion for that happy country.

I cannot tell you how much this departure of our much-loved missionary has affected me. What a sacrifice, added to those she has already made! But, also, what good will result thence to the glory of God! What do we in this world, useless that we are, or at least I? Forgive me this generalisation, which reduces itself to my own poor person, quite given over to 'tisanes' and other delicacies which fill up my vocation of invalid, the most barren possible in good works, except as regards those kind souls who make it the occasion of exercising their own charity.

In this way I have caused the laying up of rich treasures by my dear and most *perfect* nurse. She has so well succeeded as to have rendered me able to dispense with her attentions, which she is now going to bestow on her own soul at Gaillac for a part of Lent. They speak of a preacher from Lyons. His eloquence would require the impetuosity of the Rhone itself to sweep along with it the cold spirits of the Gaillac people. Father Bonet used to reproach them with that fault. Alas! it

* Mdlle. Elisabeth de Gélis.

is extending in many other places; charity and zeal for salvation are getting sensibly chilled. How much the world needs St. Lisbines!

Thank you for the very interesting news you give me; to me, in my desert, nothing can be more agreeable and useful than such edifying examples. There is, however, one thing more that I could wish; I allude to news of your health. You say nothing about it in this letter, your heart is so full of anxiety about mine. This affects me much, and I thank you for it, praying you to believe that I return you much of what you give me so lavishly.

Adieu, dear friend. You see that we are in Lent, and that I am correcting myself of one thing at least, I mean my indolence about writing. But I am not indolent in loving you.

**THE END.**